P9-DGS-186

Reversing
the CURSE

BOOKS BY DAN SHAUGHNESSY

Courtside
(with Gary Hoenig)

One Strike Away

The Curse of the Bambino

*Ever Green: The
Boston Celtics*

*Seeing Red: The Red
Auerbach Story*

At Fenway

Fenway
(with Stan Grossfeld)

Spring Training
(with Stan Grossfeld)

*The Legend of the Curse
of the Bambino*

Reversing the Curse

Reversing the CURSE

Inside the 2004
BOSTON RED SOX

Dan Shaughnessy

HOUGHTON MIFFLIN COMPANY

Boston · New York · 2005

Library of Congress Cataloging-in-Publication Data
Shaughnessy, Dan
    Reversing the curse : inside the 2004 Red Sox /
      Dan Shaughnessy.
      p. cm.
    Includes bibliographical references and index.
    ISBN 0-618-51748-0
    1. Boston Red Sox (Baseball team)—History—21st century.
    2. Superstition—Massachusetts—Boston. I. Title.
    GV875.B62S536 2005
    796.357'64'0974461—dc22   [B] 2004066080

Book design by Melissa Lotfy

PRINTED IN THE UNITED STATES OF AMERICA

QUM 10 9 8 7 6 5 4 3 2 1

For Marilou

and bambinos, Sarah, Kate, and Sam

All grown up, all sluggers

CONTENTS

Reversing
the CURSE

The Moon
and the Stars

FINALLY, THE PLANETS were aligned. Truly.

A lunar eclipse, the first ever during a World Series game, gave the moon a bloody hue. And while the Boston ball club seemed to be comfortably leading in the fourth and final game of the World Series, Sox fans in Dunstable, Massachusetts, and White River Junction, Vermont, wandered out of their homes to take a peek at the big red ball in the black sky.

Finally, the Boston uniforms were not too heavy. Larger forces ran the base paths with the Olde Towne Team. The Red Sox were going to win the World Series. It had only been eighty-six years.

Eighteens and eighty-sixes were all over the place. It was Wednesday, October 27, 2004, the eighteenth anniversary of the last time the Red Sox lost a World Series in a seventh game. It was also the eighty-sixth anniversary of the last time the Sox *won* a World Series, when they beat the Cubs in six games in 1918 with the help of a stout left-handed pitcher named Babe Ruth. Now, eighteen years after the '86 Series and eighty-six years after winning in '18, the Sox were going to eighty-six the Curse of the Bambino. And a giant full moon was bleeding red as it rose in the sky above Presque Isle, Maine, and North Conway, New Hampshire.

More than a thousand miles to the southwest, where the Sox were writing history, the scarlet moon was hidden by a cloud cover over Busch Stadium in St. Louis. The Sox were far from home but never alone, and the voices of the Nation could be heard in the National

League park as the Bostons took their 3–0 lead into the late innings of Game 4. The game had been decided on the fourth pitch, when Johnny Damon, the Jesus action figure who played center field for the Sox, led off the night with a home run over the right field fence. Trot Nixon added two more runs with a bases-loaded double in the third, and pitchers Derek Lowe, Bronson Arroyo, Alan Embree, and closer Keith Foulke were nailing down Boston's fourth consecutive win against the overwhelmed Cardinals. In the end, the poor Redbirds, who had defeated the Sox in the 1946 and 1967 World Series, were mere props in the runaway Red Sox story of 2004.

As the inevitable and wonderful final out neared, folks were still cynical in Great Falls, Rhode Island, and Putnam, Connecticut, and any other place where Sox fans were gathered. They'd been duped before by Boston teams who seemed to have it sewed up, only to compound decades of misery with yet another colossal fold. But this time it truly seemed different. This time the Sox were going to finish the job. After all, they'd already passed the toughest test of all. They had done what no team in the history of baseball had ever done—they had won four straight games after losing the first three games of a seven-game series. And they had done it against the hated New York Yankees, the bane of Boston's baseball existence since 1920, when Ruth was shipped to the Big Apple for one hundred thousand pieces of silver. The Sox and their fans had been paying a price ever since. Some called it the Curse of the Bambino. This was the night it was all going to end.

In Marshfield, Massachusetts, Paul and Marilee Comerford woke up their young daughters and put them in front of the television so they would always be able to say that they witnessed the event. It was the same scene in Medford, where Hank Morse roused eight-year-old Abbey with one out in the ninth. This was history, and Hank had to hold her small face in his giant hands so that the little girl's sleepy head wouldn't drop while Foulke wound up for each pitch.

Vacationing in Ireland, Steve and Karin Sheppard of Nantucket prepared a second wedding. They'd married in April of 1986 and concluded their wedding vows with "Till death do us part, or until the Red Sox win the World Series."

The full moon had dropped from the sky in Iraq. It was already Thursday morning in Saddam Hussein's hometown of Tikrit when

Captain Mike Tilton of Laconia, New Hampshire, sat in a morale welfare center watching the game on television with about forty-five other soldiers, all Red Sox fans, most from New England. All members of the First Infantry Division, they had gathered in the dark at 4 A.M. to watch Game 4. It connected them with home.

It was almost dawn in Spain, where Harvard softball player Pilar Adams and dozens of other American students gathered in a bar in Seville. A well-known local matador was buying drinks for the young Americans every time the Red Sox rallied, and when victory seemed assured, a couple of students from New Hampshire and central Massachusetts made plans to swim naked across the Guadalquivir River. They would have time. Classes didn't start until 8 A.M., and the Sox were playing more quickly than usual.

At 11:40, just twenty minutes before midnight back in Boston, with one on and two out, Cardinal shortstop Edgar Renteria hit a hard one-hopper straight back to the pitcher's mound. The ball seemed headed for center field, which would have raised anxiety levels throughout the Nation (tying run at the plate? Here we go again!). However, Foulke, who had been purchased in the previous off-season for exactly this kind of moment, leaped and gloved the ball over his head. He took seven or eight steps toward first—was he going to run all the way over there and make us wait even longer?—then underhanded a short toss to first baseman Doug Mientkiewicz, and the Red Sox were World Series Champions.

Finally. The seemingly interminable wait was finally over. The Curse had been reversed.

Catcher Jason Varitek jumped into the arms of Foulke—that would be the cover shot on *Time* magazine the week the leader of the free world was reelected. Mientkiewicz joined the happy huddle, followed by Arroyo, who had come out of the dugout. Then more teammates streamed from the bench, the bullpen, and their positions on the field. It was a giant pile of happiness and hair. Overcome, catcher-leader Varitek collapsed facedown on the infield grass while his teammates hugged and hopped around him. Within minutes, close to five thousand Red Sox road-trippers were congregated around the third base dugout, chanting "Let's Go, Red Sox!" while the players doused one another with Mount Pleasant, 2003 Brut Imperial (green bottles with orange labels). Around the globe, bottles were uncorked, church bells pealed, and car horns honked.

And in the small New England towns where the October skies are blackest, the crimson moon shone brightest. If you looked at it long enough, and maybe had some Brut Imperial coursing through your veins, the smiling image of Babe Ruth started to appear on the full face of the scarlet sphere—like a Bambino version of Jackie Gleason's fat face on *The Honeymooners.*

How sweet it was. New England's midnight moon dance, beneath the cover of October skies.

Red Sox fans needed no more signs. The man in the moon was Babe Ruth.

The 2004 Red Sox were the Laughing Gashouse Gang, a band of rogues who let their hair down, drove motorcycles, drank shots of Jack Daniel's before games, wore their shirts untucked, and smeared pine tar all over their helmets. They grew beards, shaved their heads, and braided their hair into blond cornrows. Pedro Martinez looked like he had black broccoli under his hat, and Manny Ramirez's barbershop explosion could not be contained by any cap or batting helmet. They were raggedy men who proudly called themselves "idiots," but when it mattered most, they did two things no team had ever done: They did not merely lift the Curse of the Bambino, they demolished the eighty-six-year-old pox on the House of Fenway. They had *Jesus* playing center field, for God's sake.

Sitting in bed at home in Cambridge, watching the Sox celebrate on the Busch infield, fifty-three-year-old Mike LaVigne knew what he had to do. A house painter and assistant soccer coach at Boston College, LaVigne grew up in Groton, Massachusetts, one of five children of Dr. Richard LaVigne, chief of radiology at Burbank Hospital in Fitchburg. When the LaVigne children were young, their dad would take them to work with him on Saturdays, and they'd help him by stamping some of the x-rays. Part of the routine included breakfast at the Moran Square Diner, where Dr. LaVigne was always teased about the Red Sox by its owners, Angie and Louie. They were Italian immigrants who loved the Yankees because of Joe DiMaggio. The Yankees, naturally, were always beating the Red Sox, and Angie and Louie took delight in breaking the doc's chops. When Dr. LaVigne was on his deathbed in 1979 at the Dana-Farber Cancer Institute in Boston, he made a final request of his son Michael. He said that if the Red Sox ever did win a World Series, he wanted Michael to buy the best bottle of champagne he could find, take it to the diner, and say, "This is from the doc!"

Thursday, October 28, 2004, was an unofficial holiday in New England. Not much work got done. Thousands of fans went to Fenway Park early in the morning and greeted their returning heroes by dawn's early light. Kids were late for school. Teachers were late, too. The entire Nation was functioning on a second consecutive week of late nights and early mornings. Warren Zevon's "I'll Sleep When I'm Dead" served as the mantra for the nocturnal masses. On the morning after the final late night, Boston newspapers were suddenly scarce. The *Boston Globe* had more than doubled its daily press run—from 500,000 to close to 1.2 million—but papers were still hard to find after fans hoarded stacks of the daily rags. Within twenty-four hours, copies of the 50-cent October 28 *Globe* were fetching $25 on eBay.

It was more than a sports story. It was bigger than the magnificent deed of a band of twenty-five baseball brothers. It was bigger than a Nation founded on hope. By the autumn of 2004, the Red Sox were America's team, almost global. Their championship run marked the end of an eighty-six-year quest that had consumed the lives of millions of people with roots in New England. The Red Sox connect generations. They remind you of your father and mother, maybe your grandfather, too. And they remind you of your sons and daughters and all that you taught them when they were young. Like green eyes, freckles, and big feet, love of the Sox is passed through bloodlines, and the shared passion can bridge gaps that come with maturity and growth. In every family there's inevitable distance—sometimes geographic, sometimes philosophical or emotional. But the Red Sox are common ground. They connect and unite.

In the second two weeks of October 2004, Sox fans connected as never before. Siblings who'd grown apart started calling one another. People who moved away after growing up in New England watched the games on TV from their homes in Colorado, Arizona, and Florida, as they remembered growing up with the mellow voice of Curt Gowdy pouring out of the porch radio into the humid summer nights. The citizens of this global Nation watched the games and thought of parents or spouses who had died. They thought about how much they missed Uncle Joe and Aunt Elizabeth.

Those who'd adopted Boston, millions of students who spent their college years in New England, shared the family secret. They carried with them a love of the Sox, along with memories of that first beer in the Fenway bleachers. For many of them, Kenmore Square's Citgo sign, which looms beyond the infamous Green Monster, was the lighthouse that guided them back to their dorms on those first wobbly nights of undergrad freedom.

The Red Sox, a charter member of the upstart American League in 1901, have not always been worthy of the faith and loyalty of their fans. Nor have they always been good or especially popular. They were not consistently championship-driven nor particularly well run. They were at times unlucky, inept, controversial, racist, and petty. Many years, Sox ballplayers were nothing like the fuzzy, stuffed-animals-come-to-life on the 2004 roster. They were not always perceived as gritty, clutch, and talented. At times they truly were idiots, and there was nothing lovable about them. But they have always been there, as indigenous to Boston as swan boats, clam chowder, Paul Revere, the L Street Brownies, Sam Adams (the man, not the beer), and the golden dome of the State House.

For Red Sox fans, it wasn't always about winning—that was the province of the Yankee fans. It was about wanting to win. Hoping they would win. The weight of the wait. Which is why the fans came back, year after year, even after so many near misses. There was something at once noble and naive about the dynamic between the fans and their team.

As decades passed, Red Sox Nation offered no asylum for those in need of instant gratification. Believing the Sox would win a World Series in 2004 required an act of faith not unlike one's commitment to a Higher Being. There were few lucid souls old enough to clearly recall the World Series win of 1918. Fans were required to believe in something they had never seen. And they did. Through the years, Red Sox fans developed a devotion to their team that was something like a religion. Fenway became a place of worship, and rooting for the Red Sox was a lifelong passion. Just as devout Catholics search for a Sunday mass schedule when they find themselves in a new town, Sox fans sought a lifeline to the Red Sox when they left New England. In the twenty-first century, the Internet tethered Sox Nation to the mother ship in Boston. Fans could read the *Globe* online or follow games live on MLB.com.

All of the above brings us to the Curse of the Bambino, which gave some Sox fans a handy way to explain the inexplicable. It was too deflating to simply admit that the Red Sox were not good enough to win the World Series every year. Sox fans needed a more agreeable reason for decade after decade of second-place finishes and October collapses. It's superstition over science, a trip into the twilight zone between the on-deck circle and the batter's box. Baseball, probably more than any sport, is governed by superstition. The black cat crossing in front of the dugout guarantees bad news, and you'd better cross your fingers when the team bus passes a graveyard or you'll never get another hit. You don't wash your uniform when you're on a hitting streak, and you don't tell your pitcher that he's got a no-hitter going because the next batter is certain to get a hit. For some, the Curse was easier to accept than the reality that the Sox somehow weren't good enough to win it all.

There was no published mention of the Curse of the Bambino until I wrote a book with that title in 1990. Before the book, there were various theories regarding those near misses and outright collapses. Certainly the preposterous fold of 1978 put the wheels in motion that Sox fans were destined to suffer. In that memorable campaign, the Sox led the Yankees by fourteen games on July 20—but managed to blow the entire lead and then lost a one-game playoff when Bucky Dent hit a pop-fly, three-run homer into the net above the Green Monster. But there were other frustrations. The Sox lost the 1946 World Series to the Cardinals in seven games after being prohibitive favorites. They lost a one-game playoff to the Indians in 1948 and blew the final two games in New York in '49 to lose the pennant to the Yankees by one game. Boston's Impossible Dream summer of 1967 ended with a World Series Game 7 loss to the Cardinals. A big fold in 1974 prompted the estimable Peter Gammons of the *Globe* to declare that Sox fans "won't get fooled again." But the fans always came back, and in '75 they were rewarded with another World Series, only to lose again in Game 7. Then came the mind-blowing disappointment of 1986, when the Red Sox came closer to winning a World Series without actually winning than any team in baseball history. The Sox led the Mets, three games to two, and carried a 5–3 lead into the bottom of the tenth inning at Shea Stadium. With two out and nobody aboard, the Mets came back to win on three consecutive singles, a wild pitch, and an error-for-the-ages—a ground ball that skipped through the legs of Bill Buckner and into history.

Through all that, there was no Curse of the Bambino. In '86, George Vecsey of the *New York Times* wrote a column in which he suggested that the Babe might be taking out his wrath on the Red Sox and introduced the word "curse." But nobody cited Ruth when the Sox lost Game 7 two days after the infamous Buckner gaffe.

In 1988 I received a letter from Meg Blackstone, an editor at Dutton. Ms. Blackstone suggested a dark history of the Red Sox tracing back to the sale of Ruth. She said we could call it *The Curse of the Bambino*. She'd picked up the expression from her grandfather, a Dorchester house painter named Arthur Whitfield Davidson.

The book came out in 1990. That year, the Sox marched to the playoffs but were swept by the Oakland A's as Roger Clemens imploded on the mound in Game 4, and the Curse became a handy theme for network broadcasts and headline writers across America. Over the next fourteen years, it took on a life of its own. The paperback version went through twenty-two printings and was updated three times, swelling to 248 pages from the original 207. It was a standard title on some local high school reading lists. In the final edition, released in August 2004, Red Sox general manager Theo Epstein talked about buying the original book at Coolidge Corner's Brookline Booksmith when he was home on break from Yale.

But it was the cult of the Curse, not the book, that the Sox dealt with after 1990. The Curse became a cottage industry, spawning a musical, an award-winning HBO special, rock songs, poems, board games, ice cream flavors, cookies, bumper stickers, Web sites, and T-shirts. Before the Red Sox played the Yankees in the 1999 ALCS, it was brought up on the floor of the U.S. House of Representatives when Ed Markey declared that the Curse of the Bambino was "in the same league at the Curse of Macbeth . . . In the same league as the ancient Curse of King Tut's tomb . . . and even in the same league as the biblical Curse of Yahweh." This was read into the *Congressional Record*.

The 2003 ALCS climaxed in an excruciating fashion for Red Sox fans—again to the delight of the Yankees. After a yearlong joust with the Evil Empire, the Sox led the Yankees, 5–2, in the eighth inning of the final game of the series in Yankee Stadium. It was the season-record twenty-sixth meeting of the two teams, and with Pedro Martinez on the mound, the Sox were set to win the American League pennant. But then Grady Little left Pedro on the mound too long. The Yankees rallied for three runs and ultimately won the game after midnight in the eleventh inning on Aaron Boone's walk-off homer off Tim Wakefield. In any ranking of the most painful Sox defeats of the last quarter century, the Boone game belongs on the dubious medal stand alongside the Bucky Dent game of '78 and the Buckner game of '86. Perhaps because it was most recent and it came at the hands of the Yankees, many Red Sox fans elevated the 2003 loss to the gold medal platform. And the Bambino's fingerprints were all over the place.

In 2004 the Red Sox gave up and joined the chorus. The management made Breaking the Curse part of the club's official mission statement. An eight-page manifesto at the front of the team press guide listed the goals of the organization and concluded: "To end the Curse of the Bambino and win a World Championship for Boston, New England, and Red Sox Nation."

"The Curse always kind of had an ambiguous status," admitted CEO Larry Lucchino. "It was always included as a fifth goal. We saw it as a fundamental obligation of ownership to do it. Tom Werner had talked about it at our initial press conference before we learned the political sensitivity surrounding the use of it. But we always knew our stewardship of the franchise would be judged by whether or not we won World Series championships, and that meant erasing and eradicating the Curse of the Bambino."

As the Curse became part of the language, diehard fans came to despise it. Gammons described it as "a silly, mindless gimmick that is as stupid as the wave." Spurned by knowledgeable fans, it deteriorated into something for tourists. The Cheers Bar Complex took hold. It relates to the fate of the old Bull & Finch Pub, under the Hampshire House restaurant on Beacon Street. Once a wonderful saloon, the Bull & Finch became an overcrowded T-shirt shop for camera-wielding tourists after the *Cheers* television show made the bar famous. True Bostonians fled, never to return. The Curse had suffered similarly.

After Boone's homer crushed the Red Sox hopes yet again, convincing a new generation of fans that there might really be a curse, the 2003–2004 hot stove season scalded fans in both cities. Twenty-eight big league teams sat back and watched in amazement as the Red Sox and Yanks engaged in the most ferocious and competitive stockpiling of rosters in baseball history. When it was over, they'd both acquired Alex Rodriguez (though Boston had him for only a few hours), and the rivals featured the two highest payrolls in baseball, prepared to meet another twenty-six times if that's what it took to settle things.

It did. With photos of Babe Ruth plastered in and around both ballparks, the Sox and Yanks battled again in 2004. A bloody, bench-clearing brawl at Fenway in late July furnished a photo op for the ages (Varitek stuffing his catcher's mitt into the handsome face of Rodriguez), then Pedro issued a late September, midnight confession in which he admitted the Yankees were his "daddy." You simply could not make up this stuff.

In an American League Championship Series that trumped the World Series, the Red Sox came back from a 3–0 series deficit to defeat the Yankees in the sacred House That Ruth Built. The dramatic comeback started on October 17, a few hours after the death of Ray Boone. Boone was the grandfather of Aaron Boone and a Red Sox scout for forty-four years. He'd been traded for Tito Francona (father of the Red Sox manager) in 1958, and he'd signed Curt Schilling for the Sox in 1986. He lived long enough to see his grandson bump the Sox out of the World Series, but he died the day his team kick-started the greatest comeback in sports history. Eighty-one years old, like so many others, Ray Boone died without seeing the Sox win it all in his lifetime.

The Red Sox comeback against the Yankees was better than the World Series. Epstein said, "It gave us a collective, cathartic exhale. The region dumped all its collective baggage at once."

Finally, the Big Apple was lodged in the throats of the men wearing pinstripes. This time it was the gluttonous Yankees who choked.

Exactly one week later, in St. Louis, the Red Sox won the World Series. Curse clues were all over the finale. The Sox won on the eighty-fourth birthday of Nanette Fabray (Fenway folklore holds that Harry Frazee, the Sox owner who sold Ruth, subsequently made a killing on the musical *No, No, Nanette*), and the last ball in play was hit by a batter wearing Ruth's no. 3. The Cardinals had been swept only one other time in a World Series: in that one, Babe Ruth hit three homers in Game 4.

Bruce Hurst weighed in from retirement. Hurst had been the man who almost single-handedly won the 1986 World Series for Boston. He beat the Mets, 1–0, in Game 1, just as Ruth, another Sox lefty, had beaten the Cubs in Game 1 in 1918. Among Sox left-handed pitchers, Ruth and Hurst rank fifth and sixth respectively in career victories. Ruth won eighty-nine, Hurst eighty-eight. And "Bruce Hurst" is an anagram for "B. Ruth Curse." Hurst's mom, Beth, once the owner of a Ben Franklin–Ace Hardware store in St. George, Utah, died at the age of eighty-five in December of 2003. Hurst watched the game with his family in Phoenix. "I'd never seen so many fans in prayer position," he noticed. When it was over, Mr. B. Ruth Curse said, "I'm pretty sure, knowing my mom, that she would have gone up and put her arm around Babe and said, 'Let's get this over with.'"

In the early moments after Game 4 in St. Louis, Steve and Karin Sheppard—the Nantucket couple who had sworn "Till death do us part, or until the Red Sox win the World Series"—got a call from Steve's mom: "I assume you'll be sleeping in separate beds tonight." They made plans to remarry. Hopefully in Fenway Park in 2005.

In Tikrit, Iraq, it was 6:40 A.M. on Thursday when Foulke got the final out. Captain Tilton resisted the urge to fire his weapon into the Iraqi sky. Instead, he thought of his New Hampshire home.

"I've always said that no matter how it happened, I'd make my way to Boston for the World Series," he said a few days later. "It was a little tough. You definitely wanted to be home to share it with the people you shared all the heartbreaks with. It added to the homesickness, but it sure made the month of October go by quickly. It was something we'd all been waiting for a long time. Even though we weren't with our families or friends from back home, it was good to be with a group of people from New England, sharing the moment."

In the corridor outside the visitor's clubhouse at Busch Stadium after the win, Sox owner John Henry brushed champagne from his
brown raincoat and said, "This is like an alternate reality. All of our
fans waited their entire lives for this."

Inside the clubhouse, Pedro looked into a television camera and
said, "A lot of people, if they die now, are gonna die in peace."

After work on Thursday, Mike LaVigne went to Burton's Liquors in
Newton and ponied up something north of $100 for a vintage bottle
of Veuve Clicquot. He drove to Fitchburg with his wife, Lisa White. He
wasn't sure if the place still existed, but when he turned on to Myrtle
Avenue just after darkness descended, the Moran Square Diner was
there—still standing but closed for the night. He set the bottle on the
steps with a note: "From the Doc! Richard LaVigne."

Similar rituals were carried out across New England. Cemeteries
were favorite sites of the faithful. A Boston policeman drove to central
Massachusetts to lay a red rose on his parents' tombstone. Roger Alt-
man, former deputy secretary of the Treasury under Bill Clinton, had
the front page of the *New York Times* laminated, then went to his
mother's gravesite at Walnut Hill in South Brookline and buried it
near her eternal resting place. She'd died at the age of ninety-four a
month after the 2003 playoffs, and according to her son, "Her entire
existence revolved around the Red Sox." Phone calls were made to
friends and relatives. Sox fans overloaded the Internet with messages
of joy and remembrance.

In the end, the Red Sox really are about life and death.

Reversing the Curse triggered the largest celebration in the entire history of the City of Boston when an estimated 3.2 million fans turned
out for a victory parade on Saturday, October 30. It changed the way
New Englanders felt about themselves and the Red Sox. Varitek told
the happy fans, "I feel really relieved, but so proud. All the years that
people have suffered. Every Red Sox fan from now on can walk into
Yankee Stadium with their head up."

Some people worried that older fans might give up and die when
the Sox finally won, but there was no spike in the obituary section of
the *Globe* in the days after the sweep of the Cardinals. The Nation
wondered if fans might feel empty or aimless, but none of that hap-

pened. People were just happy. Satisfied. Fans found nothing disappointing about the end of the quest. They bought up every piece of Red Sox garb and memorabilia they could find. You could buy Red Sox championship dog bones at Modell's in Medford. It seemed that every kid in New England suddenly knew how to spell Mientkiewicz.

The case will be made between these covers that the 2004 Boston baseball season was the most remarkable campaign in the history of American team sports. Crushed by the Yankees in the final minutes of their 2003 season, the Sox rededicated themselves to winning the World Series a year later. The Sox management did its job by acquiring Schilling and Foulke—before losing A-Rod in the final days of the front office's ferocious off-season war with the Yankees. The 2004 Sox frustrated their fans by treading water for more than three months before Epstein—in the boldest move since the selling of Babe Ruth —rocked Red Sox Nation by trading popular but unhappy Nomar Garciaparra at the end of July. From that point on, the Sox played like champions, demonstrating the camaraderie and selflessness that served them well in their darkest hours, when all seemed lost in the Yankee series.

In the final eleven days of October, the 2004 Red Sox were on a roll like no baseball team in history. They could have kept playing the Yankees and Cardinals into December without ever losing or even falling behind in a game. This time the Red Sox finally had the talent *and* the clubhouse karma, and the Curse of the Bambino was no match.

2

Damn Yankees Again

THE STORY OF THE 2004 Red Sox starts at 12:16 on the morning of Friday, October 17, 2003, at Yankee Stadium, when Aaron Boone's high fly ball landed in the left field seats and sent the Red Sox home without a championship for the eighty-fifth consecutive autumn. Fall, if you will.

Every end yields a beginning, and the 2004 Red Sox season—the Steppenwolf summer in which the Sox fired all their guns at once—was born in those first minutes after midnight, when the Boston ballplayers and their weeping Nation once again pledged that the next year truly was going to be The Year.

Sitting in the box seats down by the dugout, Red Sox owner John Henry and CEO Larry Lucchino had already decided they'd be needing a new field manager. Grady Little was working on the final days of his contract and hadn't done much to convince his bosses that he was the man to lead the Red Sox. All he'd done was win ninety-three games in 2002 and another ninety-five in 2003, taking the Sox to within five outs of their first World Series since 1986. Grady wasn't their guy, but it would have been impossible to let him go had the Sox made it to the World Series. Henry and Lucchino would have been stuck with Goober, the man who didn't know Bill James's name, the man who paid little heed to the meticulous scouting reports and the spreadsheets that were being provided by the best and brightest of Young Theo's army.

Young Theo Epstein is an integral part of this story, but on the night of October 16 he was just another Sox fan, crushed by the disappointment of the near miss. Like Henry and Lucchino, he was in the sad Sox clubhouse after the game, consoling the devastated players and knowing that he was going to have to search for a new manager. Making a change was okay with Theo; he'd been bothered by Grady's old-school style. And now, because of how the Red Sox had lost, the Sox could fire the manager without fearing fan revolt. Red Sox Nation wasn't going to lobby for Grady. Nope. Grady was already in the Red Sox Hall of Shame, alongside Buckner, Bob Stanley, Calvin Schiraldi, John McNamara, Mike Torrez, Don Zimmer, Denny Galehouse, Harry Frazee, and the rest. Closing time was still hours away in New York saloons when Grady and his defeated Red Sox walked to their buses outside the press gate at Yankee Stadium.

Yankee fans, ever arrogant but now emboldened by the latest heroic comeback against the cartoon characters from Boston, were waiting to taunt and torture the Red Sox. Piling it on. Merely winning and going back to the World Series—that routine destination of pinstripe entitlement—was not enough for these people. Yankee fans wanted to pour vinegar into the newly opened gash. They wanted to watch the Red Sox cry. Yankee vice president Randy Levine was overheard saying, "Take that, you 1918 pieces of shit!"

If not for a police presence, the New Yorkers no doubt would have rocked the Sox buses, like the angry Venezuelans attacking Vice President Richard Nixon's motorcade in 1958. And standing out there with them was none other than George Steinbrenner.

"Go back to Boston, boys," said the Boss, a man who could get furious at the idea of New England clam chowder on the menu at Yankee Stadium. "Good-bye . . . I didn't enjoy Boston, to be honest with you. It was a very difficult series because it was so intense. I don't believe I've ever been involved in any athletic event that had that much pressure. But we get the last laugh. I'm happy they're at home and we're playing . . . The Curse still lives."

Three days later, Steinbrenner would tell *USA Today:* "That was as much emotion as I've ever been through in any series. It was truly the greatest sporting event I've ever been associated with. It would have been devastating to lose to the Red Sox. They were devastated by the loss. The whole city [Boston] was devastated by it."

Devastated.

On the bus, Wakefield sat and fretted. Thirty-seven years old, he'd been with the Red Sox longer than anyone else on the team. He'd pitched with Roger Clemens and played with Wade Boggs. A Florida native, he'd recently married, settled in the area, and poured his heart into local charities. More than any of his teammates, save Framingham's Lou Merloni, Wakefield knew what the Red Sox meant back home and around the world. He knew the history. He knew how crushing this loss was going to be in Sox Nation. And he thought about one man . . . Buckner. Wakefield feared he'd just picked up the torch from the most infamous and unfairly disparaged character in recent Red Sox history. Wakefield was on the mound when Boone rounded the bases. It was a Wakefield knuckler that sailed into the seats. The first pitch of the bottom of the inning. The last pitch of the season. Walk-off nightmare.

"I was terrified," he said months later. "I was afraid I wouldn't be able to show my face in Boston. I saw what happened to Bill Buckner, and I knew how unfair that was. One play ruined him as a Bostonian. I just didn't know how the fans were going to react."

No problem. Wakefield had beaten the Yankees twice in the series. He had had a long and meritorious career in Boston. He was a Jimmy Fund champion and a standup guy. And on that fateful night, he was pitching in relief. There would be no Bucknerization of Tim Wakefield. Grady Little was going to take the fall for this one. All the way.

But it was bigger than the soul-searching of one man or the blame that would be heaped on another. Wakefield was not the only person who wept when Boone hit the home run. Around the world, chairs were thrown, containers of liquid were hurled, fists were pounded into armchairs, and tears were shed. People had gotten on airplanes, secure that the Sox finally beat the Yankees, only to land and learn that the cruelest of jokes had been played once again. On this night, the tears of Red Sox Nation would have filled the Quabbin Reservoir with salt water.

It had happened similarly in 1978 (Bucky Dent) and again in 1986 (Buckner), but this was a new story, another ghoulish ending etched in people's minds. The way baby boomers recite what they were doing when JFK was shot, citizens of the Nation remember every detail of their day whenever the Red Sox produce another mind-bending playoff loss. In the fall of 2003, the young people were most distraught, most damaged. New England teenagers and twenty-somethings had no personal memory of Dent or Buckner. They'd heard about those moments from their parents or seen them on lowlight reels of Red Sox history. It was like reading about the battle at Gettysburg or the Alamo.

The collapse of a favorite sports team can be like a terrible illness or divorce: the sadness is abstract and relatively painless until it happens to you. Fans come to love their teams unconditionally, the way they love their family and pets. In some cases, sports fans' investment of time and emotion exceed what they are giving loved ones at home. They care more about Nomar Garciaparra than about their brother. They study box scores and batting averages when they should be working at their desks or getting in touch with friends. They develop superstitions and start to believe that they can actually affect the outcome of a game by sticking with routines that have worked in the past. They blame themselves for a Sox loss because they weren't sitting in the right chair or they moved a lucky pillow or went to the bathroom at an unlucky moment. It's entirely irrational—hence the word "fan," which is an abbreviation for "fanatic."

And so it was that young Red Sox fans got their naturalization papers on the night of October 16, 2003, when the Red Sox were stunned again by the Yankees.

Kevin McHale played thirteen seasons for the Boston Celtics, and his five children grew up to love the Red Sox. When the All-Star forward went home to Minnesota to run the NBA Timberwolves, his children continued to root for the Sox. So the McHale kids cheered and held their breath in anticipation of the ultimate victory over the Yankees when their dad walked into the TV room in the eighth inning and told them, "They're going to blow it. The Red Sox always blow it. You guys just don't know." The tall dad left the room and heard the calamity in another part of the house as the Sox unraveled.

"I never saw my son that upset," McHale said a year later. "Not even when his dog died."

On Willard Street, in the Hunnewell Hill section of Newton, Massachusetts, high school senior Pat Sviokla hosted ten of his pals for a Thursday night "beat the Yankees" celebration. Watching a sixty-one-inch television screen in the big basement rec room, the teens drank cola, ate popcorn, and laughed as the Sox built their insurmountable lead. When glee turned to horror, the big room with the big TV fell silent. No one knew how to react. These kids had never lived through such a thing before. Pat's mom watched them file up the stairs and out of the house. Big teen shoulders slumped. Wordless. She thought to herself, "They look like POWs."

Down the street from the Svioklas', Cheryl Welch taped the game for her son, who was at work. Not a baseball fan, the dutiful mom noticed that the Sox were impossibly ahead, and she left the room while the machine recorded the rest of the game. Her son had left specific instructions that he did not want to be told how it ended, but his clueless mom let it slip that the Sox had won. She'd heard celebrating in the street, which must have come from Sox fans who'd jumped the gun or visitors from New York. So Peter Welch, annoyed that his mom had told him the outcome—watched and experienced the double mindfuck. The weight of being a Red Sox fan knows no limit.

The college freshmen Shaughnessy girls were not spared. One at Boston University, one at Harvard, both softball players and Sox fans, they'd attended many of the postseason games at Fenway and were certain that this was the year. Separated by fourteen months, two miles, and one river, they watched with their college teammates in their respective dormitories and were initiated with all the other young people when the New York nightmare unfolded in front of them. When it was over, they went out to the street, walking, talking to each other on their cell phones, crying a river on opposite sides of the Charles. It simply could not have happened. The tracks of the girls' tears traced back through the streets of Groton, Pepperell, and Cambridge, Massachusetts, where their parents and grandparents had first learned the fundamental rules of Red Sox allegiance.

Older fans had been conditioned. They'd been through this before. Like Kevin McHale, many of them had a sense that the Sox might blow it again. And it's not just the losing. It's not just the near miss. There's the added element of the championship team in New York, the bullying big brother annually squashing the hopes and dreams of the Red Sox. It is Red Sox Nation's obsession with the Yankees that colors everything the ball club does in its quest for a championship.

Universally, greatness and achievement are measured in relation to competition. Winning naturally beats losing, but a worthy adversary enhances the victor. It goes back to the beginning of recorded history. Only the strong survive. It's jungle law. When men hunted for food, being bigger, faster, and stronger was always an advantage. The first and everlasting rivalries are rooted in warfare, too often in the name of religion. Groups conquered other groups as civilizations evolved and were destroyed. It goes back to the Bible, when the Babylonians got the better of the Israelites. It goes back to Homer, when the Spartans fought the Trojans. The French and the Germans have hated each other for centuries, just like the Basques and the Spanish, the Turks and the Armenians.

Individually, we're introduced to rivals in earliest childhood. It can be a little brother or sister, a kid down the street, or the nattering nemesis in the front row of your first-grade classroom. Your parents tell you that you're the brightest or the fastest or the best-looking, and all of a sudden there's the kid who is smarter, faster, and more hand-some or beautiful. You have a rival, and the quest to beat him makes you better. Any victory makes the win that much sweeter.

Rivalries also polarize people, creating the unfortunate "us vs. them" mentality that permeates religious, social, and economic group-ings, too often making the world a harder place in which to live. American politics in the twenty-first century demonstrates the worst manifestation of this dynamic. Serious, well-thought-out proposals designed to make life better are tabled and torched by partisan politics —by people who believe but no longer think independently. You are Red State or Blue State and you stick to the agenda, disregarding the potential merits of other positions.

The world of arts and entertainment features rivalry in a more frivolous form. We can have fun comparing the Beatles to the Roll-ing Stones or arguing about the merits of Frank Sinatra vs. Johnny Mathis. It gets a lot more serious at the corporate level: Hertz battles Avis, Coke duels Pepsi, and Macy's checks to see what Gimbel's is doing.

But the most natural, least harmful, and most productive rivalries are part of athletic competition. It is where bigger, faster, and stronger mean a quest for trophies and championship rings instead of commercial gain or life and death. Was there ever a better matchup than Bill Russell vs. Wilt Chamberlain? Russell won eleven championships in thirteen seasons with the Boston Celtics, and he will tell you that the achievement was enhanced by the strength of his competition. Wilt Chamberlain was Goliath, larger and stronger than any player in the history of the NBA. When he first came into the league, people believed that Chamberlain would be unstoppable, winning a long string of championships. But Russell somehow neutralized his powerful rival, and the Celtics annually beat Chamberlain's team en route to a championship.

Golf had Arnold Palmer vs. Jack Nicklaus. Palmer was the god of the links when young Nicklaus came on the scene. Their cold rivalry brought golf into the mainstream, attracting a new generation of fans and players. Is there any doubt that the greatness of Muhammad Ali was firmly established by his three-bout battle with Smokin' Joe Frazier? A look at the career of horse racing's Seabiscuit is incomplete without his historic race against War Admiral. If horses could talk, Affirmed would toast Alydar as the reason he won the triple crown. We know that sprinters and marathoners run faster when a rival nips at the heels of a leader.

Team sports take rivalries to a higher level. College football has Ohio State–Michigan, Auburn-Alabama, and Texas-Oklahoma. College basketball has Duke vs. North Carolina. These are not one-day-a-year contests for bragging rights. They represent a culture and a lifestyle. Your school or team sweatshirt tells the world who you are. Without any words being spoken, colors and logos frame your résumé.

Professional sports in America may not top the passion of regional collegiate rivalries, but a sports archaeologist looking under rocks would do well to start with the Dallas Cowboys vs. the Washington Redskins of the NFL, the Celtics vs. the Lakers of the NBA, and the Cardinals vs. the Cubs or the Dodgers vs. the Giants of Major League Baseball. To take the argument to hideous heights, we can step back and include the frightening soccer rivalries, such as Argentina vs. Brazil, or Pakistan vs. India in cricket. Check out an Olympic baseball game between Korea and Japan. Unfortunately, these matches too often represent political positions or grudges under the guise of sports competition and therefore fail to fit our search for the best sports rivalries.

But the feud between the New York Yankees and the Boston Red Sox has been called by many the best rivalry in sports today.

The first obstacle in that argument would be the literal definition of the word "rival" and the inherent flaw in its application to the hundred-plus years of competition between the two teams. According to *Webster's*, "rival" represents "one that equals another." Certainly the Red Sox have been competitive with the Yankees through many of the last eight and a half decades, but since 1918 the Yankees have won twenty-six World Series compared with only one for the Red Sox. Hardly the definition of equal. Wise guys have been known to dismiss the rivalry as the eternal battle between the hammer and the nail. The script of the classic film *Casablanca*—appropriately written by Theo Epstein's grandfather and great-uncle—contains dialogue that perhaps best explains the New York take on the rivalry between the Red Sox and the Yankees. A criminal (Peter Lorre) sits across a table from a nightclub owner (Humphrey Bogart) and says, "You despise me, don't you?" Barely looking up, Bogie says, "If I gave you any thought, I probably would."

This dismissiveness and arrogance—always aimed at Sox fans—explains in part the irrational hatred Sox fans hold for the Yankees. It also highlights the imbalance of the Red Sox–Yankee fan dynamic: the Red Sox and their fans think a lot more about the Yankees than the Yankees think about the Red Sox. Through the decades, it's been too easy for the Yanks to treat the Sox like wannabe younger brothers.

The author knows what he's talking about. In the 1960s, Bill Shaughnessy was the best young athlete in Groton, Massachusetts. He was good enough to start for the high school varsity baseball team when he was in the seventh grade. He pitched and won the league championship game when he was only a sophomore. He was a four-year starter in basketball, averaging over 20 points a game and winning another championship in an undefeated season. His jump shot was deadly, his prodigious home runs instant folklore. Throughout his scrapbook teens, he tutored the author in one-on-one games in our backyard. Six years older, a foot taller, forever far more gifted, it was easy for Bill Shaughnessy to win every time. Naturally, the boy was bored. He loved to tease and had sadistic tendencies, so he'd let the author *almost* win. They'd play basketball—first to score 20 wins. Bill Shaughnessy would let the author rush to a 19–0 lead, then make a dramatic comeback and crush the spirit of the little kid, making him cry.

It's not unlike how the Yankees have treated the Red Sox for the better part of eight decades. Right up until 2004, that is.

The New York–Boston rivalry is rooted in geography and American history. Boston fancies itself the Hub of the Universe, but New York is the Capital of the World. Like a great athlete, that venerable city has more size, power, and speed than any other town. A city so nice, they named it twice: Gotham, the Big Apple. If you can make it there, you'll make it anywhere. Considerably smaller and more provincial, two hundred miles to the northeast, Boston comes naturally to its inferiority complex toward New York. America's best and brightest go to school in Boston, then go to work and live in New York. The Hub is quaint, cultural, and alive with fresh new ideas. Boston is Apollo. New York is Zeus.

Through the years, Boston developed into a triple-A farm club for New York. Plays would audition in Boston, then open on Broadway. Boston has the Pops, New York the Philharmonic. Boston has swan boats. New York is where the *Queen Mary* docks. Boston has the Museum of Fine Arts. New York has the Met. Boston has the Cheers bar selling T-shirts. New York has Times Square selling everything. Red Sox owner Harry Frazee—who sold Babe Ruth to the Yankees—loved and lived in New York City. His best friend was New York mayor Jimmy Walker. He cared more about Broadway than baseball, and he liked to say that the best thing about Boston was the train to New York. Frazee's comment and actions played to the worst fears of Bostonians, making the sale of the best ballplayer in history doubly damning. The respective successes and failures of the two baseball teams have only fortified the anxiety New Englanders feel toward New York, and in recent years institutional takeovers have hammered home the point. The *New York Times* bought the family-owned *Boston Globe*. Macy's devoured Jordan Marsh, a venerable Hub department store. And then the Radio City Music Hall Rockettes bounced *The Nutcracker* out of the Wang Center at Christmastime. Nothing is sacred.

The 2003 Red Sox collapse was hardly the first such loss. The franchises are forever linked, and it seemed—at least until 2004—that the Yankees had been getting the better of Boston since Frazee sold them Babe Ruth after the 1919 season. The Red Sox led the Yankees in championships, 5–0, when the deal was made, but Ruth launched a championship run that carried the pinstripe gang through the remainder of the twentieth century. Naturally, much of New York's success came at Boston's expense—thus the Curse of the Bambino.

Ruth's sale was only the beginning, however. The Yankees next hired Edward Barrow, the field manager of the 1918 World Champion Red Sox, making him general manager. Barrow knew all the talent in the Boston organization, and Frazee was only too happy to strip-mine his ball club in exchange for Yankee cash. Waite Hoyt, Harry Harper, Wally Schang, Mike McNally, Everett Scott, Sam Jones, and Joe Bush were next on the Boston–New York shuttle. When the Yankees won their first World Series in 1923, in the brand-new House That Ruth Built, eleven of their twenty-four-man team were former Red Sox. Is there any wonder that generations later, Sox fans bristled at the sight of Wade Boggs and Roger Clemens going to New York and winning championships for the Yankees? And then there was Alex Rodriguez, the Yankee the Sox almost had.

The DiMaggio-Williams debate typified the Yankee–Red Sox rivalry. Joltin' Joe DiMaggio was considered the best ballplayer, Ted Williams the best hitter. DiMaggio played in World Series and won championships, Williams did his best work in All-Star Games and played in only one World Series, hitting .200, all singles. The year Williams hit .406—the last time anyone would hit .400 in the twentieth century, DiMaggio upstaged him by hitting in fifty-six consecutive games and winning the American League MVP Award. Late in his life, DiMaggio insisted on being introduced at all public functions as "baseball's greatest living ballplayer." Williams could not object. Even in death, DiMaggio retained a measure of dignity while Williams's image was forever sullied by two of his children, who had his head severed and his remains frozen in a lab in Scottsdale, Arizona.

The 1949 American League pennant race encapsulated the teams' rivalry in the DiMaggio-Williams years. The Red Sox trailed the Yankees for most of the summer, got hot at the finish, and went to New York for the final two games of the season, needing only one win to clinch the pennant. Boston lost both games, crushing Williams in what would be his final chance to play in another World Series. Broken-hearted Red Sox owner Tom Yawkey did not go back to Yankee Stadium for nineteen years.

There was no parity, no real rivalry for more than two decades after the 1949 season. The Sox simply could not compete. The monster Yankee teams of Mantle, Maris, Berra, and Ford went to the World Series almost every year; the Red Sox battled for the basement rung of the American League along with the likes of the Kansas City Athletics and the Washington Senators. The Yankees laughed at the Sox. Typically, Boston pitcher Tracy Stallard was the foil for Maris's sixty-first homer, in 1961.

The respective fortunes of two teams flipped in 1967 when the hundred-to-one-shot Red Sox stormed the American League pennant while the Yankees floundered in the second division. But one event in '67 opened old wounds and rekindled the dormant rivalry. In June, the Sox and Yankees engaged in a beanball war and bench-clearing brawl at Yankee Stadium. The best part of the show was watching Red Sox shortstop Rico Petrocelli try to get at Yankee pitcher Thad Tillotson while Rico's brother, a New York City policeman, attempted to restore order on the field. Even when one team was down, the passion was still there.

In the early 1970s, both the Sox and Yankees were good again, and you didn't need to dig hard to find the new faces of the rivalry. They were behind the plate, where Yankee Thurman Munson desperately tried to show the world that he was better than Boston's pretty boy Carlton Fisk. The matchup had a Richard Nixon vs. JFK flair to it, with Munson playing the overachieving, sweathog who made himself an important player through hard work and iron will. Mickey Morabito, a Yankee publicist when Munson came of age, observed the best demonstration of Munson's hatred for Fisk. At the start of a Sox-Yankee series, Morabito put together a comparative stat sheet indicating that the Yankee catcher was leading his Red Sox rival in just about every category imaginable. In fact, the only stat in which Fisk led was assists, a relatively minor gauge of a catcher's prowess. Trailing Munson in batting average, homers, RBI, runners thrown out stealing, and everything else, Fisk had two more assists. Enraged at the perceived slight, intent on beating Fisk in *everything,* Munson went to work, dropping third strikes the first three times Red Sox batters struck out. He would let the ball roll loose, pick it up, and fire to first for . . . an assist. The third one put him on top of Fisk in everything, and he turned toward the press box and shook his fist.

Now *that* is a rivalry.

In August of 1973 at Fenway Park, Fisk and Munson brawled after a collision at home plate. Three years later, at Yankee Stadium, fists flew again after Lou Piniella barreled into Fisk at home plate. In that fight, Bill Lee was cheap-shotted by Mickey Rivers and Graig Nettles. Lee's pitching shoulder was shredded, and he called the Yankees "Nazi brownshirts." By this time the Yankees were on their way to the first of three consecutive World Series appearances. Much of their success was rooted in the bullpen, where Sparky Lyle won the Cy Young Award in the championship season of '77. Like Ruth and so many before him, Lyle came to the Yankees from the Red Sox. In exchange, the Sox got Danny Cater, a typical "Fenway hitter" who came to Boston and fell on his face. Can't-Miss Cater never hit more than eight homers in any of his three seasons with the Sox.

The epic 1978 pennant race convinced Red Sox fans that no lead would ever be safe against the Yankees. The Monster-mashing Sox had finished only two and a half games behind in '77 but bolted to a fourteen-game lead by July 20 of '78. New York surged after Billy Martin was fired and replaced by Bob Lemon. Meanwhile the Sox, managed by Don Zimmer, choked like no team in the history of baseball. In September, the storming Yankees came to Fenway and beat the Sox in four straight by an aggregate score of 42–9, pulling into a tie after winning the series finale. The panicked Zimmer refused to start Lee, who had called him a gerbil. Instead, he started rookie lefty Bobby Sprowl, a man who would never win a single game in the majors. When the Yankees beat the Red Sox in the first two games of a series at Yankee

Stadium the following weekend, Sox shortstop Rick Burleson said, "The abuse we have taken and the abuse we must be prepared to take for the entire winter, we richly deserve."

More than a quarter of a century later, those '78 Sox are still taking abuse, particularly Zimmer and pitcher Mike Torrez. Torrez had been a World Series hero with the 1977 Yankees. Naturally, the Sox signed him, and naturally, he disappointed once he put on the Boston uniform. Torrez was the man who threw the home run pitch to Bucky Fucking Dent on October 2, 1978. The *Boston Globe,* which had an evening edition in those days, went to press after the sixth inning. When the Red Sox fans walked out of Fenway after the excruciating 5–4 loss, they saw green *Globe* news boxes that featured the headline RED SOX AHEAD over a six-inning line score. Double ouch.

The Sox and Yanks went their separate ways after the 1978 season. There was little remarkable interaction until the late 1990s, when they established the pattern of one-two finishes at the top of the American League East, with the Yankees taking the first spot in six consecutive seasons. Boston's best chance to even the score came in 1999, when the Sox and Yankees both won division series and faced off in a seven-game ALCS, but the much-hyped bout was a dud, with the Yankees taking the sloppy Sox four games to one. Twice in that series, umpires delivered public apologies after making wrong calls against the Red Sox. But that was the only drama.

Fortifying the Hub's paranoia, Pedro Martinez lost the 1999 American League MVP Award when two writers refused to vote for him anywhere in the top ten because he was a pitcher. One of them was George King of the *New York Post,* who had voted for pitchers in the past.

Sox fans continued to howl and chant "Yankees Suck" at every possible moment, but the charge had little validity as the Yankees kept winning World Series. Yankee fans could always come back with "1918" and send Bostonians on their way, their tails tucked between their legs like Mookie Wilson three-hoppers.

Nothing was going to change the history, it seemed. The old stuff was old stuff—just more muddy water under the Tobin and Willis Avenue bridges. But a new intensity, a new hatred, was evident in 2003

—a spillover from twelve months of insults and competition that truly took the rivalry to a new level. On and off the field, the Red Sox–Yankee conflict was elevated to a story of biblical dimension.

The notion that the teams would meet in a seventh game at Yankee Stadium featuring starting pitchers Pedro Martinez and Roger Clemens was almost too much for fans to grasp. It was one of those rare athletic events that could not possibly be overhyped. It was the first Game 7 of any kind in Yankee Stadium since 1957, and it featured the irresistible story line of Cowboy Up Red Sox, finally ready to overtake the Evil Empire in New York.

On the afternoon of October 16, the Fenway Park groundskeepers foolishly painted the 2003 World Series logo into the grass behind home plate. They would explain that the crew needed to get the field ready early because there would be a Friday World Series workout at the site of the American League champ. But the Yankees had the same dilemma, and they had no intention of painting the logo on the field in the Bronx. A photograph of the embellished Fenway lawn made the rounds at Yankee Stadium while the teams prepared to decide the championship. It was more bad form from Boston.

The Sox brass was behind the batting cage before the game. John Henry talked about the ultimate moment. Young Theo brushed his hand across his scalp, feeling for hair that was no longer there (most of the Red Sox players and front office had shaved their heads for luck and solidarity). Larry Lucchino and his wife, Stacey, stood by the dugout. She was carrying a tiny pool ball in her purse, no. 11. Stacey searched for Grady Little, who had rubbed the ball in his palm before all the other games. For good luck. Stacey asked a reporter to deliver the ball to Grady for the lucky touch. It was done. She put the ball back in her purse.

At the start, it was almost too easy. Clemens had nothing. There was every possibility that this was his final game in the big leagues, and he was rocked for six hits and four runs before he was lifted without getting an out in the fourth inning. Nixon ripped a two-run homer in the second, and Enrique Wilson's error allowed another Boston run. Millar led off the fourth with a homer to make it 4–0. Then Nixon walked and Bill Mueller singled to center, sending Nixon to third. It was Game 7 of the ALCS, and the Sox led, 4–0, with base runners on first and third and no outs in the fourth. Oh, and Pedro was on the mound for Boston. Call off the dogs, piss on the fire—this game was over. Joe Torre came out to get Clemens. There was no discussion. Mike Mussina came in from the bullpen. It was his first relief appearance in a thirteen-year major league career (through 2003, that would be four hundred starts and one trip out of the pen, including postseason). In the stands, the Yankee fans were breaking chair backs in anger. They knew it was over.

Not so, Boston. That's a palindrome, composed by *The New Yorker*'s Roger Angell after the 1986 collapse.

What happened next has been forgotten by most Sox fans. They'll forever wail about Grady and Pedro and roads not taken. But what if the Sox had done the right thing and put the Yanks away when they had the chance? Mussina struck out Varitek on three pitches, then got Johnny Damon to ground into a double play.

These were unforgivable sins. With a runner on third and no outs, Varitek failed to put the ball in play. Then Damon, a speedster, was doubled up. He had grounded into only five double plays all season.

Varitek would carry it with him all winter. The following spring, when an innocent asked Varitek what he did in Game 7, he started with, "Well, I didn't get a guy in from third with less than two outs."

A couple of solo homers off Pedro by Jason Giambi in the fifth and seventh innings cut the lead to 4–2. New York had two men on base and two out when Pedro struck out Alfonso Soriano on the final pitch of the seventh. It was a mid-90s fastball, away, and Pedro reacted as if he had thrown his last pitch of the night. He pointed toward heaven, came to the dugout, accepted the congratulations of his teammates, put on his jacket, and watched David Ortiz homer off David Wells (the third starting pitcher used by Torre in Game 7) to make it 5–2. Physical therapist Chris Correnti told Pedro he was done for the night.

Mike Timlin was warming up in the bullpen. Timlin had been almost perfect in the postseason. He'd allowed one hit and struck out ten in 8.2 innings. That's practically a no-hitter. He was hot. He was ready. The Sox led by three runs. And fragile Pedro was up past his bedtime and had given up three hits and a run in the seventh.

Incredibly, Pedro came on for the eighth. It started innocently enough when Nick Johnson popped to Garciaparra. But then Jeter hit a double to right (misplayed by Nixon) and scored on a single to center by Bernie Williams—5–3. Pedro was up to 115 pitches. Finally Grady went to the mound. Had he checked the stats provided by Young Theo's minions, he'd have known that batters hit .363 off Pedro when he's thrown 105 pitches.

After a short conversation, Grady patted Pedro on the back and left him in the game. John Henry resisted the urge to become the first owner to fire a manager in the eighth inning of a game. In the Great Plains of Lawrence, Kansas, the home of stat guru Bill James, there were reports of spontaneous combustion and silos on fire.

"Pedro Martinez has been our man all year long, and in situations like that, he's the one we want on the mound over anybody we can bring out of the bullpen," Little said later.

Hideki Matsui was next and roped a ground-rule double to right, sending Williams to third. Finally, Posada batted. This was the same Posada Pedro had threatened to hit in the head during Game 3, the guy Pedro called "Dumbo" because of his big ears. The Yankee catcher blooped a double into no-man's-land in shallow center, scoring both runners and knocking Pedro out of the game.

"It was a fastball inside," Posada recalled six months later. "Broke my bat at the handle. It was a 1–2 pitch, and usually he throws me a curveball or changeup. I was trying to stay back. I kept going for second because there was nobody there."

Sox fans didn't need a map to know where this was going. Grady finally went to the pen, but it was too late. The game was tied. Joe Torre had Mariano Rivera (who would throw forty-eight pitches over three innings), and it was just a matter of time before some Yankee hit a walk-off homer. While Wakefield warmed up for the bottom of the eleventh, Jeter whispered to Boone, "Magical things happen here in the Stadium. Ghosts come out in October."

Boone had come into the game as a pinch runner in the eighth. Red Sox scout Ray Boone, his grandfather, was watching the game in his living room in San Diego when he saw Wakefield throw a high knuckleball. "Easiest knuckleball to hit," thought the old scout.

Aaron Boone turned on the meatball and whacked it high and far toward the left field seats. Like John Updike's description of Ted Williams's final homer in 1960, Boone's blast "was in the books while it was still in the sky."

A lot of books. Books about the Red Sox. Books about the Yankees. Books about Curses and Impossible Dreams.

Books like this.

3

A-Rod A-Yankee

T HE 2003 RED SOX ALCS blame pie was never cut into pieces. There would be no slice for Pedro Martinez, even though the Sox dropped to 10–16 against the Yankees in the games started by Pedro. Even though he blew leads of 4–0 and 5–2 in Game 7. Even though he surrendered hits to seven of the last nine batters he faced. No blame for Pedro. Same for Wakefield. Who could find fault with the veteran knuckleballer? He'd beaten the Yankees twice. He was pitching on short rest. He got them out in order in the tenth. Not his fault.

The Boston Cream Blame Pie was hurled into the kind, folksy face of Grady Little. The whole thing. One Nation. One goat. Grady was the Buckner of the new century.

It turns out that Buckner was on Grady's mind when he made his nonmove in the eighth. Before and after the game he recalled players who were worried about a tragic error at the defining moment. He even noted that one of his relievers, Scott Williamson, was showing stress. Williamson had a cold sore on his lip. Months after he was fired, Little told *GQ*, "I had players come and tell me that when they're on the field, they're thinking about those ghosts. They think about Bill Buckner—and not wanting to be a Bill Buckner. And if I got a couple of players tell me that face-to-face, then I know in my heart I got twenty thinking that."

Pulitzer Prize–winning photographer Stan Grossfeld was with Buckner in the goat's new hometown of Boise, Idaho, during the 2003

ALCS. Buckner backed Little's decision, telling Grossfeld, "I probably would have done the same thing. What manager wouldn't stick with his best guy?"

In New England, the Buckner-Grady argument carried into the winter and lives on today. The question was, which ending was more painful? Was it coming within one strike of winning the World Series and then watching the Mets score three runs on three hits and a wild pitch and an error in the bottom of the tenth? Or was it watching the Yankees snatch defeat from the Red Sox in the seventh game of the ALCS? Those who answered '86 rightfully noted that the collapse at Shea was the World Series and, therefore, more devastating. But there was something about having it happen at Yankee Stadium, against the Yankees, that made it doubly painful for Red Sox fans. And many cited Grady as the reason. In '86, the Sox lost because the players did not perform as they were supposed to perform. In 2003, it felt as if the Sox had it taken away by a decision made off the field. Grady didn't make the move and the Sox lost. In many ways, it seemed worse.

Boone's shot triggered perhaps the most remarkable off-season in the history of baseball, a nuclear winter when the Red Sox and Yankees eyeballed each other much like the Americans and the Soviets during the Cuban missile crisis of 1962. It was a Nation vs. an Empire, and it set the table for the stunning events of 2004. It was the hottest of hot stoves, a scalding series of strikes and counterstrikes that eventually left both teams with All-Star rosters and the two heftiest payrolls in baseball history. It drew commentary from the president of the United States and almost every schoolchild in both regions. And who knew that Aaron Boone—who started the whole thing with his walk-off shot in October—would trigger the most remarkable trade of all time in an off-season game of pickup basketball?

The 2003 World Series was anticlimactic, just like the 2004 version. The Sox and Yankees finished their business in the first hour of Friday, October 17, and when the Florida Marlins and Yankees gathered to work out later that day, all the talk was of what had happened in that final hour of Game 7. It was the same story around the cage before and after the first and second games of the World Series in New York. Spotting a reporter from Boston, one he'd never met, director Spike Lee was compelled to say, "They committing suicide up there in Boston still?"

The commissioner of baseball had the same reaction. Bud Selig sidled up to me and said, "What was Grady thinking?"

Outside Yankee Stadium, the World Series T-shirt hawkers were having a field day with the departed Red Sox. There was little talk about the World Series or the Marlins, but there were T-shirts highlighting the New York "Bs" who've tortured the Red Sox over the years —Babe, Bucky, Buckner, and Boone. The most noise generated in Yankee Stadium during the first two games of the Series came when the video board flashed a replay of Boone's homer.

Back home in Brookline, Larry Lucchino said, "Before Game 7, I braced myself for triumph or disaster, but it's become a little more painful as I get a better sense of how unbelievably close we came. I've lived with other disappointments in my life, and I'll live with this, too. With a little heartache. The weather outside now feels like the depths of fall, a metaphor for the baseball season—cold and over for us . . . After that loss, I vowed not to watch the World Series or eat solid food until the World Series was over."

John Henry, as is his custom, communicated via e-mail. Although he once owned the Marlins and had 1 percent of the Yankees, he wrote, "I have no interest in watching this Series. The only interest I currently have in baseball is to prepare for next season. The supportive communication I have received from fans has been shocking and has stirred me greatly—emotionally. Initially, I thought New Englanders would just finally throw up their hands. But their level of commitment and resolve is astonishing and deserves our full attention to moving this franchise forward without a break. It shows you how little I know about the toughness of this region. And it shows me how tough I need to be in making sure we accomplish our goals . . . There isn't anything we wouldn't do for these people. You know, there isn't anything these people wouldn't do for the Red Sox. We owe them."

And so they went about the process of reloading the team for an even bigger push in 2004.

The first move was to fire the manager. Everyone knew Grady was history, but the Sox brass remained respectfully quiet during the

World Series. They weren't happy when Little granted an interview to the *Globe*'s Gordon Edes during the Series and said he wasn't sure he even wanted to come back. Little concluded, "If Grady Little is not back with the Red Sox, he'll be somewhere. I'll be another ghost, fully capable of haunting."

Clearly, Grady knew he wasn't going to be in Fort Myers with the team in February. He'd seen the writing on the clubhouse wall for several months, and he wasn't about to start sucking up to the owners just to keep his job. In September, after one of Manny Ramirez's stunts (Manny called in sick, then went out to the Ritz with Yankee Enrique Wilson), Little complained about Lucchino during a conversation with me in his office. "People have no idea what goes on around here," he said. "The stuff I put up with in that room [clubhouse], most people wouldn't last five minutes in this job." He recounted a conversation with Lucchino in which he'd told the CEO that he didn't like people who listened to sports talk radio. He knew Lucchino was a listener. The CEO made regular appearances on one of the shows that was most critical of Little. Grady didn't care anymore. He wasn't going to beg for his job. He'd averaged ninety-four wins over two years. Take him or leave him.

Respecting the wishes of the commissioner—a commissioner who handed the franchise to them in one of the more outrageous bag jobs in sports history (more on that later)—the Red Sox waited until after the World Series to fire Grady. But they didn't wait long. The Series ended on a Saturday night and Grady was gone by Monday, October 27—which happened to be the seventeenth anniversary of the Red Sox Game 7 World Series loss to the Mets. It also turned out to be the same date on which the Sox would erase the Curse one year later.

Not bothering to hang around for his dismissal, Grady had already gone home to Pinehurst, North Carolina. The Sox forwarded his mail, and Grady chuckled when he opened an envelope (no name, no return address) that held World Series tickets for Fenway games never played. An attached note said, "Thanks, Grady."

Joseph Mazzone, a graduate of Notre Dame and a Sox fan who worked at the Pine Street Inn, a homeless shelter in Boston, found his own way to deal with the Red Sox manager. Drawing on Voldemort, the bad wizard of the Harry Potter books, he decided that Grady Little forevermore would be "He-Who-Must-Not-Be-Named."

"I just couldn't take it anymore," said Mazzone. "Just the mention of his name sent me into fits. So I decided this was the best way to deal with that."

Two days after He-Who-Must-Not-Be-Named was fired, the Sox dropped another bomb, placing Ramirez on irrevocable waivers. The maneuver was telling. It sent word that the Red Sox were fed up with their obtuse slugger, and it dared the power-poor Yankees to snatch him without giving up any players. The price was $95 million—what Ramirez had remaining on the final five years of his contract. There was speculation in the media that the Sox waived Ramirez to accommodate Manny and his greedy agent, Jeff Moorad. Whatever the motive, no team claimed him, which enabled the Sox brass to tell Ramirez and his agent, "We can't even give you away. So stop talking all this nonsense about playing for the Yankees."

In late November the Sox still hadn't named a manager, but they made headlines with the announcement that the club had come to terms on a contract extension with Arizona Diamondback Curt Schilling, completing a trade for him in exchange for young pitchers Casey Fossum and Brandon Lyon plus a pair of minor leaguers. It was a stunning development in the Red Sox–Yankee wars. All of baseball knew that Schilling was on the market, and the Yankees had made a pitch for him—he'd been instrumental in beating New York in the 2001 World Series. When it first became clear that the D-Backs were going to trade him, Schilling said he would pitch for only the Phillies or the Yankees. But when the Yanks talked with Arizona, owner Jerry Colangelo sent word that he wanted Alfonso Soriano and Nick Johnson in exchange. It was a preposterous demand, aimed at making the Yankees disappear from the Schilling sweeps. Why? Retribution. A year earlier, Arizona had come to terms on a deal with free agent lefty David Wells, only to see Wells back out of the agreement after a last-minute, big-dollar push by the Yankees. This turned out to be one instance in which Steinbrenner's steamroller operation came back to bite him in the butt.

Naturally, there was glee throughout Red Sox Nation. Getting Schilling meant that Boston would have a top-three pitching rotation of Pedro Martinez, Schilling, and Derek Lowe. Even though Pedro had melted down against the Yankees and Lowe's win total was largely thanks to tremendous run support, the Sox suddenly could face an opponent with three All-Star pitchers who'd been twenty-game winners in the big leagues. The idea that the Sox had stolen Schilling from the Yankees only made the deal that much sweeter. Plus, Boston had given up very little for the five-time All-Star righty.

Moving to Boston completed the circle for Schilling. Born in Anchorage, Alaska, he went to high school in Arizona and was scouted and signed by Red Sox scout Ray Boone. Boone saw Schilling pitching for Yavapai Junior College in Prescott, Arizona. "He was 6-5 and only about 185 pounds, but he threw in the high 80s back then," Boone remembered in the spring of 2004. "I figured he'd throw harder when he put on some weight, but I never thought he'd be throwing in the high 90s like he did."

Schilling was the Red Sox second-round pick in the 1986 draft and remembers watching the final game of the '86 World Series at a Hooters restaurant. As part of the Boston organization, he figured he might be in for some World Series loot if the Sox won it all. Schilling was a late bloomer, even in the minors, and when the Sox were going for it all in 1988, GM Lou Gorman dealt Schilling and Brady Anderson to the Baltimore Orioles in exchange for established starter Mike Boddicker. Both Anderson and Schilling went on to become All-Star players, but Sox fans never bashed Gorman about that deal because Boddicker pitched well for two Boston teams that finished first in the American League East.

The 2003 Schilling negotiations, like everything else that happened over the winter, involved the voice of Uncle Bud Selig. Needing to know if they could entice Schilling into a long-term deal before giving up any players for him, the Red Sox asked Selig's permission to negotiate with Schilling while he was still under contract with Arizona. Ever accommodating to the Red Sox, Selig allowed a short window of opportunity; then, at the request of the Red Sox, he extended the time by twenty-four hours when the deadline neared. Young Theo reached a contract agreement with Schilling during a Thanksgiving visit to his home in Paradise Valley, Arizona. The Yankees and their fans cried foul, again citing Selig's favoritism toward the Red Sox, but they could do nothing to stop the trade. It was far different from the contentious Jose Contreras talks in Nicaragua one year earlier, when Young Theo allegedly trashed his hotel room after the Yankees topped his bid. This time it was the Yankees breaking up the furniture.

Again it was USA-USSR, circa early 1960s. Sox fans tried to imagine Steinbrenner's removing his shoe and banging it on the dinner table at Malio's in Tampa—the 2004 equivalent of Soviet premier Nikita Khrushchev's tantrum during a meeting of the United Nations General Assembly in 1960.

A big part of the agreement involved getting Schilling to waive his no-trade clause. The Sox wanted Schilling, but they also wanted to stay flexible. If the Sox gave Schilling a no-trade, it would have prohibited them from dealing Ramirez. Manny's pact included a clause stating that he could not be traded if the Red Sox extended a no-trade clause to another player. Since the Sox were already in talks with the Rangers about a trade for American League MVP Alex Rodriguez, there was no way they were going to limit their possibilities—not even for Schilling. Learning of the club's dilemma, the veteran pitcher relented. He agreed to a two-year extension with an option for a third year that could be triggered if certain performance levels were met. The total was approximately $38 million. Schilling also asked for a clause that would pay him a $2 million bonus and trigger the third year if the Red Sox won the World Series. Epstein agreed, and the clause was approved by Major League Baseball, but it has since been banned as an incentive. Months later, when the Sox were happily paying the $2 million World Series bonus, Epstein remembered seeing a copy of *Negotiating for Dummies* in Schilling's den.

At his introductory press conference on November 28, Schilling got off to a great start with Red Sox fans when he said, "I guess I hate the Yankees now."

Thus began a yearlong ride of unbridled popularity for the big righty. Different from other big league ballplayers in almost every way, Schilling charmed Red Sox Nation by visiting fan Web sites during his negotiations with Epstein. He was online with fans at the height of the contract talks and noted their tone, saying, "They all had their motives. Most of them being screwing the Yankees . . . I have been a part of a Yankee matchup with other clubs, but the Yankee–Red Sox rivalry transcends sports. It's so much bigger than everything else in sports, and being a part of that was certainly an attraction in all of this . . . I want to be part of bringing the first World Series in modern history to Boston."

Schilling made still more friends when he immediately donated a half-million dollars to the Jimmy Fund. He also expressed reverence for Pedro Martinez, even though he had called Pedro a "punk" after witnessing Martinez's antics in the third game of the ALCS. No doubt about it, this guy was going to be an interesting character to have at Fenway Park in 2004.

He turned out to be a power broker in the Red Sox managerial search as well. Schilling had played for Terry Francona in Philadelphia, and he made it clear that he would embrace the prospect of pitching for Francona again. The son of Tito basically locked up the job the day the Schilling trade was announced.

In their short search for a skipper, the Sox interviewed Francona, Dodger coach Glenn Hoffman, Anaheim bench coach Joe Madden, and Texas coach DeMarlo Hale. They may have also interviewed the Mets' former manager Bobby Valentine, but the stories vary. Lucchino placed a call to Valentine while the Sox were engaged in their search. According to Lucchino, it was not a job interview. Valentine, who was already committed to managing in Japan, claimed he took himself out of the running by refusing to answer Lucchino's question about what he would have done with Pedro in the eighth inning at Yankee Stadium. Valentine claimed his reluctance to malign Little's judgment put an end to his talks with Boston. Lucchino said the question was asked, but he denied that it was any kind of a litmus test for managing the Red Sox in 2004.

Epstein would later send a missive to the Red Sox owners in which he explained, "We were looking for a manager who would embrace the exhaustive preparation that the organization demands . . . By using video and computer simulations, we attempted to discover how each candidate would react to game-speed strategic decisions . . . Given the demands of the media and our players, we sought a manager who would be able to communicate with all constituencies in a positive and intelligent manner . . . We were looking for a 'partner' not a 'middle-manager.' . . . Terry Francona quickly emerged from the applicant pool. His experiences (Philadelphia manager, Cleveland front office, Texas/Oakland bench coach) gave him a remarkable understanding of our vision. His preparation, energy, integrity, and communication skills are exceptional."

A week after Schilling was acquired, the Red Sox again called the media to the 406 Club, on the fourth floor of Fenway Park, and announced that Francona had been hired as the forty-fourth manager in ball club history (giving the Sox one more manager than U.S. presidents). Francona characterized the moment as "the most exciting day of my baseball life."

It was polite of the Red Sox to interview other candidates, and the session with Hale fulfilled Selig's demand that minorities be considered for all managerial vacancies, but ultimately Francona was the only candidate. By Epstein's admission, "He blew us away." Francona was young (forty-four) and embraced the stat sheet game plan that was so important to John Henry, Young Theo, and the minions. He'd been a bench coach with Billy Beane's Moneyball Oakland A's in 2003 and attacked the game with the kind of preparation that was so important to Boston's new front office. He also had the advantage of having managed Nomar Garciaparra (along with Michael Jordan) in the Arizona fall league in 1994. On the downside, Francona had compiled a 285–363 (.440) record with the Phillies in his only major league managing stint and was perceived as too soft. The day he was hired, Epstein admitted that his only question about Francona was, "Is the guy too nice?"

Francona initially donned Red Sox jersey no. 16. It was made famous by Jim Lonborg in 1967 and was also worn by the Nutty Professor, manager Joe Kerrigan, during the dark days of 2001. When the season started, Francona switched to 47. But Francona's jersey was almost always covered by a sweatshirt.

The new manager, asked about the unique pressures of the Red Sox job, answered, "Think about it for a second. I've been released from six teams. I've been fired as a manager. I've got no hair. I've got a nose that's three times too big for my face, and I grew up in a major league clubhouse. My skin's pretty thick. I'll be okay."

The day the Red Sox named Francona, the Yankees traded first baseman Nick Johnson, outfielder Juan Rivera, and lefty Randy Choate to Montreal for right-handed starter Javier Vazquez. The Yanks had also acquired two former All-Star relievers in Paul Quantrill and Tom Gordon (also both former Red Sox). And they were close to getting free agent speedster Kenny Lofton and slugger Gary Sheffield. New York was hardly standing still while the Red Sox made plans. But with all the additions, there was considerable subtraction from the Empire roster. Clemens had officially "retired" and was never part of the plan, then big-game lefty free agent Andy Pettitte stunned his bosses, taking less money to return home and pitch for the Houston Astros. In the end, Pettitte got $31.5 million over three years. The Yankees had offered $39 million in the final hours, but it was too late. Pettitte was hurt that the club hadn't made more of an effort sooner and committed to going home. It was a major blow to the Yankees. Pettitte had been one of the great postseason pitchers of his generation and had been part of the Yankee championship run that started in 1996. He went 13–8 in thirty postseason starts. He was homegrown. He was left-handed. And the fans loved him.

Later it was learned that the Red Sox had polluted the waters for the Yankees by offering Pettitte $52 million over four years at the start of his free agency period. Pettitte refused to even consider the offer. He said he couldn't do that to his teammates and he couldn't do it to Yankee fans. But it's likely that the whopping offer from the Red Sox further convinced him that he was unappreciated in the Big Apple. The New York press blasted Steinbrenner for letting Pettitte get away.

The Yankees responded by trading Jeff Weaver for Dodger righty Kevin Brown. Brown had 197 career wins but had been on the disabled list nine times since 1990. He had two years left on a seven-year, $105 million contract.

Vazquez, Pettitte, Brown, Weaver, Johnson, Quantrill, Gordon, Lofton, Sheffield. These were big names, proven stars with hefty contracts. Meanwhile, the Sox were trying to persuade Oakland free agent closer Keith Foulke to come to Boston. It was a frenzy. The Sox and Yankees were in a league of their own, and the winter stove was too hot to touch. It was dizzying for New England sports fans, who'd been trying to concentrate on the local NFL team, which was on its way to winning twenty-one straight games and the Super Bowl for the second time in three years.

The magnificent backdrop, of course, was the (at first) clandestine, then very public, courtship of Alex Rodriguez.

Red Sox–Yankee folklore holds that owners Tom Yawkey and Dan Topping got drunk one night and agreed to swap Ted Williams and Joe DiMaggio. The clarity of the morning light KO'd the deal—which would have been the biggest trade in baseball history. In the winter of 2003–2004 the Sox came close to making the biggest trade in baseball history, backed away over several million dollars, then watched in horror as the Yankees pulled the trigger quickly on a deal for the same guy.

Boston's winter-long hunt for Rodriguez started just three days after Game 7 in New York. While the Yankees were getting ready to play the second game of the World Series, Texas Ranger owner Tom Hicks called the Red Sox and asked if they would be interested in parting with Nomar and some young pitchers in exchange for Rodriguez. Hicks was trying to get out from under A-Rod's ten-year, quarter-billion-dollar contract.

Coming off an MVP season, Rodriguez was without a doubt the best player in baseball—he was only twenty-eight, a Gold Glover, a seven-time All-Star, and he'd reached the three-hundred-homer plateau faster than any player in history—but he carried the richest contract in sports history while the Rangers kept finishing last. Hicks wanted out.

After the World Series, the Sox told Hicks they would not part with Nomar in any deal for A-Rod, but they'd like to trade Ramirez, wanting to free themselves from the weight of Manny's $160 million contract. Trading Nomar for A-Rod was out of the question because the Sox would end up paying two players, Ramirez and Rodriguez, $45 million per season. No team, not even the Yankees, wanted to take on the contracts of both Rodriguez and Ramirez. Meanwhile, the Yankees had already told the Rangers that they had no interest in A-Rod. They had a shortstop named Derek Jeter. Texas's options were limited. Virtually no other team in baseball had the need and the resources to assume Rodriguez's contract.

The Red Sox were not confident about signing Garciaparra. He'd turned down one offer (four years, $60 million) in spring training and again at the end of the season. When subsequent Nomar negotiations deteriorated, the Sox renewed their quest to trade for Rodriguez, asking the commissioner for permission to negotiate with Rodriguez. It was another extraordinary request by the Boston brass, but Selig agreed for two reasons: he wanted to get Major League Baseball's best player out of the dead zone in Texas, and he'd do anything to help the men he'd anointed to lead the Boston Red Sox. On a Sunday in early November, Alex Rodriguez and his wife, Cynthia, had lunch at John Henry's Boca Raton mansion. In early December, when talks intensified between the Sox and the Rangers, Hicks leaked details of the Henry-Rodriguez meeting, and the media jumped on the story. A wounded Garciaparra took time out from his honeymoon (he had married soccer star Mia Hamm) to call sports radio talk station WEEI in Boston. He again claimed he wanted to stay in Boston, even though he and his agent had repeatedly turned down offers from the Sox. Host Dale Arnold asked Garciaparra if he considered the Sox talks with Rodriguez a "slap in the face." Nomar said, "The best way to answer that is to ask you guys if you wake up one day and start reading your station is interviewing people to take your spot, to replace you. How would you feel about that? How would I take it? Am I right?"

Garciaparra was not totally forthcoming. He pretended to be surprised by the news, even though the Red Sox had kept him informed from the beginning. The Sox pursued Rodriguez only when it was clear Garciaparra was not going to sign, but Epstein had dozens of conversations with Nomar's agent, Arn Tellem, throughout the process. At one point Garciaparra even got involved, warning Epstein to be careful, claiming A-Rod could be two-faced.

After Nomar's public plea, Tellem went on the offensive and spoke of the shoddy treatment his client had received from Red Sox management. He used the word "disingenuous." This provoked a surprisingly strong response from John Henry, who characterized Tellem's complaint as "the height of hypocrisy." Inside the walls of Fenway, it was known that Henry was not enamored of Garciaparra's dour personality. The owner found himself repeatedly rebuffed in his attempts to get to know his star shortstop, and signals from Tellem indicated that Nomar was going to be impossible to sign. It was presumed that Garciaparra wanted to play on the West Coast, far from the prodding Boston media that interrupted his routines.

After Thanksgiving, Hicks and Lucchino agreed that Henry would be the best man to talk with Rodriguez about restructuring his contract to make it more favorable to Boston. While Henry was with Rodriguez, Epstein was busy working on other important matters. On December 13, he announced that Foulke was on board. He had courted the closer with great gusto, even taking the hockey-loving Foulke to a Bruins game. It all paid off, and the Sox filled one of their big holes, picking up the man who'd led the American League in saves. Then Theo went to the baseball winter meetings in New Orleans and worked out a deal to send Garciaparra and Williamson to the White Sox for slugging outfielder Magglio Ordonez and a couple of pitching prospects. There it was: A-Rod at short and Ordonez in left instead of Nomar at short and Manny in left.

On Wednesday, December 17, the Sox had everything in place. The A-Rod–Manny trade was done, pending approval of the Major League Baseball Players Association and the commissioner. Uncle Bud would pose no problem. He was dying to get Rodriguez out of Texas and back on national television. But union lawyer Gene Orza was another story. A likable fellow and a student of baseball trivia, Orza was maniacal in his devotion to the basic agreement and considered the devaluation of any player contract to be something on a par with amputation. Orza looked at what Henry, Lucchino, and Rodriguez had done to the $179 million (over seven years) remaining on A-Rod's deal with Texas and held his nose. In an effort to avoid paying a luxury tax and with the help of Rodriguez, who wanted out of Arlington, the Sox had creatively lowered the annual value of Rodriguez's contract from $27 million to $20.75 million. It was not going to fly.

No way.

"He is subject to the rules of the association," said Orza. "We cannot allow clubs to downwardly negotiate contracts . . . I like A-Rod. I've known him since he was a draftee, but it makes no difference."

Orza made a counterproposal. His offer and what the Sox wanted represented a gap of $16 million. Lucchino ripped the union. Orza thought the Sox CEO was trying to drive a wedge between the union and the union's best player. Hicks was furious that the Sox wouldn't

budge. Selig closed the seventy-two-hour window of negotiations be-
tween the Red Sox and Rodriguez. Two days before Christmas, the deal
was dead. Hicks sent a letter to Texas season-ticket holders stating that
Rodriguez would be the Rangers' Opening Day shortstop in 2004. The
Rangers later held a press conference, naming A-Rod team captain.
Happy New Year, Texas baseball fans.

Then, on January 16, 2004, Yankee third baseman Aaron Boone
went to a gym in Newport Beach, California, to play some pickup basketball. Boone hadn't played any off-season basketball to that point
but felt he needed a workout. Early in the game, while leaping to tap
the ball to a teammate, another player crashed into him, rupturing the
anterior cruciate ligament in his left knee. To his credit, Boone did not
lie or attempt to hide the injury from the Yankees. Citing a violation of
his (standard) contract, the Yankees terminated his $5.75 million pact
for 2004 and paid him a required buyout of $917,553. They immedi-
ately started looking for a third baseman. In the meantime, their new
slugger Sheffield offered to play third.

While all this was going on, another major sports story was devel-
oping in New England. The Patriots were putting together the longest
winning streak in NFL history and were en route to a second Super
Bowl victory in three years. On the last Sunday in September of 2003,
while the Red Sox were playing their final game of a magical regular
season, the Patriots had lost to the Redskins at FedEx Field in Washington. They would not lose another game (excluding preseason) until
after the Red Sox won the 2004 World Series.

The Patriots started their streak on the day the Red Sox were beating the A's in the 2003 Division Series. The crowd at Foxborough's
Gillette Stadium was truly conflicted. In the middle of a 38–30 win
over Tennessee, the New England fans cheered when a penalty nulli-
fied a touchdown by the Pats' Troy Brown. Why? Because the fans were
watching Johnny Damon homer against the Oakland A's on their
mini-TVs at the same moment the touchdown was recalled. Later,
when the Titans regained the lead on a Steve McNair touchdown, the
fans cheered again because the Sox had just taken a 5–4 lead at Fenway.
"They can't cheer when the other team scores," complained New England's All-Pro lineman Richard Seymour. "I love the support, but
they've got to flip it around a little. Cheer when we score."

It was not the last time the baseball team would steal the Patriots' thunder. The A-Rod trade talks consumed a few months of the Super Bowl campaign, and the Pats repeatedly found themselves digging out from under the avalanche of Red Sox coverage. A Patriot official sent a letter to the editor of the *Boston Globe,* requesting more coverage, but there was nothing the team could do about the burning phone lines on local sports talk shows. The Red Sox were in season, even though it was December, and the Patriots were on their way to winning twenty-one consecutive games and another Super Bowl. At the baseball meetings in New Orleans, Epstein—feeling a little guilty about all the news he was generating and perhaps trying to make some progress under the radar—implored the baseball scribes to tell their editors to devote more space to the Patriots. Boston was bracing for what would be the coldest January in 106 years, but baseball's winter fires were hotter than ever.

Patriot quarterback Tom Brady didn't mind the region's Red Sox fixation. He went to the same California (Junipero Serra) high school as Barry Bonds and had been drafted as a catcher by the Montreal Expos in 1995. He frequently wore a Red Sox cap to work and was following the A-Rod negotiations just like every other member of the Nation. Two days before winning his second Super Bowl MVP, Brady was asked if another Super Bowl trophy would make up for what had happened to the Red Sox in October.

"I think baseball's a different thing in New England," he said. "For as much as we won last time, it's still Red Sox country."

New England needed a lift, and the Patriots delivered. They were the anti–Red Sox. They eschewed the star system. They refused to celebrate until the final game was won. Not since Larry Bird's Celtics of 1984–1986 had a Boston team won two championships in three seasons. (The Sox, of course, had turned the trick in 1916 and '18.) No ego. No entitlement. The Pats furnished every coach, parent, and teacher with a championship model to define the essence of team play. Their 32–29 last-second Super Bowl XXXVIII victory over the Carolina Panthers was rewarded with a million-fan march at City Hall Plaza.

Ten days later, Bostonians woke up on a Saturday morning to hear of an odd rumor that had appeared on a *Newsday* Web site. It was

February 14, and the Long Island paper was claiming that the Yankees had acquired Alex Rodriguez in exchange for slugging second baseman Alfonso Soriano. The paper said A-Rod had agreed to play third base. By early afternoon the story had been confirmed by several major league sources. It made for instant folklore. Ruth to the Yankees. Lyle to the Yankees. Dent into the screen. Clemens to the Yankees. New England burning while Grady slept. And now A-Rod to the Yankees all because Aaron Fucking Boone decided to play a little pickup basketball. There were broken hearts throughout Red Sox Nation . . . on Valentine's Day.

"It's clearly a blow," said Lucchino, who was being universally whipped in the media as the man who bolloxed the A-Rod–Boston deal. "I think it clearly keeps the Yankees as the favorite . . . It just looks like the Yankees have no limit."

Worse, the Yankees pulled off the deal in four days of secret talks after the Red Sox fumbled a public negotiation that lasted over two months and insulted Boston's two best everyday players. Kevin Millar was already on record, talking about A-Rod's being an "upgrade" over Nomar. Now A-Rod was in New York, and Millar and Nomar were together again in the Boston clubhouse. Meanwhile, Oakland's Miguel Tejada got six years and $72 million from the Orioles, and suddenly Garciaparra was holding the hammer again.

Tim Kurkjian of ESPN called A-Rod for Soriano "the biggest baseball trade of all time." In Boston it was viewed as the greatest blow since Babe Ruth was shipped to the Yankees for cash. In Texas, Rodriguez had even worn the same number as Ruth. Everyone had an opinion. On hand to start the Daytona 500 in Florida, President Bush, a former owner of the Rangers, told ESPN, "I was just as surprised as the Yankee fans and the Boston Red Sox fans when I opened up my paper today. It obviously is a big deal . . . A-Rod's a great player, and the Yanks are going to be a heck of a team with him in the infield."

Yeesh. The Yankees and Rangers had a pulled off a megatrade, and even the leader of the free world knew that it was all about the Red Sox.

ESPN's Chris Berman, living in the Connecticut-Switzerland zone where Sox and Yankee fans meet, noticed the different versions in the next day's newspapers. "It was like reading World War II battle accounts from French and German newspapers—two completely different takes on the same event," he said. "In Boston, it was the St. Valentine's Day Massacre and in New York it was *Field of Dreams*." Berman put a rubber band around the newspapers and stored them for posterity.

The Red Sox had some explaining to do to their fans, but there was no blaming Grady this time. According to Lucchino, Boston broke away from the A-Rod blockbuster over a difference of $25 million to $30 million. The New York papers were claiming that the Sox walked over $12 million. Peter Gammons was running around ESPN saying that Lucchino blew it by insulting Orza and attempting to put A-Rod at odds with the union.

"That's ludicrous," countered Lucchino. "The only issue was expense. The deal was what we could afford and what we couldn't afford."

Ultimately, John Henry, who holds the purse strings, was the one who'd killed the deal over money, and it was the Sox owner who came forward with the strongest reaction when the A-Rod trade to New York was officially approved by the commissioner. Lucchino had never believed the A-Rod–Boston deal would happen. That's why he kept his A-Rod trade notes in a file labeled "Hail Mary."

After the deal was announced, the Sox were ridiculed from coast to coast. Randy Galloway of the *Fort Worth Star-Telegram* wrote, "The biggest doofus organization in all of this turns out to be the Boston Red Sox. Those people had A-Rod locked up and locked away before Christmas. That deal was done, period . . . But somehow, some way, Boston blew it. A very doable deal died. And then, in the ultimate Curse of the Bambino, A-Rod ends up in the hands of the hated King George."

The *New York Times* weighed in with a front-page story by Murray Chass: SUMMER OR WINTER, THE YANKEES SHOW THE RED SOX HOW TO WIN.

The acquisition of Rodriguez was a tremendous boost to the Yankee lineup, but it also fortified the long-standing fears of Red Sox fans, trained to believe the Yankees would always win. And the Sox had no one to blame but themselves. No one could have predicted that by the time the 2004 season ended, it would seem the deal actually worked to Boston's favor.

On February 18, Henry made his first public comments in the form of an early morning e-mail sent to the media. He said that baseball needed a salary cap "to deal with a team that has gone so insanely far beyond the resources of all the other teams . . . Baseball doesn't have an answer for the Yankees."

From Tampa, Steinbrenner blasted back with both barrels. "We understand that John Henry must be embarrassed, frustrated, and disappointed by his failure in this transaction," said the Boss. "Unlike the Yankees, he chose not to go the extra distance for his fans in Boston . . . It is time to get on with life and forget the sour grapes."

By 5 P.M. that day, for the second time in just over a year, the commissioner ordered both parties to stop insulting each other. After talking with Selig, Henry described him as "apoplectic."

It was a not a proud day in Red Sox Nation. The absurdity of Henry's complaint was boundless. His memo accomplished what was thought to be impossible: he'd made Steinbrenner look reasonable. The idea of the Red Sox complaining about Yankee spending was ridiculous to the other teams in baseball. Boston was able to outspend other teams to acquire Schilling. They outbid the A's for Oakland's closer, just as they'd taken Johnny Damon from Oakland years earlier. The Sox would have a $124 million payroll by Opening Day. They were not the ones to carry the torch for the have-nots of baseball.

Steinbrenner honored the quote embargo, but that didn't stop him from going on *Letterman* that same night with a top ten list of his own. Among the top ten good things about being a New York Yankee was George's saying, "With me, there's very little pressure to win."

Three days after his unfortunate e-mail, Henry strolled into the Red Sox minor league complex, at the dead end of Edison Road in Fort Myers, Florida, and said he was amused by Steinbrenner's remarks. "I don't want to equate him with Don Rickles, but when Don Rickles insults you, you laugh . . . I think he takes everything personally. It's one of the differences between us."

The *New York Post* reported Steinbrenner's reaction: "I consider it a great compliment because Rickles is somebody I really like. He is funny and a warm and caring person. As far as Henry is concerned, he reminds me of Ray Bolger, the scarecrow in *The Wizard of Oz*."

Brian Cashman, the young, measured Yankee GM, shrugged and said, "It's real. The old guys talk about the seventies, when the players hated the players on the other team and the fans hated the fans. In the eighties and nineties, the rivalry was there, but it wasn't as dramatic as it is now. You see the banter back and forth between the ownership groups and whether it's a groundskeeper getting involved or the fans or the owners, the bottom line is that everyone on either side of the fence is extremely passionate about their club, and that's certainly carrying over in the public arena now with comments. The comments normally haven't been in the front office in the past, and that's certainly turned up the heat even that much more."

Alex Rodriguez, the cause of this series of insults, did little to make Red Sox fans feel better. After his first workout with the Yankees in Tampa, he fielded questions about the Red Sox bid and Henry's reaction.

"I'm sure there's frustration there," he said. "They've built a wonderful team over there, and they've made some great moves. We got close. A couple times. All I can say is that I really enjoyed meeting Theo and spending time with Mr. Henry . . . but I'm glad I'm a New York Yankee."

He admitted that the Sox had greased the skids for his trade to New York. "I think a lot of the landscape was already in place. We already knew the obstacles going into it. I wouldn't blame Boston for this, it was just more of a novel experience for everyone involved with Texas, Boston, and our group. And I think New York benefited some from that."

Cashman seconded that emotion: "No doubt, the Red Sox negotiation helped us. Their negotiation, which was very public, made it very helpful as a guideline, knowing what concessions were possible with the union about what would and would not be prudent."

He might as well have just said, Not only are you fat, you're ugly. It was as if the Red Sox had struggled mightily to loosen the top of the bottle, only to watch the Yankees grab the A1 and pour it over the choice porterhouse.

Diplomatic Rodriguez talked about how much he loved East Coast baseball: "If you didn't like watching New York–Boston last year, there's something wrong with you. I can remember jumping out of my couch three or four times in that series. It was just awesome to watch. I wished and dreamed about someday being able to play in games that meant that much. And the dream is here sooner than I thought . . . I love Boston. I hope if they boo, I hope they don't boo too loudly because all my in-laws will be there. That was almost. Almost. We almost went there."

Ten months later he would get his wish. The perfect player with the Whitney Houston smile would be in the middle of the perfect storm of a Red Sox–Yankee seven-game playoff series. And he would be involved in a couple of key plays, one that would tarnish his reputation and convince Sox fans that there was a new Curse—the Curse of A-Rod.

But on that splendid February morning in Tampa, the presence of Rodriguez in pinstripes was a mighty blow to Red Sox Nation. The wild winter of 2003–2004 was over. It was time for both teams to get back to work on the field.

4

Spring Break for Young Theo

T HE RED SOX EQUIPMENT truck pulled out of Fenway Park
on Monday, February 16, two days after the Nation had been
stunned by the A-Rod trade. Across the land, Sox players were
issuing diplomatic quotes about the unfortunate development. They
knew it would affect the competitive balance in the American League
East. They also knew it would dent the fragile psyche of a fan base still
in shock from the season ending in October. It was not the boost the
ball club wanted at the start of the 2004 season.

Still, Theo Epstein wasn't panicking. His whole life—all thirty
years—had prepared him for this moment, and he felt ready for the
challenge. He'd never quite get over the way it ended in 2003, but the
feeling-sorry period had long expired. Epstein and his twin brother,
Paul, were born on December 29, 1973, the same year that the American League introduced the designated hitter. The boys were the proud
progeny of Leslie and Ilene Epstein and grandsons of Philip Epstein,
who wrote *Casablanca* with his identical twin, Julius. Leslie Epstein is a
novelist and the director of the creative writing program at Boston
University. He moved to Boston in 1978, just in time to witness the
great Red Sox fold. He is also an avowed Yankee-hater, not above taking a few broadsides at Steinbrenner. He has said that rooting for the
Yankees is like voting Republican. Theo's mom, Ilene, is also a twin,
and runs The Studio, a fashionable women's clothing store in Brookline, Massachusetts, with her sister, Sandy, and their friend Marcie
Brawer. Theo is fond of telling people that he saw a naked woman for

the first time at The Studio. Theo's older sister, Anya, is a screenwriter who wrote scripts for the NBC series *Homicide: Life on the Street.* She is married to a Yankee fan, and their son, Theo's nephew, wears both Red Sox and Yankee garb. Taller and balder than his famous twin, Paul Epstein is a social worker at Brookline High School.

Children of learning, children of some privilege, Theo, Paul, and Anya grew up in a spacious apartment on Parkman Street in Brookline, not far from the Beales Street birthplace of John Fitzgerald Kennedy. It was closer still to Fenway Park, where the Red Sox of the 1970s featured sluggers named Rice, Lynn, Fisk, and Evans. The twins attended about fifteen home games a year, earning their citizenship in Red Sox Nation before it was recognized in the U.N. Charter. When they couldn't go, they watched on television, and their sister remembers battling for TV time to view her one hour of *Little House on the Prairie.*

It was not unusual for Theo and Paul to disrupt the neighbors downstairs during a game. More than once, the folks in the apartment below banged on the pipes to get the twins to calm down. One such night was Saturday, October 25, 1986, when the Red Sox were on the verge of beating the New York Mets to win the World Series. The twins were twelve, and Leslie and Ilene were down the street at a dinner party while the boys watched in the den, waiting for that final out.

"We'd been to Game 3 of the World Series and Game 7 of the ALCS," remembered Theo. "We were biting our nails with every pitch. In the last inning, when we got the first two outs, we talked about what we'd do for the final out. The plan was to be in midair, unconnected to this earth. We had a little couch against the back wall of the den and we stood on that, waiting for the final out. We figured it would be a popup or something like that, and we could be in midair for the celebration when the ball came down. We were on that couch for about forty minutes, and when the ball rolled through Buckner's legs we just crumbled to the floor, holding our stomachs in disbelief. We sat for a few minutes and then the phone rang, and it was my dad's cousin Jimmy calling from California to taunt us."

The twins never had a yard because the Epsteins didn't live in a single-family house. They could walk to the Amory Street playground, but more often they improvised, creating a ballpark out of the back lot of the nearby Beacon Street Holiday Inn. Sam Kennedy, who would later join Theo in the executive offices at Fenway, was a boyhood pal who found joy in the parking lots of toney Brookline. The boys played in the standard youth baseball leagues and were Brookline Pony League city champs, playing for a team called the Yankees. It was in soccer that Theo enjoyed athletic success in high school. The Brookline Warriors made it to the state tournament in Theo's senior season (1990–1991). His baseball career was just about over by then. He was a .250 hitter on Brookline's JV teams at Amory Street, but at the varsity level he was usually on the bench, occasionally pitching or sometimes subbing in the middle infield for his pal Kennedy.

"Mostly he coached third base," recalled Kennedy.

In the fall of 1991, Epstein enrolled at Yale, continuing on the path that led to his being the youngest general manager in the history of baseball and the architect of the 2004 Red Sox. He claims his greatest athletic accomplishment was kicking a wind-aided 53 yard field goal while goofing around with Padres associates at La Jolla High School.

To understand Theo, one must know something about two institutions and two individuals: Yale University and the Baltimore Orioles, and Larry Lucchino and Dr. Charles Steinberg. These places and people seem unrelated, but the learning curve of Theo Epstein connects the dots, making them the places and people most responsible for his development.

Certainly Yale needs no introduction, not even in a book about baseball. Founded in 1701, it ranks on any list as one of the top five universities in America. Both presidential candidates in 2004, George W. Bush and John F. Kerry, graduated from Yale. Moreover, Yale has an impressive baseball tradition. Thomas A. Yawkey, who rescued the Red Sox in 1933 and rebuilt Fenway Park, graduated from Yale in 1925. In 1948, a dying Babe Ruth visited the campus to donate his papers to the university. There's a familiar photo of the great Bambino presenting his documents (no one seemed sure what Babe's "papers" would be —hot dog wrappers, perhaps?) to Yale's captain and first baseman, George Bush, who went on to become president of the United States in 1988. In 1989, George H. W. Bush invited baseball writers to the White

House before the postseason and talked hardball in the Roosevelt Room for an hour. Asked about the photo op with Ruth, the president recalled, "I was captain of the ball club, so I got to receive him there. He was dying. He was hoarse and could hardly talk. He was hollow. His whole great shape was gaunt and hollowed out. I remember he complimented the Yale ballfield. It was like a putting green, it was so beautiful."

A. Bartlett Giamatti, the seventh commissioner of baseball, graduated from Yale in 1960 and served as its president for seven years before he took a job that represented his true love. It was Giamatti who said, "The ultimate purpose of baseball is to bring pleasure to the American people." Like John F. Kennedy's, Giamatti's term in office was cut short by an early death, but his days as commissioner are remembered fondly by all who embrace baseball. He wrote lovingly about the game and was an incurable Red Sox fan. He died near his home on Martha's Vineyard in 1989, just a few days after banishing Pete Rose from baseball.

Longtime major league pitcher Ron Darling is another Yale man. Darling's eleven innings of no-hit pitching in a twelve-inning, 1–0, NCAA tourney loss to Frank Viola and St. John's is still considered one of the best-pitched games in college baseball history. Played in May 1981 and witnessed by Smoky Joe Wood, the game was immortalized in *The New Yorker* by Roger Angell. Darling went on to pitch for thirteen years in the big leagues and was the Mets' starting pitcher in the infamous seventh game of the 1986 World Series.

As a college freshman, Theo didn't have to look far to find a baseball team with roots in New Haven. The Orioles were owned by Eli Jacobs, a Yale man. Another Yalie was in the Oriole front office, former NFL running back Calvin Hill. Hill, an African American, had been hired by Edward Bennett Williams after Al Campanis's racist interview on *Nightline* in 1987. As vice president of administrative personnel for the Orioles, early in 1992 Hill walked into the office of Dr. Charles Steinberg with a letter from an eighteen-year-old Yale freshman. Jacobs and Hill were happy to promote a Yale undergrad.

Steinberg had no agenda. He'd gone to the Orioles in 1976 as a seventeen-year-old intern from the Gilman School in Baltimore, recommended by Jack Dunn III. Dunn was the grandson of the Jack Dunn who originally signed Baltimore orphan George Herman "Babe" Ruth to his first professional baseball contract. Remarkable. The grandson of the man who signed Babe Ruth signed Charles Steinberg, who gave Theo Epstein his first job in baseball. Like reading a mystery with too many clues, tracking degrees of separation was always part of New England's obsession with the Curse of the Bambino.

While earning his high school diploma, a bachelor of arts degree from the University of Maryland, and a doctorate from its dental school, Steinberg worked for veteran Oriole public relations director Bob Brown—perhaps the best and most innovative baseball PR man of his time. Steinberg's first important task was keeping statistics for Hall of Fame manager Earl Weaver. Today, major league ball clubs' data banks overflow with information, but in the 1960s Weaver pioneered in the field by keeping index cards of how his batters fared against the pitchers from other American League teams. It was left to Steinberg to compile the numbers. An unimposing, bespectacled figure, Steinberg went virtually unnoticed in the Oriole offices until the night of the first game of the 1979 ALCS, which featured Jim Palmer starting against California righty Nolan Ryan. Late in the game, the Angels summoned reliever John Montague. Weaver found no Montague card in his file. The veteran reliever had been picked up late in the year, and Steinberg had neglected to put his numbers into the stack of cards. The Oriole dugout placed a call to Steinberg in the press box. The intern quickly produced the numbers, which were relayed to Weaver just in time for John Lowenstein (who had the best numbers against Montague) to hit an extra-inning walk-off homer. In the winner's clubhouse, Weaver toasted Steinberg and gave him credit for the win. He even offered him a beer. Alas, Steinberg was only twenty.

It is therefore no surprise that Steinberg took an interest in the young Theo Epstein. By 1992, he was the Orioles' director of public affairs, overseeing four departments. He'd reviewed ten thousand résumés and interviewed more than a thousand young candidates when Epstein went to see him during spring break in 1992.

"It was immediately obvious that this young man had unusual

thinking," remembered Steinberg, now an executive vice president with the Red Sox. "And he could put it into words. I remember thinking, Whoa, this one's unusual."

Epstein first interned in Baltimore in the summer of 1992, the Orioles' first season at Camden Yards. Young Theo arrived with a plan. He suggested a project that would pay tribute to the long-neglected Negro Leagues of baseball. Again, Steinberg was bowled over. "It was one of the most thoughtful, well-written proposals I had ever seen. He took the idea to a new level. He was impatient to get it done that summer, but we suggested taking an extra year and making it part of our All-Star celebration in 1993. And that's what he did. He came back the next summer and executed a five-day tribute to the stars of early black baseball. It was stupendous. And it resulted in Leon Day's getting elected to the Baseball Hall of Fame."

He could not help but get the attention of Larry Lucchino. A native of Pittsburgh, Lucchino loved old-timey ballparks—he'd grown up rooting for the Pirates at ancient Forbes Field. He was a good high school baseball player and made All-City in basketball, which took him to the Ivy League. At Princeton, he played on a team led by Bill Bradley, which made it to the 1965 NCAA Final Four. Lucchino graduated in 1967 and went on to Yale Law School. In 1974 he worked with a law school classmate, Hillary Rodham, on the Senate Watergate impeachment committee.

Perhaps that is where he first earned the wrath of George Steinbrenner, who had been tagged with a felony conviction (later pardoned) that involved illegal campaign contributions to Richard Nixon. Lucchino joined the law firm of Williams and Connolly in 1974, and to this day he cannot speak for more than ten minutes without bringing the name of his mentor, the late Edward Bennett Williams, into the conversation. Williams bought the Orioles for $12 million in August 1979 and made Lucchino club vice president and general counsel. Lucchino became president of the Orioles in 1988 and was a part owner by the time Young Theo appeared in Baltimore.

When not working summers for the Orioles, Epstein was a sportswriter for Yale's student paper, and he wasn't afraid to tweak the athletic department and veteran coaches such as football legend Carm Cozza. In a preview of the 1993 Harvard-Yale game, Epstein wrote a gameday piece, "Is It Time for Carm to Go?" He wrote that the coach "just doesn't get it" and blasted his motivational tactics. Epstein wrote, "His lack of passion has reached a new low" and "Cozza isn't the man to bring the program out of its problems. More and more it is becoming clear: Cozza is responsible for the problems . . . Class, integrity, and genuine feeling for one's players doesn't win championships these days — only respect."

The day of the game, Epstein bounded into the Yale press box, handing out copies of his story, and introduced himself to me — I, who had been blasting Red Sox GM Lou Gorman for almost a decade. Theo said he had an interest in being a sportswriter and had read *The Curse of the Bambino*. Yale beat Harvard that day, 33–31, and Cozza did not retire until after the 1996 season. Two months after Epstein's diatribe, however, Gorman was replaced by thirty-five-year-old Dan Duquette, then the youngest general manager in the history of the Red Sox. Less than a decade later, Epstein would replace Duquette to become the youngest GM in the history of the game.

The Orioles were sold after the 1993 season, and Lucchino joined the Padres a year later. In 1994, Epstein was a public relations intern for Steinberg in Baltimore. When Steinberg joined Lucchino and the Padres in 1995, he took Epstein with him. When Epstein graduated from Yale in 1995, he was hired by the Padres to work in the club's entertainment division. Steinberg made him promise to attend law school. Epstein said he didn't want to be a lawyer, but Dr. Charles explained that the degree would help Theo get where he wanted to go. In his early days in San Diego, Epstein's duties included preparing the goofy birthday messages and marriage proposals posted on the Jumbotron and monitoring the movements of a superfan named "Flag Man." Too busy spending his youth getting into baseball, he still didn't have a driver's license. Steinberg would pick him up in the morning, take him to McDonald's late at night, then drop the kid, exhausted, at his apartment. On weekends, his friends drove him around. A year later, Epstein was a PR assistant, writing and handing out press notes to members of the media during the Padres' division championship season. To this day, cranky national baseball writers find it difficult to be sufficiently reverent to a thirty-something GM who used to say "Excuse me, sir" in the press box. Epstein is sensitive about his early days in baseball. He does not like to be reminded of his days in public relations, and he bristles at the notion of Steinberg and Lucchino's taking credit for his success.

He got his driver's license in January 1997, at the age of twenty-three. Independent at last.

In 1997, Padre GM Kevin Towers made Epstein a happy man by moving him into baseball operations. It was important that he work in baseball operations before getting a law degree: the reverse order would have made him a target of old-timey baseball people. Nobody likes a young lawyer sticking his nose into baseball operations. But the law degree would still be important. The best general managers don't like to rely on club counsel. So Epstein went to the University of San Diego law school while he was involved in the baseball operations of the San Diego Padres. He made the dual role work nicely, offering his classmates free Padre tickets in exchange for detailed notes of the classes he was skipping. After getting his law degree and passing the California bar (on his first try), Epstein was courted by the Anaheim law firm of Gibson, Dunn & Crutcher, which offered him a starting salary of $140,000—almost five times what the Padres were paying him. That gave him the hammer to get a promotion: Towers made him director of baseball operations and bumped his salary to $80,000.

"I never had any intention of leaving," said Epstein. "I was a summer associate for two months, and at the time I thought Popov was top-shelf vodka. The one thing I learned that summer was that other vodkas exist that are more expensive and taste better. I called Kevin when I was drunk and said, 'They're offering $140,000. I don't know if this baseball thing is going to work out.' Then I told him I was kidding, but I asked him to try and get me more money. What I had been making was embarrassing."

When the Padres went to the World Series in 1998, Epstein, Steinberg, and Lucchino were a big part of the championship effort. Theo stayed on when Lucchino left after the 2001 season.

And then came the bag job of a major league franchise sale that ultimately brought Epstein back home to Boston.

In October 2000, John Harrington announced that the Red Sox were for sale. The keeper of the Yawkey Trust said he hoped to turn the club over to a local group, people who would understand the Red Sox and their fans. Thirteen months later, he was mulling offers from six prospective bidders who'd been qualified by Major League Baseball. What only few knew at the time was that one group had already been anointed the winner by Commissioner Bud Selig. Cable billionaire Charles Dolan had the money, but he had no chance. Boston concessionaire Joe O'Donnell and developer Steve Karp had money, land, and local connections, but they had no chance. Uncle Bud wanted the group of Tom Werner, Larry Lucchino, and a billionaire latecomer named John Henry.

Henry owned the Florida Marlins but wanted to get out. Werner, a millionaire TV producer, had sold the Padres and wanted to buy the Red Sox but had an underfinanced partner in Les Otten (a friend of Duquette's who seemed to owe money to most of the residents of New Hampshire and Vermont). Lucchino was done in San Diego. At the request of Selig, he had agreed to help Henry with ballpark and ownership issues in Florida. At the same time, he was working with Werner to help him buy the Red Sox. It was Lucchino who put Henry and Werner together. On November 3, 2001, Lucchino was in New Haven at the Brown-Yale game when his cell phone rang. It was John Henry.

"Larry brought me in," Henry remembered. "I was working on buying the Angels. He was working on the Red Sox deal. At one point, it became apparent to me that we weren't going to be able to make a deal for the Angels. I called Larry on his cell phone and said, 'How's it going in Boston?' And he said, 'We're dialing for dollars.' And so I asked him if there was a possibility for an investor to come in. I told him that I was only interested if I could be the lead investor, and he said, 'That would be great. Let me talk to Tom.' That's how it happened."

These were Uncle Bud's guys. Selig wanted to eliminate some major league teams as part of his contraction plan. Henry and Werner were in favor of revenue sharing between franchises and were on board with Selig's contraction plan. Selig was happy to make sure Henry could sell his Florida interest to Montreal owner Jeffrey Loria, setting up the Expos for their move to Washington, D.C., in 2005. Meanwhile, Harrington was not a Red Sox owner as much as he was director of the Yawkey estate. He had the keys to the house, and he alone would decide who'd buy the team. Ever appreciative of his place at the table of Major League Baseball, Harrington would do whatever Selig wished. Five days before Christmas in 2001, Harrington announced that the team would be sold to the Henry group (which had been bolstered by $75 million from the *New York Times*). Dolan and O'Donnell cried foul—and they were right. The fix was in, but it didn't matter. Selig would later say, "I had nothing to do with any of that" before adding, "but someday you'll thank me for it." The deal was sewed up in February of 2002, and Duquette was fired the morning after all the papers were passed. Mike Port, already in place, was named interim general manager. He was not the man for the future, but the sale was closed just as spring training was starting, and there was no time to put a permanent management team in place for 2002. Port was a veteran baseball man, well versed in the mechanics of running a team, and he would serve with dignity until the Sox found a permanent general manager.

Lucchino, the new CEO of the Red Sox, called San Diego in an effort to bring Epstein back to Boston as an assistant general manager. Epstein had been offered a similar position under J. P. Ricciardi in Toronto, but he turned it down, waiting for the call from the Sox. Initially, San Diego owner John Moores denied the Sox permission to talk to Epstein. There was lingering bad blood between Lucchino and Moores, and the Padres were not about to let the Sox raid their young front office. During spring training, however, the Padres gave the Red Sox a forty-eight-hour window in which to negotiate with Epstein. Lucchino went west and brought his prodigy home to be assistant GM of the Red Sox.

When the Sox finished out of the playoffs, Lucchino and his friends pursued Oakland's young general manager, Billy Beane—Mr. "Moneyball"—the hottest executive in baseball. Beane accepted the Red Sox job in late November, then changed his mind a few hours later. Epstein, who was prepared to work under Beane, spent some restless hours wondering about his future when he got the word that Beane had reneged on his decision. Within a week, Lucchino was offering Epstein the job, and on November 25, 2002, twenty-eight-year-old Theo Epstein became the youngest general manager in the history of the game.

"What's all the fuss about?" his dad, Leslie, asked. "When Alexander the Great was Theo's age, he was general manager of the world."

Theo Epstein's first Red Sox team came within five outs of making it to the World Series.

He was a more confident, less candid executive when he arrived in Florida in the spring of 2004. Flexing his muscles at the ripe age of thirty, Epstein moved into a house with eight of his assistants in Cape Coral. Francona called it "Animal House." Sox clubhouse chief Tommy McLaughlin went with "Phi Sign-a Playa."

It was the Real World Fort Myers, featuring the best and brightest of Gammons Youth, young men who worshipped at the altar of plate approach and on-base percentage. It's where Theo and his minions hatched their plan to win the 2004 World Series.

"It's actually pretty boring," said Epstein, rush chairman of Phi Sign-a Playa. "We barely see each other. We go to work, come home, and go to sleep. The neighbors told us that we're the most boring tenants ever."

Francona, a fossil at forty-four, thought otherwise. He went to the house several times during the spring, sometimes taking a couple of coaches, once his eighteen-year-old son. Nick Francona was bound for the University of Pennsylvania, where he would be a left-handed pitcher. He was closer in age to Theo's pals than his dad was, and that got him a seat at the poker table. The Stat Pack played Texas Hold'em, just as on ESPN. Losers left the table and went to play pool. The place was stocked with potato chips, bottled water, and Mexican beer. The manager sent his son out to fetch ice cream for the gang.

"It's actually pretty awesome," said Francona. "They're just a bunch of good guys. They got a lot of energy, they got a lot to offer. Everything's going at once. They're yelling at each other. Fuckin' fighting. It was fun to be around. I enjoyed it."

The house had nine laptops and nine cell phones, a washing machine and two dryers. No one cooked. There was a giant TV screen and two regular TVs, plus a pool table, a Jacuzzi, and a swimming pool with basketball. And a fountain. (The Sox baby brass rejected the Jet Ski option.) According to Epstein, who had lived in a house with ten guys at Yale, the Fort Myers rental saved the Red Sox $30,000 in spring-training hotel expenses.

Located on a canal, the house had been discovered by Red Sox director of player development Ben Cherington. Epstein and Cherington were tenants along with Jed Hoyer (assistant to the general manager), Galen Carr (advance scouting director), Peter Woodfork (director of baseball operations and assistant director of player development), Craig Shipley (special assistant to the GM, player development, and international scouting), and Brian O'Halloran (coordinator of the major league administration). The eighth bedroom was alternately occupied by Amiel Sawdaye (scouting assistant) and Jonathan Gilula (special assistant to the president and CEO). Most were in their late twenties or early thirties, and all of them were former college boys. Only two, Cherington and O'Halloran, were married. Cherington's bride was Wendi Nix, an emerging sports reporter for the NBC affiliate in Boston. She was one of the few women allowed to spend the night at Phi Sign-a Playa.

There were no toga parties in Cape Coral, but on a night when Hoyer went to bed too early, Theo and his friends roused him, yelling "Fire," and blasting him with the fire extinguisher when he burst out of his room.

Times certainly had changed. It was hard to imagine Dan Duquette hosing down Mike Port in his pajamas at 2 A.M. Long gone were the days of Pinky Higgins and Dick O'Connell downing brown liquor in a smoky hotel bar. Instead, the 2004 Red Sox were designed in a wrinkle-free, smoke-free house where laptops never slept. Nobody would be fired if the Sox didn't win it all. The worst that could happen was Double Secret Probation.

In the first week of his second spring training, Young Theo admitted that the Red Sox would not be able to keep all five of the veteran stars. Thanks to abysmal management by Harrington and Duquette, the 2004 Sox faced a situation in which Garciaparra, Martinez, Lowe, David Ortiz, and Jason Varitek were all going into the final years of their contracts. Epstein also hinted that the club would allow them to play the entire season without extensions. This idea was extraordinary. Valuable players in the final year of their pacts are usually extended or traded. The risk is clear. Let them play out the contract, and they can leave you with nothing but a compensation draft pick. It was how the

Sox lost Roger Clemens and Mo Vaughn, and Boston fans blasted management both times.

"To do good business and execute a successful plan, at times you have to be prepared for players to go into the last year of their contract," Epstein said in his first 2004 press conference in Florida. (He wore a blue Patriot cap, saying, "It's the least I can do.") "It's not a panic situation for the player, it's not a panic situation for the club . . . It's unrealistic to think we could sign every one of them. The finances don't add up. That's life. There's change sometime. Do the math yourself. It's not financially possible to bring back every player. And when you say we get nothing for him [Clemens, Vaughn], that's overlooking a major factor, which is that the 2004 club is going to be very good and has a chance to win the World Series, and you can't quantify that. You can't quantify what it means to have the player here this year."

No one needed Bill James to discern that this was the blueprint for 2004. Forget about 2005 or 2007. The Sox were going for it in 2004. Heavy Metal Thunder. This is when management set the tone for a freewheeling season of fun and success. John Henry, Larry Lucchino, and Theo Epstein were not going to get caught up in how it all ended in Yankee Stadium or how they had mishandled the A-Rod deal. They were not going to stand on sentimentality. They were going to do what needed to be done, even if it meant trading a superstar or allowing stars to leave at the end of their contracts. These owners weren't going to worry too much about public perception. They were a management team thinking about the present, and by the end of the year they would be smiling over a team that played in the moment and made the best of those moments.

For the most part, baseball players know little about baseball history. Most of the 2004 Red Sox had heard about the Curse of the Bambino but didn't understand its deep and tangled roots. Certainly none of them knew how this history poxed other Sox teams who tried to come back the year after *almost* winning. The 1947 Red Sox fell from first to third place, a shocking drop from 104 to 83 wins. Boston's top three starting pitchers all came down with sore arms and finished fourteen games behind the Yankees a year after winning the pennant by twelve games. This collapse established a nasty "year after" nosedive pattern for some of Boston's best teams. One year after the Impossible

Dream summer of love, the 1968 Sox fell to seventeen games behind the Detroit Tigers to finish in fourth place. The year got off to a bad start when Cy Young winner Jim Lonborg ruined his knee in a skiing accident, and the Sox never got back on track. In 1976, the year after Freddie Lynn, Fisk, and their friends almost won the Greatest World Series of Them All, the Sox were sidetracked when Fisk, Lynn, and Rick Burleson held out for more money and sabotaged the season. The '76ers never contended and finished third. Tom Yawkey died in midsummer, some said from a broken heart. Finally, the Nightmare at Shea in '86 ensured that the 1987 Red Sox would not recover. They finished fifth, playing sub-.500 baseball in a train wreck season.

All of which explains why Boston fans had a right to be nervous when the Sox arrived in Florida in 2004. How would the players respond? How could they come back from that horrible disappointment? They'd come *so* close. And now, here they were, all the way back at the beginning again. Could they endure another season?

Pedro and Nomar made their first appearances in camp on February 24 and gave back-to-back press conferences, which were predictable. Pedro said he was in the best shape of his life and was in no rush to sign a contract extension. He was in a good mood, not the least bit guilty about coughing up the lead in New York in October. He made jokes about Steinbrenner but also made it clear that he'd pitch for whoever wanted him if the Sox expressed no interest. Nomar was not in a good mood. He said, "When I heard about [trade talk], I was thinking, well, the priorities are obviously not for me. They're obviously for someone else . . . I was definitely hurt by a lot of it."

Epstein's plan seemed blessed when Jesus showed up to play center field. Johnny Damon arrived with a beard, shoulder-length hair, and a new attitude. He claimed that Grady sat him out of some games in 2003 because he believed Damon had been partying too late and too hard. Damon, recently divorced, claimed he had his nightlife under control. He was about to become engaged to Michelle Mangan, a dancer from Houston.

Epstein, a rocker at heart, told Damon to keep the hair and beard if he wanted. It was the 2004 equivalent of the Beatles' appearance on *The Ed Sullivan Show* in February 1964. Just as America was never the same after the Fab Four invaded our shores, the new identity of the

Red Sox was established when Epstein told Damon it was okay to keep the wild and crazy look.

Manny wheeled into camp wearing a smile and a Jeremy Shockey New York Giants jersey. There was a tense moment when he refused to shake the new manager's hand and skipped the early portion of Francona's first team meeting, but the superstar slugger quickly regained his good humor. He spoke briefly with reporters and said he was going to have his sister take charge of a Manny Web site. It was the beginning of a year in which he would emerge as a Boston cult hero. John Henry insisted that Manny had called him during the height of the A-Rod talks and begged to stay in Boston. Manny had said he felt as if he had nine toes in Texas and one toe in Boston, but nevertheless, he seemed remarkably happy to be back.

In the early days of spring, the always-large media contingent from New England was joined by a posse of reporters from New York, no less than five a day. *New York Newsday* decided to include a new feature as part of its comprehensive baseball coverage—a report on the Red Sox, which for the entire season would be headlined THE MISERY INDEX.

The Yankees were a constant topic, and Kevin Millar said, "It's almost getting too big. There's too much of a hate sometimes." Reliever Alan Embree added, "It's Russia and the U.S. going at it again."

And then there was the first spring training game between the Red Sox and Yankees on Sunday, March 7, at City of Palms Park in Fort Myers. It had been 143 days since the seventh game of the 2003 ALCS, and coverage went beyond anything spring training baseball had ever seen. More than 250 media members covered the game—about ten times the number at a typical Red Sox exhibition game. Tickets were scarce, so some fans slept outside the park on Saturday night, lining up for standing room. On the Net, eBay offered a pair of seats for $500. Sox fans were aware that A-Rod and Jeter were both making the two-hour, fifteen-minute bus trip down Route 75 from Tampa, and the exhibition was billed as Game 8 of the ALCS.

Historian David Halberstam explained how Sox fans felt about their team: "It goes beyond other teams in other sports . . . The great affection and loyalty is an unusual kind of virus or condition that they have . . . A lot of it is dislike of the Yankees. If you don't like the Yankees, and it's pretty easy not to like them, particularly in the age of Steinbrenner, who do you root for? You root for the Red Sox, because they are the one team that's between the Yankees and the American League pennant."

Most of the Red Sox and Yankees took the high road, but Varitek wasn't afraid to say, "I dislike the Yankees. I respect a lot of their players and what they've done. But it's getting old, and it's time for us to win."

That Sunday, the cover of the *Fort Myers News-Press* sports section featured a doctored photo of Steinbrenner, with devil's horns sprouting from his head. In a City of Palms parking lot before the game, there was a fight involving two young women, one a Sox fan and one a Yankee fan. Souvenir stands sold $6 commemorative pins marking the historic event. Millar fired up his teammates around the batting cage, shouting, "Game 7 rematch! Let's go! Let's go!" Reggie Jackson held court, telling anyone who'd listen that the Red Sox blew it by not making the deal for A-Rod ("We got A-Rod because you fucked it up"). Meanwhile, a Sox parking attendant, Dave McHugh, got into a dustup with Yankee PR director Rick Cerrone, who said, "Don't you know who I am? I'm the public relations director of the American League Champion New York Yankees, and you know what? You are a typical Boston Red Sox employee." Perhaps even more absurd, a Boston television sportscaster asked Nomar Garciaparra (who wasn't playing because of a mysterious bruised heel) if he worried about the perception that he'd "backed out" of the game. Garciaparra made a face, said nothing, and left the dugout in disgust. In the stands, Lucchino chatted with Yankee GM Brian Cashman. When he saw that their picture was being taken, he reminded Cashman that the photo op might not be a good career move. Standing by the batting cage, Yogi Berra said, "Boston has never been able to beat us." Hawkers sold T-shirts outside the park. Many had images of the Evil Empire, but one said, "Zim had it coming," a reference to the brawl in Game 3 of the ALCS when Pedro shucked a charging Zimmer, and the old man landed on the ground face-first. Even Manny got into the act, saying, "If we don't win today, it's over."

"I'd prefer not to play them in spring training at all," said Cashman. "We're going to be knocking heads with them nineteen times during the regular season as it is. We used to play the Blue Jays four or five times in the spring, but I've taken that down to two because it's too many times to play them."

In the bottom of the first inning, facing Jose Contreras, Sox leadoff man Gabe Kapler hit a grounder toward center field. Moving to his left, Jeter made a nice scoop, but his throw was wide of first and he was credited with an error. On the UPN-38 telecast in Boston, announcer Sean McDonough immediately said to sidekick Jerry Remy, "Well, let's start it right now, Jerry. A-Rod should be at short and Jeter should be at third. The more we can do to stir up controversy for the Yankees, the better." McDonough was being funny, but Sox fans loved it. When Boston blew out to a four-run lead, Michael LaVigne got a call from his wife, Lisa White, who was watching the game at home. Lisa, who had managed to survive her first winter of heartbreak as a new Sox fan, told her husband, "We're beating them, 4–0." When Michael reminded her that it was only an exhibition game, she said, "Yes, but we're sending them a message." Unfortunately, the Yankees hammered Sox relievers Jason Shiell and Ed Yarnall for ten runs to beat Boston, 11–7. So much for sending messages. It turned out New York had an instant message of its own.

Some Sox fans were dismayed to see Garciaparra walking around and hugging many Yankees, including Jeter and Rodriguez. Hearing the Sox fans taunting "Nomar's better," Jeter turned to the stands and said, "Don't worry. He's gonna be with us next year."

Aaron Boone was not on the premises. Jeff Horrigan of the *Boston Herald* reached him at his home in Newport Beach, where Boone sounded worried about the wrath of Red Sox fans. "It's an extremely hot rivalry, and it has only grown with that series and what's happened in the off-season," he said. "It's at an all-time high now, which is great, but you don't want people hating each other. It's one thing to beat your rival, but hopefully it doesn't get to life-and-death and bad things happening. I think they should just appreciate that this is the greatest rivalry in sports, and at the end of the day it's baseball, nothing more and nothing less."

On the Yankee bus going home was a backup catcher who hadn't seen any action in the sloppy game, Jon-Marc Sprowl. It's a significant name in Red Sox–Yankee history because his dad is Bobby Sprowl, and Bobby Sprowl was the rookie lefty tabbed by stubborn Sox manager

Zimmer to start the fourth and final game of the infamous Boston Massacre in 1978. Sprowl didn't get out of the first inning, the Sox lost again, and Sprowl retired with a career record of 0–3. Jon-Marc Sprowl was one player who was not surprised by what he had just seen at City of Palms Park.

Back in Boston, television ratings for the game were off the charts. The numbers were higher than the ratings for some regular-season games and more than doubled any other sports program that winter weekend. "There's no other sports franchise in the country with this kind of interest right now," said Ross Kramer, Boston's Channel 38 research director. "It's unprecedented for a spring training game."

The sad autumn and wacky winter seemed only to heighten interest in the Red Sox. In a truly remarkable demonstration of fan fidelity, Fenway Park's 2004 regular season was virtually sold out before the end of spring training. More than 95,000 hopefuls went online in an effort to secure Green Monster seats after purchase procedures were announced. Another 80,000 fans went online to register for new right-field rooftop seats, to be unveiled on Opening Day.

Fox Sports jumped on the Sox-Yankee bus earlier than ever. The network wasn't scheduled to begin its Saturday afternoon broadcasts until late May, but in March it announced it would broadcast the first Red Sox–Yankee regular-season game at Fenway Park on Friday, April 16. The starting time was shifted from 7 to 8 P.M. Ed Goren, the president of Fox Sports, said, "If it were up to me, we'd take the whole series and come back a week later and carry all their games at Yankee Stadium . . . We started thinking about this at some point after the Yankees closed the deal with A-Rod . . . This is going to be an event." Commissioner Bud Selig chimed in, calling the game "an extension of the postseason brought into April."

Schilling, who had an opinion on everything, was already talking about the Fox TV game. When he arrived in Florida in mid-February, the big righty said he'd looked ahead two months, done the math, and concluded that he would be Boston's starting pitcher on April 16. Never diplomatic, he was the perfect player spokesman for the rivalry. "If Red Sox fans weren't passionate and pissed off and angry and bitter and hated the Yankees, they wouldn't be who they are," said the ace. "And now they're my fans. So instead of looking at them and saying,

'What a bunch of dopes,' I'm going, 'That's cool.' I'm glad they are the way they are."

Schilling wore vintage old-time jerseys almost every day in Florida. Phil Esposito. Walter Payton. John Hannah. But no Yankee jerseys. Not even a "Yankees Suck" shirt.

Offensive and untrue, by the spring of 2004 "Yankees Suck" had become part of the language of New England, on a par with the Midnight Ride of Paul Revere, and parking your car in Harvard Yard. The chant is believed to have started in the bleachers at Fenway in the 1970s, just after Steinbrenner bought the New York team. In those days, the Sox and Yankees were both good at the same time, something that hadn't happened since the late 1940s. But in the early 1970s, the flames were rekindled. Those were the days of Munson vs. Fisk, Graig Nettles vs. Bill Lee, and Fenway's bleacherites vs. Mickey Rivers. Marijuana had replaced beer as the mind-altering substance of choice in the bleachers, and the first "Yankees Suck" chants emerged from the smoky haze around the same time that the redoubtable Rivers was dodging darts hurled from those same green seats. At the time, "sucks" was considered quite shocking, though by 2004 it would be deemed okay for prime-time television.

Through the years, Yankee fans replied to the chant with "Boston Sucks" or, better, "19-18." But nothing caught fire quite like "Yankees Suck." Red Sox fans are simply more tortured and frustrated than New York fans, and as the shock value of "sucks" waned toward the end of the twentieth century, the phrase reached cultlike status. Any gathering of two or more Sox fans represented a chance for a friendly "Yankees Suck" chant. The phrase started to break out in the most unlikely places. Sox manager Jimy Williams commented after hearing it while the Red Sox were playing the Astros in Kissimmee, Florida. Students at Newton North High School chanted it when they were herded into the school's football stadium during a bomb scare the day after September 11, 2001. Patriot special teams player Larry Izzo ignited a "Yankees Suck" chant in front of half a million people in 2002, when the Pats celebrated their first Super Bowl victory. Mike Barnicle, a former *Globe* columnist, claims to have heard it while waiting in a long line outside a funeral home. Fans pouring out of concerts almost never fail to start the chant. Weddings, bar mitzvahs, graduations. No event is safe.

"I heard it at Disney World when I was there with my wife and kids," said Varitek. "There were about ten or fifteen people doing it. Pretty funny. They come up and show you their shirt, and they're so proud of it."

T-shirts bearing the phrase are ubiquitous in and around Boston. At Fenway on gamedays, it's possible to see middle-class parents unloading kids from minivans with the whole family wearing "Yankees Suck" garb. It's like wearing a Hawaiian shirt to a Jimmy Buffet concert.

In his classic recap of the 2004 postseason, Roger Angell wrote of an eighty-six-year-old gent at his home in Gramercy Square, "wearing the first messaged garment of his life, a classic white cotton T-shirt with 'Yankees Suck' in 75-point blue capitals . . . The shirt summed up his convictions: Voltaire could not have put it better."

With the nonstop growth of "Yankees Suck" came the emergence of a Nation. Red Sox Nation. A search in the *Boston Globe* library showed the term first being used by the *Globe*'s Nathan Cobb during the 1986 ALCS. It's part of the language now.

"It's really very distinctive," said David Halberstam. "I don't think there's a Yankee Nation. Maybe there's a Cardinal Nation. There really is a definable Red Sox Nation. Traveling around, I have been like a psychiatrist. I have maybe gotten into the artists and writers and poets section of Red Sox Nation. The fans are quite interesting and important and different. You keep believing and you have this faith, even with all the evidence that piles up that says it's hard to have faith. There's something about New England. Maybe it's the ethnicity. Maybe it's that they come so close so often. I think the Red Sox are so star-crossed. You have the hard winter that makes baseball the signature sport there. You get through the hard winter talking about them. There's always just enough hope. And there's a sense of a whole area that by dint of modern communication with radio and television that is shaped and molded almost perfectly to be Red Sox Nation."

The author of three baseball books, two of them related to the Red Sox, Halberstam would hardly be the last literary giant to talk about the Sox in 2004. During spring training, Scribner announced that Stephen King and novelist Stewart O'Nan would collaborate on a book about the 2004 season. O'Nan, who wrote *A Prayer for the Dying,* said, "This is the year." It seemed that with all that went on in the off-season, with the stakes higher than ever, members of the Nation believed that something special was going to happen this year. One thing was certain—the 2004 Red Sox were going to be anything but boring.

Back on the ballfield, the Red Sox got some bad news near the end of spring training. Dependable right fielder Trot Nixon would start the season on the disabled list due to a herniated disc in his back. He would be replaced by muscular Kapler and (sometimes) Millar. Interestingly, every time Kapler played right, with Damon in center, fans in the bleachers saw "19 18" when they stood side by side during the anthem or a pitching change.

Nixon's injury caused concern, but more alarming was the condition of Garciaparra. He'd allegedly hit a foul ball off his heel during batting practice and developed mild tendonitis in his right Achilles tendon. With two weeks left in spring training, he was walking in a removable cast and still hitless. He finished the spring 0–8 in four games and did not play in any exhibition after St. Patrick's Day. The Sox were still talking about his playing Opening Night in Baltimore. No one even imagined he was going to miss the first fifty-seven games of the regular season.

The Red Sox and Yankees met for a second and final spring game at Legends Field, in Tampa, on the night of March 24. Happily, this contest involved little of the emotional frenzy that had accompanied the earlier game in Fort Myers. Cerrone, the combative Yankee publicist, joked before the rematch, saying, "This time it counts! Game 9!"

In truth, by late March the fans in both cities had grown accustomed to the idea of Alex Rodriguez in a Yankee uniform. Meanwhile, Rodriguez was growing more comfortable at third base, and there was no need for a daily press briefing around his locker. The Yankees weren't thinking about the Red Sox. They were thinking about Japan. A strange schedule (and a payoff of many millions of dollars) dictated that they would open the regular season in Tokyo, playing two games against the Tampa Bay Devil Rays. While the Red Sox boarded their buses in Fort Myers for the two-and-a-half-hour drive north to Tampa, the Yankees were anticipating an eighteen-hour flight to Japan the next day.

The Yankees' Japanese journey seemed curious. It was bound to take a physical toll on the team and had the potential to sabotage the start of this important season. Five days before any other team opened, the Yankees and Devil Rays would play two regular-season games on the other side of the world. They would then take five days off before playing each other in St. Petersburg. The Yankees planned to fill some of this time with a couple of exhibition games *after* they'd already started the season. Money corrupts. And sometimes, even in baseball, it doesn't help you win. Sometimes it makes it harder to win.

"We're not going to use that as an excuse," said Cashman, sounding a little worried. "We've done everything we can to alleviate those problems. I've talked to football people who've done it and former players who've done it, and I think we've structured it in a way that's going to work best for us, given the circumstances. It will be tough on us, but we'll deal with it."

The Yankees were taking batting practice when the Sox spilled out of their buses and sauntered into the dugout for the second spring meeting of mastodons. Manny was one of the few Sox regulars to make the trip, and it provided some interesting photo ops when he walked over to embrace Enrique Wilson and Alex Rodriguez. Millar, seeing Manny making his way toward Enrique, cheerfully hollered, "No, Manny, don't do it!" Too late. Ramirez hugged Enrique. Then he hugged A-Rod. There was Manny, a guy making $20 million who'd said he wanted to play for the Yankees, then been waived and later traded to the Rangers, only to have the trade nullified by the union, and he was hugging the guy the Sox had traded him for, the guy making $25 million who ultimately wound up with those same Yankees. It was a Manny Moment. Major League Baseball's circle of life. Given Ramirez's well-deserved reputation as the king of clueless, one almost expected to hear him tell A-Rod, "Hey, man, too bad we didn't get you. What a lineup we would have had!"

It didn't take much to underline the Ramirez-Rodriguez contrast. None of the Sox owners made the trip to Tampa, but they'd have certainly winced had they seen A-Rod play to the sponsors and friends of the Yankee owners after batting practice. After A-Rod was done hitting, Reggie Jackson, who had been every bit as big a star back in the late 1970s, escorted him from the batting cage to a group from Microsoft. Rodriguez smiled for the photographs, signed all the balls and shirts, and chatted up the VIPs. It was a demonstration of what the Sox had hoped to get from him—in addition to his customary forty homers. They'd wanted a fresh face for the ball club, a star who could schmooze. Instead, they had clueless Manny, sour Nomar, and Pedro, the Diva.

It was chilling to see Wakefield take the mound in the bottom of the first. The veteran knuckleballer hadn't pitched against the Yankees since . . .

Wakefield was roughed up in an 8–6 loss. The game was relatively uneventful and inspired not a single derisive chant from the stands, but a memorable moment came in the fourth inning when the Red Sox inadvertently knocked A-Rod out of the game. The kooky play started when Millar hit a shot down the left field line while Brian Daubach was leading off first base. Seeing Hideki Matsui run down the ball, Daubach rounded second and broke for third. A-Rod extended his glove to take Matsui's throw, but it caromed off Daubach's right foot up into Rodriguez's left cheekbone. It looked almost like a hockey play. "A kick save," said Daubach.

In 1993, when he was playing for Miami Westminster Christian High School, Rodriguez had suffered a broken cheekbone when an overthrow struck him in the face while he was sitting in the dugout. He said this ball hit him in the same place, and the Yankees took precautionary x-rays (which indicated nothing more than a bruise).

Epstein made the trip to Tampa for Sox-Yanks Grapefruit II, but there was no socializing with his Yankee counterpart, Cashman.

"I don't talk to Theo that much because there's nothing to talk about," said Cashman. "Our goals are the same. I know what he's up against, he knows what I'm up against. I joke that last year he almost got me fired in his first year on the job."

Joke?

The day after the Yankee game in Tampa, Pedro pitched five innings against the Twins in Fort Myers. After he struck out only one batter and gave up seven hits and three runs, he was grilled about having lost his fastball. Martinez smiled and gave thoughtful answers in front of the TV cameras and more than twenty reporters, but he was not happy with the line of questioning. Earlier in the week he'd participated in contract talks with his agent and John Henry, but he remained unconvinced that the Sox would meet his demands. Though he would make $17.5 million in 2004—an all-time high for a pitcher— he often complained about what he perceived as a lack of respect. On Friday, March 26, while most of the Red Sox were in Bradenton for an exhibition with the Pirates, two television reporters encountered an angry Pedro in the Red Sox clubhouse at City of Palms Park.

CBS4's Steve Burton and Thomas Forester of NBC-2 in Fort Myers asked Pedro if he would appear on camera for an interview. Martinez said he would make no public comments, then vented his frustrations to the two reporters, both African American. Pedro said he was "shutting it down" with reporters. He was offended by the questions about his fastball. It was, after all, only spring training. He was thirty-two years old and had never had surgery. What did the media want from him? He said he no longer wanted to be the Red Sox ace. Pointing toward Schilling's empty locker, he said, "They bring in the great white hope." Rubbing his fingers on his dark forearm, he said, "In Boston, they don't want this." He said he would play out his contract and leave at the end of the year. That night, NBC-2 (Fort Myers) reported that Pedro had told their reporter he would leave Boston at the end of the season.

While Pedro complained, the Yankees were shaking out the cobwebs from their 7,270-mile trip to Tokyo. Matsui, a Japanese god, was the primary attraction for the Japanese fans, but there was plenty of curiosity about A-Rod, Jeter, and friends. The Yankees had a history in Japan. Babe Ruth and Lou Gehrig toured Japan with the Pinstripers in 1934, and the Yogi Berra Yankees made the trip after losing the 1955 World Series to the Dodgers. Yogi claimed Whitey Ford learned his pickoff move in Japan because the locals had so many anxious base runners. Ruth's Yankees played eighteen exhibitions in Japan, and the 1955 team went 15–0–1 in front of half a million fans. This time the Yankees were going to play a couple of games that actually counted, and there was more than a little interest back in Boston when the Yankees opened their season in Tokyo on March 30.

The first Yankee game started at 5 A.M. Boston time, and John Henry was sitting in front of his television. He hadn't slept all night, and the game kept him awake as the Devil Rays pounded Mussina and the American League champs. Rodriguez struck out in his first two

Yankee at-bats, then doubled and popped up. Tampa's 8–3 victory put the Red Sox a half game ahead of the Yankees in the American League East, a stupid fact not lost on anyone in the Nation. Henry vowed to stay up again to watch the sequel. He attended a baseball forum at the JFK Library on the night of March 30 but excused himself before dinner was served in order to go home and get ready for another all-nighter.

There was some dark humor in the Yankee clubhouse after the abysmal opener. Reggie Jackson, still with the team as an honorary coach, said, "If we lose tomorrow, we won't be in a 747 going home. It will be B&O, the Baltimore and Ohio Railroad."

The Yankees came back and won, 12–1, the next day, flexing the muscles of their $182 million payroll. Posada hit a pair of three-run homers, former Red Sox Tony Clark hit a homer, but the big blow was a two-run shot by Matsui in the fifth inning. It was immediately dubbed the greatest baseball moment in the history of Japan. So while the Yankees' 2004 season began a half a world away, for the Red Sox, who tried in vain to keep their blinders on, what was happening in the Evil Empire was immediate and important.

The Red Sox finished spring training in Florida by beating the Twins, 4–3, on April Fools' Day. It gave them a 3–2 edge over their crosstown spring rivals and returned the coveted Mayor's Cup Trophy to the Red Sox. Leaving spring training is always a big moment in any baseball season. The Grapefruit and Cactus seasons have become far too long, with interminable bus rides and too much downtime. Red Sox clubhouse man Joe Cochran estimated that he ate at Fort Myers's Outback Steakhouse thirty-two times. "That's thirty-two Cinnamon Oblivion desserts—with extra whip cream—to go," said Cochran, who said he thought he'd acquired an Australian accent by the time camp broke.

The Sox went to Atlanta for two more exhibitions on the way to the opener in Baltimore. Turner Field was particularly lifeless that final weekend of the preseason. It was so bad that Millar neglected to run out a ground ball in the final game. Francona spoke to him about it afterward, and Millar managed to joke about it with—who else?—Manny Ramirez. Manny didn't say it out loud, but everyone knew what the reaction would have been if he'd performed the same stunt.

Players like Millar and Ortiz were good for team morale. It was not as easy as one would think. Twice during the spring, wealthy star pitchers chartered private jets to get to faraway games, choosing some teammates to fly while leaving most of them behind. Schilling started the trend, taking a handful of players from Fort Myers to Vero Beach for his start in Dodgertown. A few days later, Lowe took Millar, Kapler, Embree, Varitek, and Daubach on a nineteen-minute flight from Fort Myers to West Palm Beach for a game against the Marlins. Most of the guys on the three-hour bus ride were kids, so no one complained.

Thirty-nine-year-old Ellis Burks, who'd last played with the Sox back in 1992—the old days of the "twenty-five players, twenty-five cabs" Red Sox—said, "I think the camaraderie has changed a lot since I was here . . . You got a lot of guys that get along. Guys get together and have dinner and go watch games, and you didn't have that when I was here. The whole team aspect is a lot better."

The team that checked into its hotel in Baltimore on Saturday night, April 3, was not the team Sox fans expected when Young Theo was making his moves over the wild winter. Garciaparra was home in Boston, and Nixon was seeing back specialists from coast to coast. The GM was worried about his team's defense. He wanted his pitching staff to be "relentless," but it would be difficult with holes in the infield. New second baseman Mark Bellhorn would get on base more than Todd Walker, but was not strong defensively. And now Garciaparra was out and so was Nixon. The front office's stated goal was to score 900 runs and allow 700–725 runs. That formula should produce 95–100 wins.

Nixon's back had everyone worried. He claimed he first felt the pain while driving to spring training—only days after he'd signed a three-year contract extension. He was unable to play any baseball, and the Sox ruled him out at least through April. Boston sports fans remembered that Larry Bird had been forced to have surgery and eventually retire because of a similar problem. Nixon said surgery was the last option and his worst fear, but no one knew when or if he'd be able to play. He was in a rehab clinic in Miami when the Sox went north to open the season. There was some comfort in the knowledge that his father, Dr. William Nixon—who once caught Catfish Hunter in high school—was an orthopedic specialist.

Garciaparra was another story. As always, there was rampant speculation. Sox officials were already wondering about the alleged batting practice ball hit off his right heel during early spring training. What they did know was that he had developed Achilles tendonitis because of the bruise and couldn't play. Much later it would be reported that he hurt the heel playing soccer during the winter. Epstein believed he'd been hurt during his rigorous training sessions in Scottsdale. It was a mysterious injury, one with no witnesses and no true measure of severity save what the player said. Given his anger over the willingness of the Sox to trade him and the stalled contract extension, it was a particularly awkward time for Nomar and the ball club. Some Sox fans thought Garciaparra just didn't want to play, but that was ludicrous. Even if he wanted out, he was coming off the worst month of his major league career and needed a strong 2004 season to maximize his value as a potential free agent.

The contract status of Garciaparra, Martinez, Varitek, Lowe, and Ortiz was on everyone's mind when the Sox went to Camden Yards for the nationally televised opener on Sunday, April 4. Lowe had already said he planned on being elsewhere the following year, the ultrasensitive Pedro was thinking the Sox had replaced him with Schilling, Garciaparra was angry and injured, and Varitek and Ortiz were wondering why their situations hadn't been addressed.

Everyone got the message. This would be the last year that all of these talented players would be together in the Red Sox dugout. Win this year. It's Boston's last, best chance.

Still sporting his long hair and beard, Damon stood in the dugout in Atlanta before the trip to Baltimore and declared, "This year will be a failure if we do not win the World Series."

5

Pieces of April

T HE NATIONAL MEDIA regarded the 2004 Red Sox with considerable suspicion. The A-Rod acquisition, coupled with the injuries to Garciaparra and Nixon, made the Yankees favorites in most baseball publications. The cover of *Sports Illustrated*'s baseball preview issue featured a photo of Cub righty Kerry Wood and the headline HELL FREEZES OVER — THE CUBS WILL WIN THE WORLD SERIES. Ranking all the teams in the majors, the magazine slotted the Sox third (prophetic, since the Sox would finish with the third-best regular-season record), behind the Cubs and Yankees, and predicted a Cub victory over the Yankees in the World Series. Chicago fans, always dubious and still hurting from a fold in '03, had to be worrying about *Sports Illustrated*'s famed cover jinx. Alex Rodriguez was on the cover of *ESPN the Magazine*. ESPN's hardball guru Peter Gammons picked the Sox to win the American League East but picked the Cubs over the Sox in the World Series. It was more of the same in newspapers in New York, Washington, and Baltimore.

Meanwhile, there was unbridled optimism back in New England as baseball scribes predicted a pennant, and citizens of Red Sox Nation seemed more confident than ever that this was The Year. The acquisitions of Schilling and Foulke had much to do with it. By every measure, Schilling was a productive, money pitcher. He was capable of leading the league in wins, strikeouts, and innings. If healthy, given the Sox offense, he was capable of 18 to 20 wins. He was also a proven postseason winner and he had an attitude. Schilling announced that he was coming to Boston to do something that hadn't been done in eighty-six years, and fans embraced him as their savior. At the same time, Foulke gave Francona something that Grady Little never had. He led the American League in saves and games finished in 2003, a new, important weapon at the end of the game. Despite the injuries to Nomar and Nixon, nobody worried about the Sox scoring runs. Ortiz was still hitting moon shots in Florida, and Manny seemed like a happier slugger. The 2003 team had been good enough to win ninety-five games and come within five outs of the World Series. This team was better. Five of five *Boston Globe* sportswriters picked the Sox to finish first, with four projecting a World Series victory. But this had been projected before. The question was, How would the Curse present itself in 2004?

Still, skeptics wondered if such a lofty prospect was a dream only in New England, a delusional and predictable consequence of so many years of near misses. *Globe* Living section columnist Alex Beam certainly was not caught up in the euphoria. He wrote, "Never have I been so utterly pessimistic about a forthcoming sports campaign as I am about the 2004 Sox. The horror, indeed."

Beam's wasn't the only dissenting voice in New England. Angelo Cataldi, a Philadelphia sports radio talk show host who watched Francona for four years in Philadelphia, wrote for the *Providence Journal:* "As a disciplinarian Francona was laughably inept. The running joke in Philadelphia is that Curt Schilling was the first player-manager in baseball since Pete Rose . . . Calling Francona a 'yes man' for Jordan [Francona managed Michael Jordan in A ball] does a disservice to yes men everywhere. Francona should be the lead singer in Yes. He should be running the YES network."

The Sox manager was in a typically upbeat mood before the opener. He arrived at Camden Yards at 12:30 for an 8:05 P.M. start. Mr. Preparation. Boot up the computer. Theo and his minions loved it.

"When I woke up this morning, I was right in the middle of an inning," Francona told the Boston writers. "That usually doesn't happen until the season starts . . . I know that sleep as I knew it is done. That's just the way it goes. You guys may think I'm not looking too good now, but wait until the end of the season."

Terry Francona grew up in baseball. His father, Tito, was a major league outfielder for fifteen seasons with the Orioles, Indians, White

Sox, Tigers, Cardinals, Phillies, Braves, A's, and Brewers. Young Terry was in major league clubhouses from his earliest days and fondly recalled shagging in the outfield during batting practice with the likes of Al Downing and Phil Niekro. His dad never offered any advice about Terry's ball playing ("I always wondered about that," Terry said later). He thought his son would be better off if he figured things out on his own. To this day, Francona downplays his abilities as a player, but he was a sensational high school and college hitter, batting .769 in his senior season at New Brighton (Pennsylvania) High School. He was the first pick of the Montreal Expos in the 1980 amateur draft after three seasons at the University of Arizona, where he hit .401 and was named College Player of the Year by the *Sporting News*. His big league career lasted ten seasons but was largely disappointing. Eleven knee surgeries and major league pitching neutralized his strengths, and he retired in 1990 with a career batting average of .274, two points higher than that of his dad. His worst moment as a big leaguer came when he sustained a serious knee injury chasing a ball in the outfield of St. Louis's Busch Stadium — later the site of his greatest baseball joy.

Like a lot of baseball lifers, Francona had a rough time in his first months away from the game. His wife tried to take charge. In 1991, seeing her husband lying on the couch, watching *Gilligan's Island* reruns, and apparently out of baseball for good, Jacque Francona persuaded Terry to enroll in real estate class. There were young mouths to feed (the Franconas had three children when Terry retired; they now have four). Francona skeptically but dutifully went to real estate school until former teammate Buddy Bell called with an offer to join the White Sox organization as a minor league coach. The decision was fast and easy. Francona made one last trip to the school and told the instructor he was quitting. "No one's going to buy a house from me, anyway," he reasoned.

As his family grew, Francona climbed the ladder, managing in the lower minors for the White Sox. He also did stints of winter ball in the Dominican Republic, where he remembers getting hit by bottles and fruit when his decisions angered the fans. One night he pinch-hit for popular local Tony Pena, and fans waited for him outside the clubhouse after the game. Pena asked Terry what his plans were for the evening, and when Francona said he was going to dinner at a nearby restaurant, Pena said, "No, you're not! Do you hear that pounding on the other side of the clubhouse door? That's for you!" Another memorable managing stint was in the Arizona Fall league in 1994, when Francona had a young shortstop named Nomar Garciaparra and a light-hitting outfielder named Jordan. The stint with superstars served him well later in his career. In 1997, he was hired to manage the Phillies, enduring four consecutive losing seasons with skimpy rosters. Worse, he was starstruck and overwhelmed. He earned a reputation as the ultimate players' manager, which would haunt him through much of his first season with the Red Sox. Schilling was his ace pitcher and the dominant personality in the Philly clubhouse, and the Philly writers believed that it was Schilling, not Francona, who ran the team.

Oddly, Francona's first big league manager was Dick Williams, considered the last of the tough-guy managers of the twentieth century. Williams made his bones with the 1967 Red Sox and later won World Series with the A's. He was a my-way-or-the-highway guy, quick to publicly rip players. He called George Scott "cement head" and was considered a big league dinosaur by the time he stopped managing in 1988. An armchair psychologist might argue that Francona was permanently damaged by having had Williams as his manager. Certainly, by the time he landed in Boston, Terry Francona was the polar opposite of the tough guy who forever changed the fortunes of the Red Sox in the Cinderella season of 1967.

Francona's mantra throughout 2004 was "I love these guys." He made it a point never to criticize any of his players in public. If harsh words were uttered behind closed doors, no one heard about it. Unlike some recent Sox skippers (Jimy Williams, He-Who-Must-Not-Be-Named), Francona engaged the writers and tried to answer questions and explain his moves. Having been raised in baseball clubhouses, he often wandered into old-fashioned baseball vulgarity ("horseshit" is a clubhouse favorite) and could be quite amusing when he relaxed. Talking about an experience on the "quiet car" of a modern train, he said, "This woman was annoyed with me because she said I was talking and it was supposed to be the 'quiet car.' I told her, 'Okay, if this is the quiet car, then why don't you shut the fuck up?'" He also spoke of mail he got from Red Sox fans: "Some of the things they ask you to do are physically impossible. I mean, you can only shove that lineup card so far up your ass." But despite the old-time language, he was decidedly new school, usually conducting his press sessions with a laptop on his desk. Very un-Grady-like.

The 2004 season opener was disastrous. Perhaps it had something to do with the fact that it was played on the site of Ruth's Cafe, the tavern operated by George Herman Ruth Sr. just after the turn of the twentieth century. For a time, young Babe lived upstairs in an apartment over the tavern on West Camden Street, which meant that for nine innings of the opener, Johnny Damon was standing where Ruth actually was a bambino. Seven of the first nine Orioles reached base against Pedro, and Baltimore beat Martinez, 7–2, in a nationally televised (ESPN) Sunday night game. The Red Sox put nineteen runners on base but pushed only two across the plate. Pokey Reese bunted with two outs. Mike Timlin relieved Pedro in the seventh and was torched for three runs on three hits and two walks (maybe Grady was right). Damon went 0–5 and peeled away from a fly ball in right center, which landed for a cheap double. There was speculation that Damon was gun-shy because of the playoff collision in Oakland in 2003.

Worst of all, Martinez left the ballpark before the game was over.

Epstein was steaming when he learned of Pedro's early exit. When the *Globe*'s Gordon Edes asked about it, after midnight, Young Theo said, "Terry is gonna find out what happened and address it with Pedro, I'm sure."

There was no game the following day. Francona took the opportunity to confront his temperamental ace pitcher, and the two engaged in a heated argument. However, the new manager saw no advantage in publicly berating Martinez and presented a sanitized version of events to the Boston media. When he was first asked about Pedro's early departure, he said he would not bother Martinez on his day off. Then he took a bullet for Pedro, saying, "In fairness to him, and everybody else, that wasn't conveyed correctly on my part, and I take responsibility for that."

Weak. This was tantamount to saying that the manager should have to tell his players not to urinate on the dugout floor. Every player on every baseball team knows that you stick around until the game is over. Leaving the ballpark while his teammates were still trying to win,

Martinez sent a powerful and disturbing message. He also put his manager on the spot. Francona should not have had to deal with such a volatile issue on his first day on the job. Moreover, his handling of it rekindled the "too soft" charges that dogged him in Philadelphia.

Pedro continued his careless approach the next night, when he strolled into the clubhouse an hour and a half before the first pitch while the rest of his teammates were already dressed and stretching on the field. He had no comment about anything.

Schilling provided a distinct contrast in that second game, hurling six innings of one-run ball before turning the game over to a bullpen that was almost perfect. Foulke picked up his first save as a Red Sox, and Francona had his first win as Sox manager, a 4–1 win over the Orioles. The game was a nine-inning demonstration of the wisdom of Young Theo's off-season effort, right off the Bill James blueprint from Lawrence, Kansas.

When he wasn't pitching, Schilling was appearing at charity events, going online to chat on Sox fan Web sites, trashing the New England media on the radio, and generally making his opinions known about every issue of the day. He chastised those who criticized Pedro's early exit in Baltimore. Anointing himself team spokesman—annoying some veteran Sox players, given their seniority—he announced that none of the players had any problems with Pedro's behavior. Schilling wanted Martinez happy. He would leave it to others to note the contrast in the team's two ace pitchers.

The Sox played extra innings in Baltimore on the final night of that series. They lost the game when a journeyman lefty named Bobby Jones walked four batters in the bottom of the thirteenth. But that was only the beginning of a rough patch for the Olde Towne Team. Bound for the home opener, the team boarded its plane at Baltimore-Washington International Airport—and sat on the tarmac for four hours because of a defective wing flap. Another plane was summoned, but not in time to avert a sleepless overnight. The Sox saw the sun rise as they flew into Boston, and it was 7:30 A.M. on Good Friday, April 9, when they trudged into Fenway Park for the first time in 2004. Francona never bothered to go home. He slept on his office couch for an hour, then got up and made out his Opening Day lineup card. Ellis

Burks went home to his apartment, which had no curtains, and put a towel over his face as he tried to sleep for a few hours. The players had to be back at the ballpark by noon for the 3 P.M. start.

Outside the park, the fans had no idea of the travel travails. The Sox had already sold a record $2.4 million in tickets before the first game, and Opening Day scalpers enjoyed their best day ever, with bleacher seats fetching up to $125. It was a seller's market right up until Patriot owner Bob Kraft popped out of the dugout for the ceremonial first pitch.

Fenway looked terrific for its ninety-third opener. The new wrinkle in 2004 was a rooftop section above the right field grandstand. Seating four hundred, the new space featured intimate tables, a full bar area, and sparkling restrooms. A giant Budweiser sign loomed overhead, replacing the Jimmy Fund board of many decades. In exchange, the Sox were getting $14 million from the King of Beers. It was one more piece of evidence that the new owners had no intention of leaving Fenway Park. Who would make these kinds of improvements if the wrecking ball was on the schedule?

The new owners appreciated the rabid interest in the team and made no apologies for the highest prices in baseball. A spring survey of all thirty teams revealed that a family of four would spend an average of $263 for a day trip to Fenway Park in 2004. In second place was Wrigley Field, where a day would cost $70 less. The Sox were charging more than the Yankees, Dodgers, Giants, or Phillies. But almost no one in Red Sox Nation complained. The 2004 Sox would be only the fourth franchise in baseball history to play in front of a sellout for every home game (1996–2000 Indians, 1996 Rockies, 2000 Giants).

If you renovate it, they will come.

Schilling got the biggest ovation when the players were introduced. There weren't many other highlights. The Toronto Blue Jays smoked fourteen hits and beat the sloppy, sleepless Sox, 10–5. The lowlight of the afternoon was the sight of Boston reserve outfielder–first baseman David McCarty on the mound in the ninth inning. Given the thirteen-inning fiasco in Baltimore and the Good Friday rout, Francona simply ran out of pitchers. It was the first time the Sox had used a nonpitcher on the mound in a game since 1997, when Jimy Williams sent Mike Benjamin into a game and apologized to the umpire. Needing a posi-

Ghosts, curses, 1918—it wasn't so long ago that these were all part of the Boston fans' experience at Yankee Stadium.

In the wicked winter of 2003–2004, Red Sox general manager Theo Epstein (*above*) coveted and lost Alex Rodriguez (*opposite*), baseball's highest-paid and arguably best player to—who else?—the Yankees. The headline-grabbing A-Rod trade would stoke the flames of the Red Sox–Yankees rivalry all season.

Johnny Damon set the tone early in the season with his new look. A cult of idiots was born, complete with disciples.

Red Sox Nation endured more midseason taunts and horrors in New York. But Sox leader Jason Varitek (*opposite*) made a statement at Fenway in July, stuffing his catcher's mitt into A-Rod's pretty face.

Brooding shortstop Nomar Garciaparra was a common sight in the club-house until he was traded to the Chicago Cubs, a bold move that drew both ire and praise from Red Sox fans and the media.

tion player in the fifth game of the season made the Sox look down-right unprepared, but Theo rightfully explained, "These are unusual circumstances."

Pedro made everything right the next night by pitching 7.2 innings of four-hit, one-run ball in a 4–1 victory, which got the Sox back to .500 (3–3). What made this game significant was the appearance of Francona on the mound after Martinez fanned Frank Catalanotto on a 91-mile-per-hour fastball. It was Pedro's 106th and fastest pitch of the night, and Francona came out of the dugout and yanked him before Vernon Wells left the on-deck circle. Little would never have insulted Martinez by taking him out in the middle of an inning, particularly if Pedro was sailing smoothly. In this case, he was lifted after fanning a lefty hitter, with a right-handed hitter getting ready to bat. It made no sense . . . unless you were plugged into the database of the invisible man in Lawrence, Kansas. Bill James and STATS, Inc., concluded that opponents hit .231 against Martinez before he reaches 105 pitches and .364 afterward. Francona and pitching coach Dave Wallace all but admitted that 105 would be pumpkin time for Pedro. There was a new sheriff in town, and he was going to follow the orders of Bill James, Young Theo, and his minions.

Toronto general manager J. P. Ricciardi was in Boston for the opening weekend. The Jays had won eighty-six games in 2003, but their payroll put them in the bottom quarter of all the baseball teams. On Opening Day, the Jays' payroll was $50 million compared with $125 million for Boston and $182 million for New York. It was going to be difficult to compete in the same division, and the Jays were going down.

Ricciardi, a Massachusetts native, had a good perspective from his front-row seat: "The one thing you know when you're in our division is that those two teams are always going to be able to do that. Look at this year. We thought A-Rod was going to the Red Sox and he ends up going to the Yankees. If we had him, his salary would be half of our payroll. I think they've taken it to another level. It's become personal . . . We just can't take a guy with a high salary. I'm not jealous of them. I came from Oakland. In sixteen years there we were always fighting uphill, and I think it's the same thing here. I'm into player development. You don't get to tap into that potential when you have the money. Draft picks don't matter. On draft day, the Yankees just show up. For us, it's like a six-day war room, an NFL-type thing. Some year, the Yankees may not even show up for the draft."

On Easter Sunday, David Ortiz hit a two-run, twelfth-inning, walk-off homer to beat the Blue Jays and put the Sox above .500. A joyous mob greeted him at home plate and the fans stayed around to hear "Dirty Water," by the Standells. It was the first game in 2004 that felt like a Cowboy Up game from 2003. And it came just days before the long-awaited arrival of the Yankees. It would not be Ortiz's final walk-off moment of 2004. The big man who rose on Easter was just getting started.

The Red Sox had a scheduled day off after Ortiz's walk-off winner, but the players were required to attend a $400,000 fund-raising luncheon at the Copley Marriott Hotel. The ubiquitous Ben Affleck and comedian Seth Myers roasted the Sox while a thousand members of Boston's business community ate lunch and tried to mingle with the ballplayers. They had paid between $5,000 and $10,000 per table for the event, which raised money for local children's charities. Only two Sox players failed to show: Lowe, who was scheduled to pitch that night, and Ramirez. Affleck joked that Manny was probably lunching with Enrique Iglesias (a nice twist on Manny's AWOL night with Yankee Enrique Wilson in September 2003), but Lucchino and his friends were steamed. It was another demonstration of the ball club's lack of control over its superstars. These were the days they missed Alex Rodriguez. Manny could do the same job at home plate, but he could not do the meet-and-greet drill that was so important to this image-conscious Sox ownership.

While the Sox were letting their hair grow and getting used to their new manager, their alter egos, the clean-cut Yankees, were struggling, still legless after the long trip to Japan. The team with the massive payroll batted only .205 in its first seven games, and A-Rod hit .160 in the first week of the season. Mussina, who was getting roughed up on a regular basis, blamed the trip to Japan. The best news in New York was manager Joe Torre's signing a three-year, $19.2 million contract extension. It stipulated that if Torre did not want to manage the Yankees after 2007, he could spend the next six years as a special adviser. In a

New York newspaper, it was characterized as the "keep Joe out of the Red Sox dugout" clause.

The Yanks were in no condition for an April renewal of hostilities, but the schedule called for them to play four in Boston on the weekend of April 16–19, which was also Patriots' Day weekend, featuring the traditional Boston Marathon. New York's four starters for the weekend —Javier Vazquez, Mussina, Jose Contreras, and Kevin Brown—were being paid $49.2 million, almost precisely the amount of the entire Toronto Blue Jay ball club.

The night before the Yankees arrived, while Pedro was getting cuffed around by the Orioles—raising more questions about his health and his future—a prop plane flew over Fenway toting a banner: NY POST—EMPIRE STRIKES BACK—GO YANKEES! The *Post* had paid pilot Harry Nikitas $900 for a two-and-a-half-hour ad. Nikitas made it back to the Fitchburg Airport without being shot down by ground fire. Meanwhile, *USA Today* sent Chris Jenkins to Boston wearing a Yankee cap and an Alex Rodriguez jersey. Jenkins and a photographer stalked the bars and shops around Fenway the day before the Yanks arrived with predictable results, which appeared in the Nation's Newspaper.

The redoubtable *Post*, on the heels of its aerial reconnaissance, won the trophy for best pregame hype. Its front page featured a pinstripe figure wearing a Darth Vader mask and holding a bat over his right shoulder. The ever-understated headline screamed MAY THE CURSE BE WITH YOU. The back cover displayed Jeter and Manny sandwiched around the headline LET THE WAR BEGIN! Inside the bold covers, Steinbrenner told the *Post*, "It will depend on how good our pitching is because they have a tough lineup." There was also a MAY THE CURSE BE WITH YOU two-page spread, which included a story complaining about the Radio City Rockettes' wearing Red Sox jerseys during a performance in Boston earlier in the week.

Players from both teams tried to downplay the early April series. "I've run out of words," said Jeter. But Ortiz admitted, "We try to say it's not different, but it is. It just is."

The American League East standings looked familiar when the Yankees arrived in the Hub. New York was first, Boston second, a half game behind. It seemed normal, but given that the Yankees had played only nine games and the Sox ten, it was surprising not to find an early season aberration. It also made for one of those "who researches this stuff?" records. The 1–2 ranking on April 16 meant that this was the fiftieth consecutive meeting between the two teams in which the Yankees and Red Sox were 1–2 in the standings. A full three consecutive years, dating back to April 2001. It was the longest streak in big league history.

The Red Sox put an end to the streak, winning the first game of the series, 6–2, and taking three of four in a wacky weekend that featured uneven performances by both teams. The two clubs made eleven errors in the four games, and Damon and Kapler forgot how many outs there were. Most of the big-money starting pitchers failed, but the man who suffered the most was A-Rod. Much to the titillation of the 140,000 fans who filled Fenway, Rodriguez went 1–17 over the four games. He was 0–16 with six strikeouts before stroking a single in the ninth inning of the final game. He also committed a throwing error that led to the tying run in Boston's 5–4 victory on Marathon Monday. Torre joked that it might be a good idea to change A-Rod's number. Rodriguez had worn no. 3 throughout his career but had to switch in New York because Babe Ruth retired the digit after his Yankee tenure. Rodriguez took no. 13, which appeared to be giving him bad luck, and Torre suggested putting Ruth's jersey in Rodriguez's locker or perhaps changing 13 to ⅓.

On hearing the latter suggestion, GM Brian Cashman shrugged and joked, "Yeah, we're getting one-third of the production."

Hours before the first game, the Sox ensured the date's immortality by dedicating a statue of Ted Williams outside Fenway's Gate B on Van Ness Street. Williams's former teammates Bobby Doerr and Johnny Pesky participated in the unveiling, along with the Splendid Splinter's daughter Claudia. Doerr and Pesky would be back for some ceremonial first tosses before the end of October.

Near the statue, seven hours before gametime, no fewer than fifteen television trucks were beached on Van Ness Street. It looked like the OJ trial. The Red Sox public relations staff issued 250 extra media credentials, which meant more reporters for an April series than for the division playoff series against the Oakland A's. Throughout the afternoon, Curse capitalists infested the streets around Fenway. Fans were handed "Break the Curse" cookies, a molasses-clove recipe from Boston's Dancing Deer Baking Company. More sophisticated was the effort of Michael Moorby, CEO of Rebel Forces LLC and the maker of Anti-Fan Stadium Gear. Moorby was selling Yankee-hater hats. They were adorned with a logo featuring a Y and an H, layered in the familiar N-Y formation of the Yankee cap. Tiny devil horns sprouted from the letters on the hater cap. Rebel Forces sent a three-page press release to media members to introduce the product. Datelined "BOSTON, MA, April 16, 2004," it began: "Hate is good. At least to the extent that it opposes Evil. That is the basic premise underlying The Anti-Fan Line of Stadium Gear which will makes its debut at Fenway Park in Boston, MA, on April 16, 2004, when the Red Sox host their chief nemesis, the New York Yankees." The first Red Sox player to wear the cap in public was Schilling, who donned a Yankee-hater lid at a Bruins game that weekend.

The Yankees prepared for the first game by watching a tape of October's Game 7. Rodriguez had dined at the Capitol Grille on Newbury Street the night before and said he'd received a particularly vulgar welcome. He chose not to elaborate, saying, "Maybe another day. It was rated 'R.' I got welcomed, but I can't talk about it."

Jeter did talk to *Sports Illustrated* about it. He said the two, seated at a window table, received middle-finger salutes and charges of "You suck" from a parade of passersby. "It's gotten worse over the years, their hatred for us," sighed Jeter. "This was one of their better performances."

The first game against the Yankees at Fenway was also the seventh home game for the Sox. It meant that tickets were marked "Game 7," which naturally played into the fears and frustrations of what had happened six months earlier. It seemed both symbolic and symmetric that Wakefield would be the starting pitcher. Wakefield didn't learn about it until the day before. Torrential downpours had postponed two Sox-Oriole games during the week, and Francona was forced to tinker with the rotation. The fans embraced the veteran righty when he went to the bullpen to warm up for the start.

"You can't put it into words," Wakefield said later. "I wanted to show the fans my appreciation by going out there and giving everything I had. It turned out to be a win for us, and it was kind of like my thanks to them for opening their arms to me and embracing me like their second son."

The Red Sox PR department made no attempt to hide from history. When Wakefield threw his first pitch, the crack staff calculated that it had been 182 days, 19 hours, and 51 minutes between Yankee pitches for Wakefield. The tone of the weekend was set in the first inning, when ground balls went through the legs of both Jeter and Giambi and the Sox erupted for four runs off Vazquez. It the end, it was a satisfying 6–2 victory. At least thirty fans were ejected in the course of the evening.

Establishing a theme that would carry through the entire season, decisions by Francona were framed in relation to what had happened against the Yankees in October. When the Yanks loaded the bases with two out in the eighth inning, bringing Matsui to the plate as the potential tying run, Francona came out and called for lefty Embree—the same Embree who had not been summoned by Grady when Matsui came to the plate in October. It was as if Francona were wearing a WWGD bracelet. He could look at his wrist, think What would Grady do? then make the opposite choice. It once worked for former Yankee employee George Costanza, why not for the new Red Sox manager?

Francona tried to downplay the event. "I still woke up and looked in the mirror and had no hair," he said. "Some things never change."

The Sox won again the next day, 5–2, as Curt ("I guess I hate the Yankees now") Schilling pitched 6.1 innings of one-run baseball, striking out eight, including Rodriguez twice. It was a virtual coronation for the new ace righty. He said he felt the love:

"It's just energy. Emotion that becomes energy for me. It's an October atmosphere. The only regular-season game that I could equate that to was the game in Philadelphia when I pitched against the Yankees in front of sixty thousand in a sold-out Veterans Stadium. I'd never seen that before. The Yankees bring that when they travel. I didn't realize the depth of passion, not just for the team, but for this series. Obviously the media makes it out to be a much bigger deal than we do, but your emotions are heightened because there are expectations."

The manager scored points when he lifted an angry Schilling in the middle of the seventh, flying in the face of the old Philadelphia, Schilling-as-player-manager theory.

The Sox fans continued to make their presence felt. Rodriguez was routinely booed while Giambi was subjected to a more pointed attack. The Fenway legions chanted, "You use ster-roids," every time Giambi came to the plate. Caught in a web of accusation that also snared Barry Bonds and Sheffield in 2004, Giambi said he didn't hear the hooting, but players in both clubhouses disputed the notion. (In December, Giambi's leaked grand jury testimony established that he had used steroids.) Privately, Yankee officials complained that the Red Sox were stifling music over the PA system during batting practice to make sure that the Yankees heard all the insults from the stands.

Burks said, "As a professional player you learn to eliminate certain things, but when you hear chants like that out of thousands of people, how do you not let it bother you? It gets under your skin a little bit." Schilling added, "I was impressed with their ability to chant in unison."

Despite two terrible games, Jeter was in a good mood on Sunday morning. Standing in front of his locker, spotting a Boston reporter, he asked about the condition of Garciaparra. Was the Sox shortstop healthy? Would he sign again with Boston? The Yankee star wanted to know. Then he kissed his bat and called A-Rod to join him in the batting cage under Fenway's center field bleachers (visiting teams call it "the hole"). Despite rumors to the contrary, it seemed that the millionaire stars on the left side of the Yankee infield were getting along well. They were always together. They even looked quite a bit alike and could have been mistaken for brothers. They'd been together in the Ritz bar the night before, and now they were going out together to hit. They reasoned that Lowe was going to be working on ten days of rest and would be too strong. The sinkerball wasn't going to sink today. That was the hope.

The hope was fulfilled. The Yankees routed Lowe for seven runs on eight hits and four walks in a mere 2.2 innings of a 7–3 New York victory. Clearly perturbed about having to wait ten days between starts to accommodate Martinez and Schilling, Lowe shrugged and said, "I got a check sitting in my locker. I feel like I should give it back."

Starting for the Yankees the next day was Cuban righty Jose Contreras, a latecomer to the Red Sox–Yankee rivalry, but one who had inadvertently played an enormous role in the escalation of emotions between the franchises.

Epstein, who'd been on the job less than a month when Contreras sold his services, remembers it this way:

"Luis Eljaua was our director of international scouting and was on the case early. Luis is Cuban, so he had a pretty good relationship with Contreras. He was following him all around, and he was the first person of anyone in Major League Baseball to go to Nicaragua. He beat me down there by a week or ten days, and he was calling me every day. He told me that Contreras was staying in this fourteen-room hotel, the Hotel Campo Real.

"There were only five rooms left, so he suggested we buy up all those rooms to reserve the rooms for us, and as a side benefit, it would be doubly sweet to keep the other teams away from him. So I got there and it was a great hotel. There were chickens running around all over the place and a monkey tied to a rope. There were little hammocks and a covered bar. Contreras was there, and we got to know him, staying up late, telling baseball stories, and smoking cigars with him one night. He kept saying how much he didn't like the Yankees. He liked the Red Sox, and he wanted to pitch with Pedro Martinez. His agent, Jaime Torres, was there. The Yankees kept coming in and meeting with him. His agent said, 'We're gonna get it done tonight.' He alternated meetings between the Red Sox and Yankees. We reached our limit. The Yankees came in and had their last meeting with him. Luis and I were sitting at the bar. The room was about forty feet away. We could see two dark figures, Yankee scouts, going into the room. We kept seeing the door open and close. The scouts would come out. There were frantic phone calls, we assume back to either Brian Cashman in New York or Steinbrenner in Tampa, asking for more money. Then they went in and came out with smiles and handshakes."

Contreras had signed with the Yankees for four years and $32 million. He could not look Epstein in the eye when he thanked him for his efforts.

Part of the mythology of *l'affaire* Contreras has Epstein trashing his hotel room when he learned the outcome. Epstein insists that nothing of the sort happened and believes the rumor was started by Yankee officials. Gordon Blakeley, Yankee director of international scouting, and Carlos Rios, another scout, were with the Yankee entourage in Nicaragua and feared they'd be fired if they went home without a signed contract.

"From what I understand, some of the Yankee officials who were down there proactively contacted New York papers and told them that I destroyed the hotel room," said Epstein.

What is not in dispute is the reaction of Lucchino when he got the news. Reached by phone in Brookline by Murray Chass of the *New York Times,* the furious CEO first said, "No comment." But he couldn't resist. "No, I'll make a comment. The Evil Empire extends its tentacles even into Latin America."

Wham. It was the Red Sox–Yankee equivalent of the assassination of Archduke Ferdinand.

Steinbrenner went ballistic when he heard of the remark. He told the *New York Daily News,* "That's bullshit. That's how a sick person thinks. I've learned this about Lucchino. He's baseball's foremost chameleon of all time. He changes colors depending on where he's standing. He's been at Baltimore and deserted them there. When he was in San Diego, he was a big man for the small markets. Now he's in Boston, and he's for the big markets. He's not the kind of guy you want to have in your foxhole. He's running the team behind John Henry's back. I warned John it would happen to him. Just be careful. He talks out of both sides of his mouth. He has trouble talking out of the front."

There was history behind the rhetoric. Lucchino entered baseball with Edward Bennett Williams when the attorney bought the Orioles in 1979. Williams was friendly with Steinbrenner and had represented him when Steinbrenner faced a felony rap for illegal campaign contributions to Richard Nixon when he was president. In the 1980s, Lucchino was the power behind the throne in the Oriole front office and represented Baltimore's interests when both the Orioles and Yankees were American League East powers. One memorable joust involved the strike-ridden 1981 season, when the Orioles won more games than any team in the division but were excluded from the playoffs because they failed to win either of the contrived half seasons that were created

by the strike interruption. This came one year after the O's had won
100 games yet missed the playoffs because the Yankees won 103. Lucchino's efforts for the Orioles put him in conflict with Steinbrenner,
and the Boss never forgot him.

"George still sees me as Ed's bag carrier, and that's fine," said Lucchino.

In the early 1990s, Lucchino was in charge of a league committee
that inspected the Yankees' whopping new cable contract. The American League voted, 13–1, in favor of reconsidering how to distribute the
Yankees' cable money. Steinbrenner, naturally, was not pleased. By '96,
Lucchino had moved to the Padres, but he clashed with Steinbrenner
again over the services of Japanese pitcher Hideki Irabu. In the 1998
World Series, the Yankees beat Lucchino's San Diego Padres in four
straight games, and there were issues about poor seating arrangements
for the executives of both teams in enemy ballparks.

"We've clashed on issues over the years, political and economic,
within baseball," Lucchino told Gordon Edes of the *Globe*. "Then we
had the 1998 World Series [the Yankees beat Lucchino's Padres, 4–0),
when he got his pound of flesh. Now I've walked into a situation where
I've inherited a rivalry that comes quite naturally."

Lucchino never let go of his *Star Wars* reference. The Sox game entertainment staff regularly played *Star Wars* music when the Yankees
prowled Fenway during batting practice.

The Yankees won the Sunday game of the April weekend in Boston,
but a struggling Contreras was unable to stick around long enough to
pick up the win, even though he took a 7–1 lead into the bottom of
the third. It never worked out for Contreras and the Yankees. At midseason, he would be dealt to the White Sox and replaced by fellow
Cuban Orlando "El Duque" Hernandez. As it turned out, the only real
contribution Contreras made to the Yankees was to drive a wedge further between the Sox and Yanks front offices.

The Yankee team bus pulled out of the new Ritz Hotel, on the edge
of Boston's Chinatown, at 8:30 A.M. on Monday, April 19. It is not a
traditional departure time for baseball players, but in Massachusetts
the holiday known as Patriots' Day commemorates the midnight ride
of Paul Revere and the battles of Concord and Lexington in 1775. The

Red Sox always play at home on Patriots' Day and they always start at 11 A.M., an hour before the start of the Boston Marathon in Hopkinton. The Yanks, most of whom were still complaining about their trip to Japan, were less than enthused with the early time.

The Red Sox stole the final game of the series. Francona sent out a lineup that included Cesar Crespo, David McCarty, and Kapler, all playing behind the number five starter, Bronson Arroyo. Kevin Brown pitched for the Yankees and led, 4–1, in the third inning. Given all of the above, New York would generally win this game 99 times out of 100, but the Sox prevailed on a wacky morning and beat the Yanks for the third time in four days, 5–4. It was without question the most exciting game of the almost boring series. The Sox won, even though Kapler twice lost track of the outs while running the bases. It was Kapler who delivered the game-winning hit in the bottom of the eighth when he singled home McCarty, who had doubled to left.

The marathon leaders, all Kenyans, were approaching Kenmore Square outside the left field wall when Foulke came on to close the game in the top of the ninth. Across from the Green Monster, beyond the right field grandstand, black smoke spewed from a fire in the Fenway area. The biblical effect was not lost on Young Theo. He turned to the man next to him and said, "The apocalypse is upon us. The tying run is coming to the plate in the form of A-Rod, who hasn't had a hit all series. Foulke's facing him. Right field's on fire. Apparently we're all going to die. This is the end of the world."

It wasn't the last time the Sox would look in the sky and see omens. Rodriguez snapped out of his 0–16 Boston funk with a single to center, but Foulke put out the fire, getting the final out when Giambi took a called third strike, sending thirty-five thousand happy fans toward Kenmore to watch the end of the Marathon.

The seeds of doubt were planted. Was A-Rod too soft for New York?

"You can't keep a good player down," said Cashman. "The cream will rise to the top. In hindsight I should have said that he's got to go through the same process Roger Clemens did when he got here, Patrick Ewing when he got to New York, Mike Piazza with the Mets. Every star that hits New York. I think big names in the big markets, you have to walk through the fire first. It's human nature to put a lot of pressure on yourself and try to perform at a higher level. But you know the numbers will be there at the end."

Torre added, "It's so much bigger for him than anyone else right now. He's fighting it. He's patient to a point. It'll happen. It's sort of funny for us, because we know how talented he is, but it's not funny for him."

Other Yankees assessed the weekend. Mike Mussina said, "We came up here and we felt we were going to play good baseball. We're not playing the way we're capable of. That's the frustrating part. It's important to come out and win some of these ball games, and in the first two games we didn't even show enough life to put ourselves in it. We just haven't played our best baseball. We need to do it when we come to Boston. When you play the Red Sox, with all the hype and expectations, you want go out there and play the best games you can play, and we have not."

"It ain't everything," said Gary Sheffield. "It ain't the World Series. Until that last pitch is thrown, I'm not worried . . . From their end, they got the first round. There's another round."

In fact there were several more rounds, much to the titillation of the Sox.

But the next round went even worse for the Yankees. Four days after the Marathon weekend, the Sox invaded New York for a three-day weekend, which resulted in a three-game Boston sweep. In straight sets it was 11–2, 3–2, and 2–0. The Yankee fans were booing Jeter and Bernie Williams before it was over, and the tabloids had a festival of fret at the Yankees' expense. This early demolition of New York's megamillion wagon emboldened Red Sox Nation and cast true doubt on the Yankees' ability to compete with the Red Sox. It was shocking.

The scene in and around Yankee Stadium was not as zooey as in Boston a week earlier. The Knicks and Nets were involved in an early round NBA playoff series, and the NFL draft was scheduled for that Saturday and Sunday. Still, the *Post* featured a back-page fabrication of Rodriguez sitting on a dugout bench that appeared to be on fire. The headline was A-ROD ON HOT SEAT. Meanwhile, fans walking past Hudson News stands at Grand Central or Penn Station couldn't help but notice Pedro Martinez on the cover of *Business Week,* next to the headline CAN THE RED SOX BEAT THE YANKEES AND FINALLY WIN IT ALL?

The continued emphasis on the two division rivals was viewed with some amusement by the rest of Baseball America. Jim Caple of ESPN.com wrote: "By exploring the Internet and examining the sports pages . . . you will find that other major league teams still stubbornly persist in playing games outside Fenway Park and Yankee Stadium. I know, I know. I didn't realize there were still other baseball teams, either. Like you, I thought they had all been turned into farm clubs to feed the Greatest Rivalry in Sports, but apparently, that is not the case. There not only are other teams in baseball, some have better records than the Red Sox or Yankees. And some of those teams just might be better than the Red Sox or the Yankees. And some of those teams just might play in the World Series instead of the Red Sox or the Yankees. Teams like Oakland and Anaheim."

Sox players expressed little agita about the return to the scene of the hideous finale of 2003. Timlin, the man who had been warming up in the eighth—the man who should have been in the game instead of Pedro—was the first Sox player to pop into the dugout before the game. Timlin said he had no regrets. He'd wanted to pitch that night and was disappointed when the phone didn't ring, but he wasn't into looking back. He remembered being in the clubhouse when Boone hit the homer. He remembered waiting for Wakefield to come through the door. He wanted to tell his teammate that none of it was his fault.

Millar said, "It makes you tougher, makes you stronger. If you don't taste the bitterness and taste the loss, you won't realize how good the W is. This team went through that. It was miserable that night and those first couple of weeks, but you know what? That's what it's about. It makes you stronger. It's not even an issue for us."

Standing in the dugout before batting practice, Varitek said, "It'd be pretty unprofessional if we couldn't put that behind us."

Easy to say. But for fans and media members, returning to Yankee Stadium was like driving through your childhood neighborhood and passing the spot where your dog got run over when you were ten years old. The ballpark on 161st Street was still a place where something bad happened. The last time the Sox were in the visitor's dugout at Yankee Stadium, they were cursing, crying, and kicking buckets of Gatorade while Aaron Boone circled the bases. That they were able to return without much thought augured well for future visits. No longer the Cowboy Uppers of 2003, the new Red Sox had confidence and swagger without the slogans. They were in the moment, and they seemed to have a genuine fondness for one another. At this hour, the absence of the injured Garciaparra was viewed only in the context of his missing contributions at the plate and in the field, but the possibility exists that the Sox players were more comfortable in the clubhouse when Nomar wasn't sitting around with steam coming out of his ears because a reporter asked him a question or a teammate inadvertently interrupted his rigid routine.

The Sox again pounded Contreras, winning the first game in Yankee Stadium, 11–2. Boston hit four homers to reinforce the belief that Contreras couldn't pitch against the team he rejected in Nicaragua. Yankee people believed Boston was stealing signs. Millar (who homered) and Company smiled when the theory was floated. No comment. At that moment, Contreras's career numbers against Boston were 0–3 with an ERA of 18.00 (twenty earned runs in ten innings). "I don't know about the bidding war, but we've had great at-bats against him," said Millar. Yankee fans started to wonder if Contreras might be an embedded Red Sox.

A rookie pitcher named Lenny DiNardo made his major league debut for the Red Sox in the ninth inning of the blowout. The detail was lost on most people in the crowded winner's clubhouse, but Kapler approached several reporters and urged that they speak to the kid pitcher about his special day. It was a small but telling gesture. "Gabe is an awesome teammate," said Varitek. It said something about the camaraderie of the 2004 Sox, something that would take them where no Boston team had gone in so many years.

Standing in front of his dugout the next morning, Cashman said he hadn't heard from Steinbrenner. He also said he'd learned not to worry about picking up the papers during bad times. The Saturday *Daily News* reviewed Friday's Yankee stinker with YUCK! while the *Post* put the load on the Yankee moundsmen with the headline STAFF INFECTION.

Red Sox executives don't particularly like going to Yankee Stadium either. It holds bad memories, and there's a certain feeling that they aren't welcome. Yankee Stadium features a woeful selection of luxury boxes, and there's no good place for out-of-town owners to sit. Tom Werner went there rarely after he was shoved by a Yankee fan in the lower boxes while he watched his Padres play the Yankees in the 1998 World Series. Werner was not with Henry and Lucchino when the disaster unfolded in October 2003, and he was not at the first two Sox games in Yankee Stadium in 2004.

Henry's pale complexion can't take much sunshine and he doesn't like getting hooted by Yankee fans, so he watched most of the Saturday win from the Red Sox television booth next to the press box behind home plate. He was standing in the booth when A-Rod hit his first home run for the Yankees against the Red Sox.

Henry is a notorious low talker, and it was hard to hear him over the din of Yankee Stadium during the game, but he spoke about his new nonrelationship with Steinbrenner: "He's been pretty quiet, hasn't he? I'm not mad at him. We never had a social relationship. We'd sit together at ball games once in a while at spring training or here. He treated me well here."

The Red Sox won again, 3–2, in twelve innings, despite going 0–19 while batting with runners in scoring position. Boston scored all three runs on sacrifice flies. In the series finale on Sunday, the Sox won again, this time by the score of 2–0 as Pedro smothered the Yankees for seven innings, then turned the game over to a bullpen that was as outstanding as it had been in October when He-Who-Must-Not-Be-Named didn't make the call. This Sunday, the Sox went at the Yanks with an infield of McCarty, Crespo, Reese, and Bellhorn. Contrast that quartet with the Yankee foursome of Rodriguez, Jeter, Giambi, and Enrique Wilson. New York's infield was signed to contracts worth more than $560 million. Still, the Sox prevailed. Ramirez's monstrous, two-run homer provided all the offense in the New York finale, and Manny continued to speak to the media. He talked about the homer. He talked about Pedro. He talked about the Yankees. He even talked about the awkward winter.

"I never think they didn't want me or nothing," said Ramirez. ". . . I ain't going to be thinking, Oh, they put me on waivers, they don't want me. So what? They don't want me. It's a lot of things out there that I could go and play and have fun. But I'm glad I came back to Boston, and I hope I could finish here . . . The main goal for me before I leave this game is to maybe get a ring."

The emergence of Ramirez as a fan favorite and go-to guy for the media was somewhat shocking. Manny was scorned in the winter of 2003–2004. There was no support to keep him around when his name was floated in the Rodriguez trade. The front office wanted relief from his salary, and there was a considerable question about his desire to play in the wake of his wacky weekend in August–September when he bailed out of games against the Yankees and Phillies. But a month into the new season, while Pedro pouted and Nomar worked out apart from the team while his Achilles healed, Manny was suddenly the team mascot. After three seasons of Marcel Marceau Manny, the savant slugger was Manny Motormouth. In a hilarious interview with Boston television sports reporter Wendi Nix, Ramirez said, "I don't got no problem with the media. The problem is that I'm a quiet guy. I like to come, do my job, and just go home. But I want people to get to know me a little bit more, and that's why I'm talking a little bit more . . . The big thing now is everybody's getting along so good. Everybody's laughing and having fun, and that's the big key. It doesn't matter if you have a good team or a bad team as long as you go out and have fun . . . The problem is that $160 million, that don't last like they used to. I'm on a budget now. Can't be spending money. But don't worry. I'm going to take you to Taco Bell."

Manny being Manny. The phrase was used in earlier seasons to explain yet another knucklehead play or disappearance. Ramirez's unpredictability and occasional lackadaisical play could be tough on the eyes, especially for hardball purists, but in 2004 Manny served as the poster child for a band of sloppy brothers who had fun . . . and won. They could be late, unshaved, and covered in dirt, but they got the job done. It's not unprofessional when you win. With help from Jesus Johnny in center, Manny set the tone for the 2004 Red Sox team. Clearly, Manny didn't have his head in the history books, where the ghosts and curses lived.

Meanwhile Rodriguez, the man who would have been traded for Manny, stood at his locker after the last of the seven April games against Boston and said, "Everyone cares too much, and sometimes that translates into trying too hard. We have to believe in ourselves and believe in our talent and play with energy. There's a home turf we're very proud of. That's a good team over there, Boston. They're playing with a lot of energy and executing all parts of their game extremely well. They did it there and they did it here. Every facet of their game has been almost flawless."

The Yankees batted .152 in the three games. At the end of the series, they were hitting .217, the second lowest in baseball, and they led the majors with nineteen errors. Millar raised an eyebrow and said, "You know what? Those guys miss Soriano—more than anyone thought they would." Mike Vaccaro of the *New York Post* wrote: "There is an appropriate time for alarm. There is a proper place for panic. For the Yankees, that time is now, and that place is Yankee Stadium . . . If the Red Sox proved anything the last few weeks, it's that they really are, right now, a far superior baseball team."

New York's poor play didn't hurt television ratings in either city. The Yankees' YES Network set a record for a live event in the series finale while the Sox's NESN outlet enjoyed its third-highest single-game rating in history.

That Monday, Steinbrenner issued a tepid statement from his Tampa bunker: "I have a great manager in Joe Torre and GM in Brian Cashman, and I have confidence in both of them. It's in their hands."

There. Round one to the Red Sox by a knockout. The Red Sox left New York with a four-and-a-half-game lead, five in the loss column, and the Boss was issuing threats to his manager and general manager.

It kept getting better. After sweeping in New York, the Sox came home and took three straight from Tampa Bay. At month's end, Sox fans had every reason to think this truly was The Year. Of course, there had been a lot of times the Red Sox thought they were going to do it at this stage. The final gameday of April featured a doubleheader sweep of the Rays, in which the mercurial Byung Hyun-Kim pitched five innings of one-hit ball in front of the largest Fenway crowd (35,614) in fourteen years. The Sox had the best record in baseball, Boston's bullpen pitched thirty-two and a third consecutive scoreless innings, and Francona had a sixth starter to go with an already strong quintet. Their 15–6 record represented the best start in franchise history since (gulp) 1918. No ghosts. No curses. No buzzard luck. Optimism was positively boundless. The doubleheader featured a ball boy named

Dan Godfrey making perhaps Fenway's finest catch since Cleveland outfielder Al Luplow took a homer away from Dick Williams in the 1960s, as well as the sight of Young Theo and Dr. Charles Steinberg cleaning the ballpark between games of the day-night affair. The 2004 Red Sox were the feel-good movie of the new year, and the Nation had reason to believe that this year *would* be different.

6

Pedro and Johnny

A N OLD SAYING IN THE National Basketball Association holds that no playoff series has truly begun until the road team wins a game. When it comes to the Red Sox, veteran fans have learned that the season hasn't truly started until a Red Sox star starts bitching about something. And so it was that New England sports fans picked up their May 1 newspapers and read that Pedro Martinez was unhappy. He said he was done negotiating for the season. He said he would become a free agent at the end of the season. He said he felt sorry for Red Sox fans who wanted to see him pitch. He called his owners liars—those men who were paying him $17.5 million, more than any pitcher in the history of baseball.

"Right now, it's done," he told reporters after a rainout at Ameriquest Field in Texas. "It's not going to work this year . . . I just don't like people lying, trying to fake that they're signing us when they never made an effort to make us actually think about anything. They never made us an offer. I waited an extra month to actually let John Henry do whatever he promised me he was going to do, and nothing came out of it." Martinez added that he thought the Sox had tried to spread the word that his shoulder was injured "just to bring my contract down. That bothered me a little bit because that was dirty playing after I promised I was going to keep my mouth shut about negotiations. That bothered me that they did that just to bring my salary down or make things more difficult for me to go in a free agency year." He later launched into a diatribe in which he indicated that Lucchino and Henry had run their franchises into the ground in Baltimore and Florida, respectively.

It was an unfortunate but not surprising session. Already jealous over the acquisition of Schilling and insecure about his waning fastball, the ace had spent several weeks whispering to reporters that he would soon go public if nothing changed. He'd set the end of April as his deadline, and when his agent had an unproductive session with the Sox, he decided to go public. He gave the story to the *Herald*'s Mike Silverman, then spilled it to all the reporters after early editions of the May 1 *Herald* hit the streets.

His timing could not have been worse. A 15–6 record and a month of harmony and great expectations were dashed with a single morning headline. The Dominican Diva compounded his woes the same night when he was routed by the Rangers (nine hits and six runs in four innings) in the second game of a doubleheader loss in Texas. It was the beginning of a five-game losing streak that would erode the big lead the Sox had built over the Yankees in April. While the Sox were suddenly struggling and squabbling, the Yankees were winning eight straight games and pulling into a first-place tie with them.

There was considerable backlash against Pedro back in Boston. It was a first. Six-plus years of Hall of Fame pitching had built Martinez a reservoir of goodwill, and the fans had tolerated chronic tardiness, tantrums, and selfish remarks, always defending him. Even his implosion on the mound in Game 7 of the ALCS in New York was quickly forgiven. He-Who-Must-Not-Be-Named got all the blame. It was as if Pedro had had nothing to do with blowing the lead. Boston loved him unconditionally.

Martinez's remarks found almost no support on the talk shows or the streets of New England, and the star pitcher seemed genuinely surprised. Sox management offered little in the way of public reaction other than a 181-word press release by Epstein, which did not name Martinez but contended that the Sox were not lying to their players. Inside the locker room, there was some dissatisfaction with Pedro's attempt to bring Lowe, Varitek, and Garciaparra into the same boat. All declined to comment on Martinez's remarks.

One of six children (four boys) of Paolino and Leopoldina Martinez, Pedro was born in Manoguayabo on October 25, 1971. Paolino Jaime Perez, Pedro's dad, played amateur ball with Felipe Alou and Manny Mota but never made it off the island. He worked as a caretaker in the school his sons attended, but there was not a lot of extra cash for baseball equipment. Pedro and his brothers would rip the heads off their sisters' dolls and use them for baseballs.

The boys were all fine players, gifted with extraordinary throwing arms, and scouts from the Los Angeles Dodgers were keen on signing the best young players from the Dominican Republic. Pedro's older brother Ramon signed with the Dodgers in 1984, and four years later sixteen-year-old Pedro signed with the Dodgers just two months before Ramon made his big league debut in Los Angeles. After signing, Pedro went directly to the Dodger academy in the Dominican. Two years later, when Ramon was pitching in the major league All-Star Game, young Pedro made his professional debut with Great Falls in the Pioneer League. It was 1988.

Two things stood out when Pedro arrived in Big Sky to hone his skills. He weighed only 150 pounds but could throw almost 90 miles an hour. And he demonstrated a rare hunger to learn English. Great Falls pitching coach Guy Conti remembers young Pedro sitting next to him on every bus ride, demanding that he teach him new words in his new language. These bus rides through Montana, Idaho, and Utah were long and boring, and there was a lot of time for learning.

"When I left school, I had a little bit of English," he said years later. "But in Dodger school, I learned how to speak and not be afraid. My lowest grade was 98. I was straight A, all the way."

He had a good role model. Ramon, who is considerably more reserved, was on his way to a twenty-win season when Pedro was riding the buses in the Pioneer League. Within two years, they were Dodger teammates.

Pedro does not have fond memories of his Dodger days. Used almost exclusively as a middle reliever, he never found a place in Dodger blue. Los Angeles traded him to Montreal for Delino DeShields after the 1993 season. Pedro won his first Cy Young Award in Montreal in 1997, a few months before he was traded to the Red Sox. Accepting his trophy at the Boston Baseball Writers Dinner, he turned it over to Hall of Famer Juan Marichal, saying, "You are my daddy" (a quote that sounds amusing in light of another one late in the 2004 season). Marichal, a Dominican native who won 243 games but never a Cy Young Award (he pitched at the same time as Sandy Koufax and Bob Gibson), was deeply moved.

Martinez was wildly embraced when he first pitched for the Red Sox in 1998. Pedro's gamedays inspired a festive atmosphere at Fenway, with many fans waving Dominican flags. Youngsters in a splinter group in center field took to painting their faces red, wearing only red clothing, and posting "K" signs on the back wall of the bleachers every time Pedro struck out a batter. The "K-Kids" earned instant fame and started showing up at Martinez's games on the road.

His first three seasons in Boston made him a Fenway folk hero. He went 19–7 in 1998, finishing second to Roger Clemens in the Cy Young voting. The next year he performed at a level that put him in a category with Koufax and Gibson, going 23–4 with a 2.07 ERA and 313 strikeouts in 213.1 innings. Included in this run was perhaps the best game ever pitched by an opponent in Yankee Stadium. On September 10, Martinez beat the defending World Champion Yankees, 3–1, striking out seventeen, walking none, and fanning twelve of the last fifteen and the last five in order. But it was in the playoffs that he earned a place in the heart of the Nation. On the night of October 11, in the fifth and deciding game of a Division Series against Cleveland, he came out of the bullpen to stop the bleeding in a game that was tied, 8–8, in the bottom of the fourth. Despite a strained back, he hurled six innings of no-hit ball, beating the Tribe, 12–8, and sending the Sox into a best-of-seven ALCS with the Yankees. Boston won only one game in that series, when Pedro beat Clemens in Game 3. Martinez easily copped the '99 Cy Young Award and would have won the MVP if not for two voters (one from New York) who refused to list a pitcher in their top ten.

Oddly, it was in this stellar 1999 season that Boston got its first look at the "bad Pedro." Working on his own timetable, Martinez was habitually late throughout the season, and pedestrian manager Jimy Williams decided he'd had enough on the afternoon of August 14. With gametime approaching and no Pedro in sight, the never-starstruck manager sent Bryce Florie to the bullpen to warm up in place of Pedro for a Saturday afternoon start against Seattle. When Martinez strolled into the clubhouse a few minutes before the game was supposed to start, he learned that he would not be pitching. He was embarrassed, offended, and incensed. In his view, the manager was showing him up, disgracing him in front of Red Sox Nation and Baseball America. It didn't matter that Williams was correct. A man of great pride, Pedro was livid and would never forgive the perceived slight. He wound up going into the game out of the bullpen (compounding the indignity), and in the Boston sports media, the story had better legs than Heidi Klumm. Five days later, Martinez was scheduled to start against Oakland at Fenway, and TV crews staked out the Sox parking lot at the corner of Van Ness Street and Yawkey Way. Martinez was plenty early but did not appreciate being monitored like a criminal, and he voiced his displeasure to GM Dan Duquette in the clubhouse before the game. Afterward, Pedro was completely composed, demonstrating no evidence of his agitation before the game.

"I was not mad before the game," he said. "I am just a loud talker."

Perhaps. But in a page one *Globe* story recounting the evening's events, I wrote that Pedro appeared to have been struck in his "tiny butt" by a tranquilizer dart in the course of the evening. The Sox flew west after the victory, and Pedro was not amused by the phrasing in the *Globe*. Friends and teammates teased him about his "tiny butt," and somehow he was led to believe that his sexual preference was being called into question.

When the team returned from a six-game road trip, Martinez corralled me in the clubhouse and said, "Shaughn, I am not gay. Why do you write that I am gay?"

Stammering, I tried to explain the tranquilizer dart reference, allowing that something might have been lost in translation. I complimented Pedro on his command of English, but allowed that if he had seen the article in Spanish, it would not have offended his manhood.

"No," he said. "I have seen in Spanish. Is worse."

At that point, what could one say other than, "Sorry, no more lines about your tiny butt"?

The entire episode deserves mention only in that it speaks to the mindset of a world-class athlete who cares about how he is portrayed to the public. Since Martinez came to town, he had received kid-glove treatment in the media, an attitude normally reserved for Bobby Orr and Larry Bird. The Boston press (affectionately dubbed "the carnivorous Boston media" by Sox legend Johnny Pesky) appropriately worshipped Pedro and his 1999 numbers, but the lateness episode with Jimy Williams was the first indicator that even with Koufaxian numbers, Pedro could be a problem.

Martinez won back-to-back Cy's with the Sox in 1999 and 2000, and by 2001 he was vying for a statue in the Boston sports pantheon beside Ted Williams, Bill Russell, Bird, and Orr. Then his fragility reared its porcelain head. Small by major league standards, Pedro could only get so much out of that 5-11, 180-pound frame. True, his fingers were longer than Michael Jordan's, but it was impossible to ask a man of his stature to keep throwing at 97 miles an hour without sacrificing some shoulder strength. In 2001 it finally happened. The arm problems that plagued and prematurely ended the career of his brother finally found Pedro. On May 30 he pitched eight shutout innings, beating Mike Mussina and the Yankees at Fenway, 3–0, to improve his record to 7–1. After the game, he called out Babe Ruth, saying, "I don't believe in damn curses. Wake up the damn Bambino and have me face him. Maybe I'll drill him in the ass."

The Curse was not amused. Martinez did not win another game in 2001. Shoulder woes put him on the shelf until August, when the reeling Sox brought him back for three ill-advised starts while the team was imploding under the horrid leadership of Duquette and interim manager Joe Kerrigan. Pedro never liked Kerrigan. The tall redhead had been his pitching coach in Montreal and Boston, and Pedro always thought he took too much credit for the success of his pitchers. When Kerrigan became manager for the end of the 2001 season, it created an intolerable situation for Martinez. At a Fenway workout after 9/11, Pedro cursed Kerrigan, stripped off his uniform, and went home to the Dominican Republic. There were still three weeks left in the season.

The next two years, Pedro came back with strong seasons of 20–4 and 14–4 under the gentle guidance of He-Who-Must-Not-Be-Named. Pedro never had a bad moment with Grady. The manager kept Martinez mementos on the halls of his home in North Carolina. None of that mattered when Grady was sent packing.

So Pedro found another reverent skipper in the corner office in the spring of 2004. Terry Francona, a hitter who could never hit a pitcher like Pedro, was sufficiently starstruck when he took over the toughest job in Boston. He was not going to call out his ace or challenge his Cy Young candidate. Ever. Pedro could leave the park early on Opening Day and he could talk about his contract at the most inappropriate times, and Francona would never utter a cross word about him. Perhaps only his wife knows how Terry really felt about the delicate persona of his ace pitcher.

When the losing streak reached five games, Francona went against his instincts and held a ten-second team meeting before the Sox went out to play at Jacobs Field.

"Guys, I just want to let you know that you are good," he said. "I love every one of you guys. You're going to be fine. Trust me. That's it."

Hall of Fame manager Earl Weaver, so much a part of the Oriole way that Lucchino and Epstein had studied in Baltimore, despised team meetings. "The problem," he reasoned, "is that if you lose the next game after the meeting, then what do you do?"

But the Sox didn't have to worry. They beat the Indians, 9–5, that day, and the losing streak was over when Martinez pitched his next game. Pedro gave up a home run on the first pitch of the night but was spectacular thereafter, beating the Indians, 5–2, with seven innings of four-hit pitching. The recharged Sox produced a comeback worthy of 2003 on their return to Fenway on Friday, May 7. Trailing, 6–4, in the ninth, Mark Bellhorn hit a two-run homer to tie the game, then Varitek plated Ramirez with a pinch double to right.

During the game, some fans who couldn't get tickets were a few blocks west, watching *Still, We Believe: The Boston Red Sox Movie* at the Fenway 13 Theater on Brookline Avenue. One of those "only the Red Sox" productions, the feature-length film tracked the lonely lives of eight Red Sox fans during the 2003 season. Director Paul Doyle was given complete access by the ever-friendly, savvy Sox management, and owners John Henry, Tom Werner, and CEO Larry Lucchino all attended the premiere, which was held at the 100 Loews Cineplex near the Boston Common on a rare night off in April. Kevin Millar was the only Sox player at the premiere. Ramirez, who lived a few blocks away, was in the building watching *Man on Fire* and rejected an offer to join the baseball buffs across the hall. Most reviewers considered the star of the film to be Paul Costine, a legendary local sports talk show caller who went by the name of "Angry Bill." Boston sports talk radio has been described as "fellowship of the miserable" (Rick Pitino), "carnival barking" (Bill Parcells), and "nitwit entertainment for bloodthirsty shut-ins" (me), and Angry Bill was a typical sports talk get-a-lifer. It was left to Dr. Charles Steinberg to put the best spin on the unusual flick: "It's the only movie where the audience already knows the outcome but the stars don't." The filmmakers had held a contest to name the movie; some of the clever rejects were *Eighty-five Years Without a Ring and Still Married, The Passion of the Sox,* and *Kill Grady 2.*

"I had fun with the movie," said Millar. "That's the true passion. Angry Bill, man, somebody needs to shoot him. This guy is just miserable, sweating, his nose is bleeding. This is baseball, man, this is a game. I'm worried about his health. I appreciate the fans because that's why we play, that's why we do what we do. That's why you go out there when you can't even walk because these people, they come to see you play. I remember when I'd go to a Dodger game and Pedro Guerrero wasn't playing—it bummed you out. Some of the guys understand how much the fans care, but I think some don't. Some forget. Angry Bill, man, that poor guy. Somebody should put him in a straight-jacket."

While *Still, We Believe* was making its run in local theaters, no fewer than four other film projects involving the Red Sox were under way. The wishing well at the foot of Fenway was bottomless, and it seemed that everyone wanted to use the trappings of the Sox story to frame something larger. The Sox approved the use of Fenway for *Fever Pitch,* a love story starring Jimmy Fallon and Drew Barrymore, which would tell the story of an insatiable Red Sox fan interacting with a new girlfriend. Not to be outdone, John Ratzenberger, famous as Cliff Clavin on the barstool at *Cheers,* was set to direct *Bottom of the 12th,* an independent farce about thieves from South Boston stealing concessionaires' money while Carlton Fisk was hitting his historic home run in the sixth game of the 1975 Series. (Messrs. Damon and Affleck had already used Game 6 in *Good Will Hunting.*) Meanwhile, a Boston company, Silent Partners Films, was planning an indie move about a Red Sox player, and Stephen King's *The Girl Who Loved Tom Gordon* was being worked into a movie by George Romero (*Dawn of the Dead*) starring Dakota Fanning and Laura Dern.

Thanks in large part to his new hairstyle, Johnny Damon was a beneficiary of the rabid interest in the ball club. The 2003 season had been rough on him: he went through a divorce and had visitation problems with his four-year-old twins, Jackson and Madelyn. His numbers bottomed out at .273, with twelve homers and sixty-seven RBI, and Sox officials worried about his partying. Grady Little benched Damon repeatedly in 2003, citing his fitness to play, and on a *Jimmy Kimmel Live* telecast, Damon said he got over tough defeats with the help of "our friend, Jack Daniel's."

The new hair seemed to change everything. It was downright Sampsonesque. There were still concerns about his headaches due to the October collision with Damian Jackson, but Damon was a new man in every way in the spring of 2004, and his shoulder-length hair and beard made him an instant cult hero. And his hair was not just long. It was *good* long hair, nicely conditioned and highlighted. At home and on the road, fans showed up wearing wigs and fake beards, paying homage to the neon god they made. Many wore DAMON DIS-CIPLES T-shirts. Veteran Dodger broadcaster Vin Scully said Damon looked like Charles Manson, but most observers cited his resemblance to Christ.

"Johnny is the Passion," observed Manny Ramirez. Damon took to greeting his teammates with "Bless you, bless you."

Some geniuses from Gillette offered Damon $15,000 to shave his beard, so on a sunny Friday in May, more than two hundred people congregated on the Boylston Street side of the Prudential Center to watch four gorgeous young women use a new shaving product to erase Damon's beard. He donated the money to the Boston Public Library.

Damon was a Vietnam War baby, born to Sergeant Jimmy Damon and his wife, Yome, on November 5, 1973. Jimmy Damon was a 300-pound duty sergeant in D Company, 538th Engineer Battalion. A native of Peoria, Illinois, he enlisted in 1959 and was on his second tour of duty when he met Yome in Thailand in 1969. Yome was one of eight children, and she was only fifteen when she started working at the U.S. base in Satahip, polishing boots, making beds, and washing uniforms for the American servicemen. The daughter of a rice farmer, she was totally unimpressed the first time she saw big Jimmy Damon. But like two of her sisters, she married an American soldier, and two years later they had their first son, James, in Bangkok. Sergeant Damon was transferred back to the States, and a year later Johnny Damon was born in a hospital at Fort Riley, Kansas, less than two years before the fall of Saigon.

The family lived in Okinawa and Germany, then briefly settled in Illinois when Jimmy retired from the service. The former sergeant didn't like his job as an officer at the Joliet Correctional Center, so they moved to Orlando, Florida, where both parents had two jobs. Yome cleaned hotel rooms and office buildings while Jimmy worked as a security guard. In their living room was a sign, in Thai, that read WHEN YOU STAY IN THIS HOUSE, YOU'RE GOING TO BE RICH.

Johnny stuttered when he was young and was sent to a speech therapist. He did a lot of his reading at the public library (which is why the beard money went to the BPL). Most of the time he was on the run, almost Gump-like. Yome had been the fastest kid in her school in Thailand and noticed that Johnny had inherited her speed. But the Damon parents had no time for coaching Little League or putting their sons on expensive AAU teams. There was no traveling around the county to watch Johnny play ball. Jimmy and Yome hardly ever got to see their son play, and his baseball prowess was little more than a community rumor to them. Parents worked. Kids played. It wasn't until the phone started ringing when Johnny was in high school that they learned that their younger son had extraordinary baseball skills. Professional scouts and college coaches all wanted Johnny Damon.

Quite simply, Damon is a natural baseball player. He was not gifted with a strong throwing arm, but the good lord provided him with every other attribute he would need to compete with the world's best players. Damon is big (6-2, 190 pounds), fast, and powerful. He has astounding hand-eye coordination. He can catch anything that is hit, and he can hit everything that is thrown. When he was a senior at Dr. Phillips High School in Orlando, he was rated the top high school baseball prospect in the country. He didn't have to work particularly hard at any of it. It just happened.

The Kansas City Royals drafted Damon in 1992 and paid him a bonus of $250,000. As much as anyone who's ever played in the big leagues, Damon was born to play major league baseball. He was a star with the Royals, then the A's, before joining the Red Sox before the 2002 season. The fans loved him in Boston, but when he under-achieved in 2003, his name surfaced in trade rumors. His new look made him a target early in the 2004 season, but he responded by play-ing better than he ever had in Boston. With his hair flapping in the breeze, he was on his way to hitting .304 with 35 doubles, 20 homers, 94 RBI, and a whopping 123 runs scored (second in the league, trailing only American League MVP Vlad Guerrero).

When the Red Sox lost ten of seventeen at the start of May, one might have wondered if Damon's close shave and haircut had anything to do with the slump. This team would play its best when it steered clear of all razors and anything else that constituted good grooming. The May swoon put the Sox behind the Yankees again, and the organi-zation was concerned about the difficulties they were having catching and throwing the baseball. After the first thirty-eight games of the sea-son, the Red Sox had thirty-five errors, tied with the Tigers for the most in baseball. Schilling warned, "I've never been on a champi-onship-caliber club that wasn't a good defensive team and didn't pitch consistently."

They explained some of it away by saying they were waiting for Nomar. No one knew it was actually going to get worse when the shortstop returned.

A May weekend in Toronto featured the beginning of knee prob-lems for reigning batting champ Bill Mueller and the big league debut of Kevin Youkilis, the prototypical Young Theo Stat Pack ballplayer. It was Youkilis who was dubbed "the Greek God of Walks" in Michael Lewis's best-selling *Moneyball.* An unusual physical specimen, Youkilis is a 6-foot, 205-pound third baseman who did not hit homers and was already twenty-five years old when he got the call to the bigs. But he was also Mr. On-Base Percentage: he had reached base a record seventy-one consecutive times in the minors in 2003. He had a bad body for a young player.

"I've seen him in the shower," offered Francona. "And he's not a Greek God of anything."

Youkilis was with the Pawtucket Red Sox in Charlotte on Friday, May 14, when he got the call to Toronto. He immediately phoned his parents in Cincinnati and told them to fly to Canada to see his long-awaited big league debut in Skydome. Mike and Carolyn Youkilis were in the second row behind the Red Sox dugout when their son homered off Pat Hentgen in his second at-bat in the major leagues. Observing a time-honored tradition, the Sox dugout froze him out when he arrived after crossing home plate. Francona was the first to break the ice, then NESN reporter Eric Frede honored another tradition and tried to get the baseball for the kid. It wasn't easy. Frede went to the left field grandstand armed with two baseballs autographed by Pedro, but the girls who'd corralled the ball had never heard of the pitcher. It was surprising, for Skydome, like so many other American League parks, doubled as a Fenway satellite stadium in 2004. Red Sox fans were everywhere. It was the same in Tampa, Baltimore, and Oakland. Unable to get tickets in Boston, Sox fans took to the road in record numbers and dominated some ballparks ("Let's go, Red Sox!") where the home crowd was small or disinterested. The Toronto crowds were both.

Frede finally made the swap and gave the ball to clubhouse attendant Tommy McLaughlin. A longtime Sox employee who started as a groundskeeper and batboy, McLaughlin and his sidekick, Joe Cochran —who came up through the ranks the same way—took care of all the Red Sox equipment and uniforms and offered advice and counseling when asked. These were grown men who had devoted their working lives to the Red Sox, and their inside knowledge of ballplayers' personalities would fill several baseball encyclopedias. They knew that Youkilis would not be able to get his home run ball the day he hit it because Wakefield—the senior Sox player in continuous service and the official marker of all clubhouse memorabilia—was back in Boston, where his wife was delivering their first child. An "old" man of thirty-seven, Wakefield met his wife, Stacy, while playing for the Sox. Trevor Steven Wakefield came into the world the same hour in which Youkilis hit his homer. The rookie and the veteran both announced that May 15, 2004, was the best day of their lives. But with Wakefield gone, Youkilis didn't get his commemorative ball until a few days later, in Tampa.

The subsequent trip to Florida put the Sox back in the infamous Vinoy Hotel—where reliever Scott Williamson said he saw a ghost when he was a pitcher for the Reds in the spring of 2003. After his final postgame press conference in Toronto, Francona said, "Watch out for the haunted rooms," as the reporters filed out of his office. The players were dressing for the trip to Florida, and the rookies, including Youkilis, were forced to wear Hooters uniforms as part of an annual hazing ritual. While DiNardo, Youkilis, and the other kids donned the orange shorts and tight tank tops, Williamson was only too happy to recount his ghost story from a year earlier.

"I was laying on my stomach, and all of a sudden, I couldn't breathe," said the pitcher. "It was like something was pushing down on me. I turned around, when there was this guy dressed in 1920s, '30s-style staring at me. I never believed in ghosts before, but, like I said, I couldn't breathe. I told somebody about it the next day and then it was all over the news. It's just crazy stuff. One of those freaky things. I'm not one for ghosts, but I know I couldn't breathe."

Nodding, Millar added, "When we were in Baltimore at the start of this season, I heard another story about one of their infielders, Brian Roberts, when they stayed there. Supposedly he had some dry cleaning delivered to his room, and when he came back to the room the clothes were all laid out on the bed."

The ghost sightings occurred in the old section of the Vinoy, where Babe Ruth had stayed during spring training with the Yankees. At his request, Williamson stayed in the new section when the Sox returned in 2004.

The last night in Tampa resulted in another stink bomb for Derek Lowe. The last-place Devil Rays rocked him for seven runs before he was pulled in the third inning. Lowe's ERA ballooned to 6.02, and Sox watchers across the land nodded sagely and agreed that the tall righty was putting too much pressure on himself because he was in the final year of his contract. Like Varitek, Lowe was following the advice of notorious agent Scott Boras. The book on Boras was simple: he will always go for top dollar above all else. No hometown discount. No consideration for family or lifestyle or franchise or ballpark friendliness. Boras was in the business of getting record contracts. When you hire Scott Boras, you take yourself out of the equation and put your career in the hands of a bloodsucking lawyer who wants to impress his next generation of clientele by crashing through contract ceilings. Most folks who watched Lowe on a daily basis believed that Boras was a terrible choice. Lowe was simply not equipped to take pressure to the hill for thirty-five starts in 2004, and he was already cracking at the end of May. His ERA climbed to 6.84 after his final start of the month, a 13–4 loss to the Orioles. In May, Lowe was 1–4 with an 8.09 ERA, the worst among all American League starters. The ownership was taking notice. The day after Lowe's disastrous Memorial Day outing, Tom Werner greeted a reporter at the Grill in Beverly Hills and opened the conversation with: "What are we going to do about Derek Lowe?"

Werner was troubled. He didn't seem to think the organization had much chance of signing any of the Sox primo free-agents-to-be. He said that Garciaparra had turned down another big offer in the spring of 2004, and word from his camp was that the shortstop wanted to go to the Yankees and play second base. That would have given the Yankees the greatest infield in baseball history—A-Rod, Jeter, Nomar, and Jason Giambi. It was fan fodder throughout the 2004 season, but even the men at the highest levels of the front office were taking the notion seriously.

David Ortiz, one of the Sox stars who'd been in the final year of his contract, broke ranks and signed a two-year contract extension the day after Lowe's implosion in Tampa. Considered a second-tier priority, not quite in the fab foursome of Pedro, Nomar, Lowe, and Varitek, the big slugger's new deal guaranteed him an aggregate $12 million in 2005 and 2006. Oddly enough, it was Martinez who recommended that his countryman stay in Boston. Greeting the media after signing the deal, the twenty-eight-year-old Ortiz said, "It's a great situation, especially when you're still young, have a great chance to play for a winning team, and to win a World Series. The fans here always wish you the best, and it makes you want to do your best."

Before the year was over, Ortiz would shine brighter than any of the other members of the free agent class of 2004. But at the time he came to terms, he was a mere footnote, and the Sox fans wondered if they would ever hear any appreciation of Boston management from the mouths of Martinez, Garciaparra, Lowe, or Varitek.

By the end of May, Garciaparra's situation had become downright absurd. When the team was home, Nomar came to the park every day, hit against live pitching served up by some Harvard right-handers, ran the bases, took grounders, and sat with his teammates during the games. He didn't travel with the team, and he worked out at Fenway when the club was on the road. He sometimes had his wife, soccer star Mia Hamm, hit him grounders at Fenway. He continued to smile and say all the right things about his plans to return and his love for the Red Sox and the city of Boston, but Henry, Werner, and Lucchino were beginning to wonder if their star shortstop was repaying them for their cold attempt to deal him during the off-season. The trio remained tightlipped whenever the issue was raised in public, but privately they had the same concerns and suspicions that were being raised on sports talk radio nearly every hour. No one ever saw Nomar hurt himself in spring training when he said he hit a ball in the batting cage that somehow wounded his right Achilles tendon. Athletes who'd suffered similarly weighed in with opinions about the seriousness of the injury, but it was hard to escape the feeling that Nomar was taking his time coming back. Teammates took to asking the media: "How'd he look to you?" No one would come out and say it, but there was suspicion in the clubhouse. Meanwhile, Pokey Reese was demonstrating that he was clearly a superior shortstop, and the Boston papers started speculating that perhaps Nomar might consider moving to second base when he did return. It was something of a hot button, because the Sox never considered keeping Nomar and moving him to second when the club was trading for Alex Rodriguez. Henry had posed the question to Young Theo and been told that the Sox would not make such a request of Garciaparra. It was just not done—until, of course, the Yankees did it.

Nomar smiled and did numerous interviews when his teammates and other assorted stars gathered at a bowling alley for the fifth annual Nomar Bowl on May 24. The fifth annual event was a tremendous success, raising money for charity and generating positive publicity for Garciaparra. Alas, Nomar announced that there would be no more Nomar Bowls. It was only May, but it was hard not to read something into that. The Sox wanted him to rehab in Florida, but Garciaparra insisted on staying in Boston. When he was finally ready to play, he went to the triple-A Pawtucket Red Sox and got his first hits in his second game at Toledo off a pitcher named Jung Keun Bong. It was a big story back in Boston, but *Globe* headline writers resisted the urge to write NOMAR GETS TWO HITS OFF BONG over the game account.

Other minor league news involved the Red Sox. The Brockton Rox of the Northeast League promoted a Grady Little bobblehead doll night for May 29. The unusual twist was that the dolls featured the manager touching his left arm with his right—the international sign for a call to the bullpen. The back of the doll carried statistics lauding Little's 194 wins (including postseason) in two seasons with Boston, but it also read: "October 16, 2003, 11:03 P.M." the exact time He-Who-Must-Not-Be-Named failed to pull Pedro. The Rox had a thousand dolls packed in a warehouse when they got word that many fans —including Grady—were not amused. Rox team president Jim Lucas canceled the promotion, saying, "I thought that the wounds would have healed seven months later. I underestimated how raw this still is for people." The cancellation only made the dolls hotter, and the Rox pondered how charities could perhaps benefit from them. Eventually they were sold, with Grady's blessing, the proceeds going to veteran big league scouts.

On May 31, Lowe was thrashed again as the Orioles beat Boston, 13–4. The loss dropped the Sox into a first-place tie with the Yankees. After all the early season euphoria, the Red Sox were right back where they started, neck and neck with the Yankees. The Bronx Bombers were getting hot while the Sox struggled. After batting just .227 with twenty-one home runs in twenty-one games in April (an 11–10 record), the Yanks smashed forty-two homers in twenty-six games in May, batting an aggregate .293 and scoring 6.6 runs per game. It was a different Yankee team than the one the Sox had beaten six times in seven tries in April. The race was on.

7

Summertime Blues

AN EARLY JUNE ISSUE of *The New Yorker* featured a cartoon of a bearded, grizzled, long-haired man wearing a sackcloth and sandals and carrying a sign on a city street corner. Typically, the message on the cliché character's signboard would read: THE END IS NEAR. But this peasant prophet had other ideas. His sign read: THIS IS THE YEAR, and he was wearing a Red Sox baseball cap.

Meanwhile, the Sox tried something that had never been done in baseball history. In September 2003, Showcase Cinemas' Randolph theater had received twenty-five thousand requests to watch the Sox play the Yankees on the big screen. As a result, the theater company contacted the Sox during the off-season and worked out a deal to broadcast seven 2004 Sox games at select cinemas. For $5, fans could go to theaters in Randolph, Worcester, Springfield, or Providence and watch the games on high-definition, 58-by-25-foot screens. Vendors roamed the aisles of the theaters calling, "Bee-ah, hee-ah!" selling 12-ounce cups of Budweiser on tap for $4.75. Hot dogs (Nathan's instead of Fenway Franks) went for $3.50 (compared with $3.75 at Fenway).

Farming out the live broadcasts to movie theaters spoke to the sad reality that Fenway had become a province for the wealthy. The cost of going to watch the Red Sox was prohibitive for middle-class families, and tickets were almost impossible to find. The Sox regularly advertised "Tickets Still Available," but the disclaimer at the bottom of the ad indicated that the club was unloading returns, standing room, and

119

obstructed-view seats. Why not? Supply and demand were totally out of proportion. The Sox were charging the highest prices in baseball because they could get them. There seemed to be no ceiling, not during the good times of 2004. The Giants, Indians, and Rockies, other franchises that had sold every ticket for a season, owed much of their draw to trendy new ballparks—nothing like the ninety-two-year-old relic in the Back Bay.

Interjecting some harsh reality into this horn of plenty was a phone call made to the *Globe* by social worker Eileen O'Brien. Ms. O'Brien was the director of the Boston Medical Center's Elders Living at Home Program, which rented space at the Pine Street Inn, a homeless shelter for men. The program was designed to help men move from homelessness into housing, and O'Brien was working with a group of elderly men who wanted to share their opinions on the Red Sox. And so they did. Melvin, Pablo, David, and John invited a reporter and photographer to join them in the community room on the second floor of the shelter. Watching the Red Sox was a nightly ritual for these men without homes, and they were remarkably well versed in the condition of the team. John, who hailed from Pittsfield and did not want his last name used ("That's on a need-to-know basis, and not everybody needs to know"), was commander of the 17-inch overhead television and went behind it at 7 P.M. to make the cable switch, allowing the fellows to tap into the Red Sox (NESN) network. All the men sat in regular seats, and Melvin, a sixty-four-year-old Boston native who walked with a cane, took his usual spot on the left side of a sofa in the middle of the room. Melvin grew up in Roxbury and said his dad took him to Fenway in the 1950s. David, a native of the South End, remembered sneaking into the park during the 1975 World Series. Pablo, who grew up in Puerto Rico, said he'd been to the ballpark a few years earlier, adding, "It used to be if you got some money you could get a ticket, but I can't afford it now. Now, if you get a little money, you'd better hang on to it."

David, who'd been homeless for thirty years, said, "I'm one of the lost legends that didn't make it. A lot of people look down on you, but you can't judge a person. There are people who care about their lives and do want to help themselves. It's not all lost. There's hope."

Hope. Even for the Red Sox. "I believe we learned from our mistakes last year," said David. "We're definitely going to do something this year."

After the story ran in the *Sunday Globe*, the residents of Pine Street were peppered with offers of tickets and bigger televisions. Nomar sent over a new TV, and within a week the elderly gentlemen were sitting in box seats, enjoying the Red Sox in person with the hoi polloi. Looking out at the perfect Fenway lawn, John sighed and said, "People found out we love baseball and started sending all these TVs and tickets. If we'd known that was gonna happen, we'd have said we like women and beer!"

When John's quip was relayed to Garciaparra, the shortstop laughed. Nomar was standing at his stall in the visitor's locker room at Yankee Stadium, and it seemed as if it was the only time anyone saw him smile during the 2004 Boston baseball season.

The San Diego Padres and Los Angeles Dodgers made their first-ever trips to Fenway Park in early June. The Brooklyn Dodgers played in Boston in the 1916 World Series, but those games were played at Braves Field because the Hub's National League ballpark offered more seats. The Sox won that series, and the Dodgers no doubt had revenge on their minds when they finally set foot in baseball's oldest park.

In Boston, there was considerable fanfare and curiosity regarding both West Coast clubs. A good portion of the Red Sox front office—Werner, Lucchino, Epstein, Steinberg, Kennedy, and publicist Glenn Geffner, to name a few—had worked for the Padres before moving to Boston. Even Grady Little had made a favorable impression on his future bosses when he was a Padre coach under Bruce Bochy for a season. The Dodgers came to town after the Padres and brought with them the regal likes of Sandy Koufax, Vin Scully, and Tommy Lasorda. All had Boston stories. Koufax remembered pitching briefly ("and not all that effectively," he added) at Fenway in the 1961 All-Star Game, and Scully said his career was launched when he covered a Boston University football game from a Fenway rooftop on a freezing November afternoon.

The Dodgers were under the new ownership of South Boston native Frank McCourt, who had been one of the jilted suitors in the Bud Selig–John Harrington fixed sale of the Red Sox. McCourt was ubiquitous throughout the Fenway weekend and hosted a massive postgame party at a trendy new restaurant in Kenmore Square after a nationally televised game on Saturday afternoon. But nothing detracted from the return of Garciaparra. Sox fans had been waiting patiently, expecting that the return of Nomar was going to propel the ball club to a higher level.

Nomar spent the first week of June playing triple-A games for the Pawtucket Red Sox and reportage of his first steps was something normally reserved for Neil Armstrong's moonwalk. Ever one to take himself seriously, Garciaparra did nothing to discourage the notion that this was the most important thing happening to the Red Sox. Meanwhile, the Sox were starting to lose ground to the Yankees in the AL East.

By this time the Nation was divided on Garciaparra's relative worth and his desire to play for Boston. One faction questioned why it took so long for him to return. Both Lucchino and Werner were grumbling about the length of the shortstop's stint on the shelf, and Boston's sports talk radio was peppered with callers asking, "Where's No-mah?" The entire Sox organization expected his return to coincide with the Padres' arrival on Tuesday, June 8, but Nomar opted to go to Pawtucket for another game of rehab. *Herald* baseball columnist Tony Massarotti took this as a sign that he was indeed "sticking it to" the front office in retaliation for the club's public attempts to deal him during the off-season.

Nomar said he was ready to play against the Padres the next day and met the media in midafternoon on the day of his long-awaited return. When one reporter started a question with, "Nomar, you said you wouldn't come back until you were 100 percent," the shortstop cut him off, claiming that he'd never said those words and that he would never be 100 percent. When another reporter asked about charges that he was "sticking it to management" by delaying his return, Garciaparra laughed and said, "Who said that? Give me a name and I'll address it." Alas, no one stepped forward. Later in the session, Nomar added, "If I was taking my time, I'd see you in August."

As always, he received a Lindberghesque welcome from the Fenway sellout crowd. He tipped his cap to the grateful fandom but spent the rest of the night doing what he always did, stalking around the clubhouse with a touch-my-stuff-and-I'll-kill-you look on his face and going at his work like a man in the on-deck circle at a root canal clinic. He batted only twice, getting one hit before rains delayed an 8–1 Red Sox loss. He also short-hopped a throw to first base, which resulted in a couple of Padre runs. He was not charged with an error, but the misplay validated the feelings of the fans who had already forgotten Garciaparra's gifts and were anxious to keep flossy veteran Pokey Reese at shortstop. The throw did not go unnoticed by Epstein.

Reese was a Fenway golden child early in the summer of 2004. He hit an inside-the-park homer on a Saturday afternoon, a dashing excursion that secured his position as a fan favorite. It was easy to fall in love with his fielding. He had better range than any shortstop in the American League, with the possible exception of Cleveland's Omar Vizquel. He was a better shortstop than Nomar, just as Yankee third baseman Alex Rodriguez was a better defensive shortstop than Derek Jeter. But Francona and friends couldn't entertain the idea of playing Garciaparra at second and leaving Reese at short, even if it would have made the Sox better. The Sox had already insulted Garciaparra and were not about to further alienate their five-time All-Star, who was clearly playing his final games in a Red Sox uniform.

The contrast with Reese was striking. A veteran of seven seasons, Calvin "Pokey" Reese still went about his work with the exuberance of a ten-year-old Little Leaguer at his first game with a real uniform. Just as you couldn't hit the ball past him, you couldn't wipe the smile off his face. Born in Columbia, South Carolina, he'd been handed plenty of hardship. The name "Pokey," like so many lifelong handles, came from his family. Reese was a chunky little boy (hard to believe, given his gaunt adult frame), and his grandmother took to calling him "Porkie." Anyone who's been around South Carolina won't have a hard time understanding how southerners can make "Porkie" sound like "Pokey." And so a lifelong nickname was born. Pokey's dad, Calvin "Slick" Reese Sr., was a truck driver afflicted with the tragic thirst that destroys so many families. Slick was gone much of the time, and the Reese children grew up on a dirt road in a house with no running water. Pokey learned to carry water from his great-grandfather's well half a mile from home. An extended family of eight to ten relatives shared the two-bedroom shack. Three Reese brothers and a cousin shared bunk beds, two boys per mattress.

With little equipment, the Reese brothers improvised to play baseball. They learned to field balls with their bare hands. They ripped
Pepsi cans apart and attached them to their shoes to pretend they were
wearing baseball spikes. They tapped into their grandparents' flour
sack to draw lines for a batter's box, a luxury that usually resulted in a
spanking. For organized games, Reese borrowed friends' mitts until he
finally got his own when he starred at Lower Richland High School.
He must have been pretty good. He was a star quarterback at Richland,
throwing passes to future Patriot David Patten, and the Cincinnati
Reds made Reese the twentieth pick of the 1991 draft, just seven picks
after the Indians drafted a New York City high school slugger named
Manny Ramirez.

Reese's professional money did not put an end to his life's hard-
ships. He fathered a son and a daughter by two different women. The
mother of Reese's daughter died in a car crash, and the mother of his
son died in childbirth, delivering the child of another man. Reese's
son, Naquawan, went to live with his maternal grandmother and
great-grandmother, but both women were murdered on Christmas
Eve in 1997. The boy then moved in with Pokey's mom, who was living
in a house that Pokey had bought for her in Charlotte.

But none of the tragedy and poverty showed on his face when he
played baseball. He was gifted with a name and a game that made him
a natural favorite with children. "Pokey" shirts were flying off the
shelves at the souvenir store across from Fenway by the time Nomar
made his so-serious return. In a nationally televised Sunday night
game against the Dodgers, Reese pulled off one of the more memorable plays of the season, leaping more than three feet in the air
("'Scuse Me While I Kiss the Sky") to snag a certain gapper by Dave
Roberts—who would soon join the Red Sox and be involved in one of
the most important plays in Boston baseball history, a stolen base in
the playoffs against the Yankees. Meanwhile, Reese's leaping catch triggered Pokey chants and more Pokey mania.

The downside was the inevitable groaning of "Pokey would have
had it" anytime Garciaparra made an error or failed to get to a ball
in the hole or up the middle. POKEY WOULD HAVE HAD IT bumper
stickers started appearing on cars around Boston.

Nomar was not amused. He had only three hits in his first fifteen at-bats, and when he spoke with the *Herald*'s Silverman before a game in Denver, it was clear that his wounds had moved from his Achilles tendon to his tender psyche. "I've been judged on one month—I've got eight years," Nomar started. "Think about what I've done. What would you rather have: eight great years and one bad month or eight bad months and one good year? I think those years count—they will somewhere, to somebody . . . I can't win—twenty-one ABs [of rehab] but no, 'You're faking it' and 'C'mon, what are you waiting for?' Then I come back, they are still going to say, 'See—he sucks. He's not good. You were bad last year, you're bad this year.' It's a no-win situation."

It was an odd, ill-timed outburst, one that had Lucchino and friends scratching their heads. Few players in the long history of the Red Sox had been more warmly received than Garciaparra. He was universally worshipped by fans from the first day he came to Boston late in the 1996 season. Young fans learned to spell his name and immediately started imitating his obsessive-compulsive routine between pitches of every at-bat. Every citizen of the Nation knew that his unusual name was "Ramon" spelled backward, in honor of his father. He played harder than any superstar in Red Sox history. He ran out every grounder and every pop-up. He took time to sign autographs before almost every game. At home plate, he attacked the baseball like no middle infielder in franchise history. Ted Williams adopted young Nomar as his favorite charge and compared Garciaparra to Joe DiMaggio (both were righty sluggers who wore no. 5). Garciaparra was one of Boston's most eligible bachelors and became a *Saturday Night Live* skit. "Nomaah" became synonymous with the Boston accent, a new twist on the old "Paaahk Your Caaah in Haavaahd Yaahd."

Ever reluctant to cooperate with the media (a posse that he detested as too large, negative, and intrusive), Garciaparra still received well-deserved glowing coverage throughout his days with the Sox. The writers may not have enjoyed trying to draw words out of him, but there was no denying his effort and his talent, and the reportage reflected his many attributes. All of which made it difficult to identify the anonymous few critics who were bothering Nomar when he came back from his injury. He could have been talking about talk show instigators, or maybe it was the suggestion that he took too long to come back. More likely, he was taking out his frustrations on upper management. His comments were not the words of a player who planned on agreeing to a hometown discount and finishing his illustrious career with the Red Sox.

Two unrelated events coincided with Garciaparra's outburst. On the same night, Trot Nixon made his return after missing sixty-three games. It was also the night that the Sox fell a season-low six games behind the Yankees in the loss column.

The Yankees were smoking. They had the look of the 1978 Yankees, who recovered from a fourteen-game deficit and passed the Red Sox after Billy Martin was replaced by Bob Lemon in midseason. The Pinstripers already had twenty-seven come-from-behind wins by mid-June. On Sunday, June 13, playing at home against the Padres, they trailed, 2–0, in the bottom of the ninth with two out and nobody aboard, then sent the game into extra innings with two homers. They later fell behind, 5–2, in the top of the twelfth, only to score four to win in the bottom of the inning. A-Rod, back from the dead zone of his early season struggles against Boston, said, "There's an aura on the team that we think we can win every game no matter how far down we drop." New York moved to twenty games over .500 in the middle of June.

Steinbrenner issued a statement in which he gloated and took credit for filling up ballparks. It read, in part: "2004 will be recorded as the Year of the extraordinary Yankee fan! As the team demonstrates its enormous talent and heart on the playing field, Yankee fans throughout the tri-state area are responding by coming out to the stadium in record numbers. But it's not just Yankee Stadium that is seeing capacity crowds. Our team is helping fill ballparks throughout the country when we play. This turnout is simply unprecedented and speaks to the excitement of our New York Yankee team. Who knew you could hear a Bronx accent in Seattle, Texas or so many other ballparks?"

Murray Chass of the *New York Times* wrote: "The Red Sox are to be pitied. As vigorously and as expensively as they have worked to overtake the Yankees, they still find themselves second best."

During this stretch of uninspired baseball, Young Theo uttered a remark that indicated trouble in the Nation. Sitting next to me in the Sox dugout during batting practice on a warm late afternoon in June, he looked straight out at the Fenway lawn and said, "If we don't get going, your book is gonna suck."

Thinking again, he added, "No, we're gonna be okay. The book is gonna be okay."

Then the Red Sox went back to New York to finish out the month. This time, there was no Boston domination. This time the Yankees were ready, and they fashioned a three-game sweep that effectively ended the 2004 American League East race while reminding Red Sox Nation of all past horrors in the House That Ruth Built.

Things were wrong for the Sox from the start. Before the return of the Red Sox, the ever newsworthy Contreras had the best day of his life, beating the Mets with six innings of ten-strikeout pitching. More than that, he got to pitch on American soil in front of his wife and two daughters, who'd been smuggled out of Cuba only days earlier. With Brown on the disabled list and Mussina struggling, it was the kind of emotional lift the Yankees needed. Plus, any success for Contreras still stung the Boston brass.

On June 29, when the Red Sox rolled into New York on the train, the Yankees were 39–15 since the Sox had left town. The Red Sox were 30–26 over the same span. The Yanks were suddenly the team everyone expected them to be when Rodriguez was acquired. They were playing like a team with sixteen (former or current) All-Stars, a team on track to become the biggest road draw in baseball history. The 1993 Colorado Rockies drew (home and away) 7.17 million fans, and the Yankees were on a pace to smash that record and become the most watched team in history. Their only problems involved two players' intestinal parasites. Both Jason Giambi and Brown (who also had a lower back strain) were weakened by the unusual malady, and it naturally gave all New Yorkers something else they could blame on the Yankees' trip to Japan. The Yanks could ill afford losing any more starting pitchers. New York used thirteen different starters before the All-Star break. In contrast, the Red Sox would have the luxury of the same five starters all season.

The *New York Post* greeted the Red Sox with a back-page quote from Steinbrenner: IT'S PAYBACK TIME. Steinbrenner later denied having made the threat, but who cared? It made for a great headline and perfectly set the table for the new millennium's edition of the Boston Massacre. These were dark days, in which the Sox were ridiculed and exposed. Their clubhouse threatened to splinter, and there was rampant speculation regarding the impending, once-unthinkable trading of Nomar. It was not a happy time.

Things got off to a rotten start in New York. More than three hours before the first pitch, Timlin was playing catch with his seven-year-old son in front of the Yankee dugout when he was approached by a security official and told that the child was not allowed on the field. Angry and embarrassed, Timlin waved his son into the dugout and disappeared into the runway, muttering, "Great city."

Minutes later, while the Yankees were in the middle of batting practice, Cashman talked about the midseason acquisition race.

"I hope the Red Sox don't improve themselves, they don't need any improving. We talked about Carlos Beltran [who had been dealt from Kansas City to Houston a week earlier], but I made recommendations that we don't participate there because it's not an area of need. Bernie's turned it in the right direction and—"

Cashman's phone rang. He took the call, spoke briefly, ended the call, then said, "Can we talk a little later? I've got to go see George."

Much of the pregame buzz concerned the impending arrival of Vice President Dick "Big Time" Cheney, who was preceded by a team of Secret Service agents large enough to protect a few city boroughs. The vice president made it in time to visit both clubhouses, and we can only imagine what it would have been like had he struck up a conversation with Citizen Manny (Ramirez had recently earned his U.S. citizenship).

When Schilling did not attend a routine pitchers' meeting before the start of the Yankee series, Varitek chided him afterward. Schilling was not pitching in the series, and Francona, as always, said it was okay that "Schill" wasn't there, but none of that stopped *Newsday*'s Jon Heyman from printing an item in his column contending that there had been a serious and harsh exchange between the catcher and the ace.

"I was there," said Heyman. "They can cover it up all they want, but Varitek was mad at Schilling. And he should have been. Schilling's got great numbers against Sheffield. Why not be at that meeting and help the other pitchers?"

The Yankees routed the Red Sox that night, 11–3. The Sox made three errors, two by Nomar, the second of which was a killer: it advanced a Sheffield three-run homer when the inning should have been over.

"After they manhandled us the last time, you're wondering how you stack up," said Torre. "Basically, what we wanted to do was hold our own."

Wednesday's Gotham newspapers had a field day with the Sox woes. Two *Post* headlines: YANKS ROUGH UP ROTTEN RED SOX and SOX BUILT FOR BEER LEAGUE. The *Daily News* led with APRIL FOOLS over a full-page photo of Nomar's second error. Even the venerable *Times,* which has $75 million invested in the Sox, couldn't resist a taunt: WITH BRIDESMAIDS BACK, YANKEES EXPLOIT THEIR HELP. It was only the beginning of a three-day mugging in the Big Apple.

Varitek called a players-only meeting before the second game. He was furious about being asked about the alleged dispute with Schilling (it had become a steel cage match by the time the players got to the stadium), but the meeting was held because of what was happening on the field, not in the clubhouse. Francona certainly wasn't going to get tough with the players, and there wasn't a single member of the Sox hierarchy in New York, so the veteran catcher took it upon himself to deliver a message. He told the press that he was calling the meeting to invite his teammates to dinner when the Sox played in Atlanta over the upcoming weekend, but nobody was fooled. All of the players attended except Diva Pedro. Martinez did not know about any meeting, and his routine kept him away from the park until about 5:30 P.M. Asked if Pedro was late when the rest of his teammates were stretching at 5:30—after the meeting—Francona said, "He's pitching tomorrow. When I know where people are and the reasons why, I'm okay with it."

Game 2 of the series was, for a short period, the most excruciating defeat of a suddenly southbound season—but only because it was played a day before the series finale, a true mindblower for the ages. The Red Sox blew a 2–0 lead in the bottom of the seventh. New York tied the game when Tony Clark hit a two-out, bases-loaded, scorching grounder to first base. Some, including Francona, claim that the baseball actually tore through the webbing of David Ortiz's glove. Ortiz wasn't sure, but Sox trainer and glove doctor Jim Rowe punctured the theory, reporting that the glove was not torn.

The odd play instantly became part of Boston baseball folklore, like Luis Aparicio's falling down rounding third base in 1972. Ortiz's error enabled the Yanks to tie the game and increased the Sox's unearned run total to sixty to lead the major leagues.

In the bottom of the eighth, Garciaparra, by now officially the loneliest athlete in the world, made another throwing error to start the inning. Kenny Lofton took second, and Jeter bunted him to third. Sheffield was next and worked Timlin through a ten-pitch at-bat, hitting eight consecutive foul balls before ripping a double inside the third base line to win the game. Mariano Rivera struck out the side in the Boston ninth. When the game was over, Francona said, "I love these guys," as fans back home threw beer cans at flat-screen televisions.

"What has happened has happened," said the manager. "We have been bad at times. That's certainly a fair assessment. We do have to make the plays and not give the extra outs. We are a team that doesn't feature a lot of speed, and when you don't hit and you make errors, your team looks slow."

Varitek said, "The effort's there. It's just not happening . . . Things need to work together, and when they don't you have chaos."

The next night, Lowe sat in the dugout and spoke about the ownership's motives and the impact of trade rumors involving the big four: "They can do what they want. They were trying to trade me a month and a half ago. When I was really struggling, I know they tried to get rid of me then. Now I think it all depends on what happens in the next month. These guys, they know who they want to sign and who they don't want to sign, and if we start falling out of this thing, then I think the guys they don't want to sign, they'll listen to trade talk. They already tried to trade me once. Why won't they do it again? And they could trade more than one of us. You hope it doesn't come down to that and we don't fall out of it . . . But if the right deal comes up, I think anybody could be traded at any point.

"It's a weird situation . . . There's no doubt about it. This year is definitely different. The main question is: 'Why aren't we doing better?' We can debate that for days on end. The atmosphere at Fenway this year is great, but everyone is very impatient, more than ever. Say we don't perform well this year. What's to stop them from getting rid of everybody? Who knows."

Regarding Garciaparra's obvious unhappiness, Lowe said, "It's not the most pleasant thing when you see the writing on the wall and you know where your future's headed. If he has a feeling they don't want him back, and if they're just trying to get rid of you, how much fun are you going to have at your job?"

"The clubhouse is the same," countered Wakefield, who'd survived his haunting return to the mound at Yankee Stadium only to see his victory erased by a freak play. "We're just frustrated with the way we're playing, but it's the same core of guys. A lot of fun. We just need to start playing better. To look at us on paper, you wouldn't think we could play under .500 this long. It's like an engine. All the parts got to be running at the same time to make it perform well."

A few hours later, Sinatra's "New York, New York" was again blaring out of the Yankee Stadium loudspeakers, and the usual fifty-five thousand were running to the subway, full of excitement and conviction that they'd just seen one of the best regular-season games in the history of baseball.

That it was. The final game of the Red Sox–Yankee midseason series in New York, a thirteen-inning, 5–4 Yankee win—a game played the day before a full moon on the first of July—was one of the best regular-season games anyone could remember. It was a game in which once again we were reminded that the Red Sox have been put on this earth to test the patience and loyalty of their always expanding fan base. Fans were treated to yet another demonstration of why-the-Yankees-always-win.

Pedro was back on the mound for the start of this historic event. He put his stamp on the proceedings when he drilled Sheffield with a pitch after Sheffield stepped out of the batter's box in the first inning. It was an odd return to seriousness for Martinez, who'd been goofing around with Yankee fans from the top step of the Sox dugout for the first two games. He'd also attempted to shake hands with some of the Yankees before the first game of the series, but many, including Posada, avoided the awkward gesture. There was media speculation that Pedro's sudden friendliness was a contrived effort to grease the skids for an off-season bid from the Yankees. Hitting Sheffield put a stop to Pedro's feel-good campaign. (Later in the summer, the ferocious Sheffield told *Sports Illustrated* that he had allowed Pedro a "buddy pass" but would not tolerate another plunking.)

The Red Sox trailed, 3–0, after five, but it was 3–3 after seven, and the drama built when both managers went to their bullpens. Francona let Pedro pitch seven, then went to Foulke, who was followed by Timlin, then Embree, and finally journeyman Curtis Leskanic. Torre started with rookie Brad Halsey, then summoned Paul Quantrill, Gil Heredia, Tom Gordon, Mariano Rivera, and Tanyon Sturtze. Francona used a five-man infield in the twelfth, sometimes featuring a left-handed second baseman, David McCarty. McCarty changed gloves five times during the inning. Millar played first base, third base, and left field in the same inning, one in which the Sox escaped from a bases-loaded, one-out jam. The Yankees used every player on their bench, the Red Sox all but two. The Red Sox took a 4–3 lead in the top of the thirteenth on a monstrous home run by Ramirez, but the Yankees won it in the bottom of the inning on three straight hits by bench players after two were out with nobody aboard.

When the four-hour, twenty-minute epic was over, the Yankees were winners, and writers went to work on proposals to do a book about one of the greatest regular-season games in baseball history.

A-Rod said, "That was the greatest game I've ever watched, played, or been in the ballpark for." Boss Steinbrenner issued a statement: "This was the most exciting game I have ever seen in all of sports." Bob Herbert of the *New York Times* devoted an op-ed column ("A Game to Remember") four days later. Commissioner Bud Selig watched it from his home in suburban Milwaukee and said, "It was one of the great games I've ever seen in my lifetime. Are you kidding? My wife had a bad hip, and I kept running downstairs and saying, You've got to turn this game on. It's just unbelievable. People will talk about great college rivalries and great pro football rivalries—Packers and Bears—but in my judgment there is no rivalry like the Red Sox and Yankees. That game proved it."

Unfortunately for Garciaparra, the game will always be remembered for a play made by Jeter in the twelfth inning that would be elevated into the Willie Mays 1954 World Series genre.

The Sox had already blown incredible scoring opportunities when the Yankees took the field in the twelfth. They'd failed to score with the bases loaded and no outs in the eleventh. In the twelfth, the Sox had runners on first and third and one out. After Mark Bellhorn popped up for the second out, Trot Nixon was sent up to hit for Gabe Kapler. He lofted a soft pop-up into the Bermuda triangle behind third base. The ball was tailing toward the foul line and had a chance to land inside the line for a potential two-run double. Jeter was the only Yankee who had a chance. He streaked to his right to glove the ball on the dead run, and his momentum carried him into the seats along the third base line. After crash-landing in the third row behind a second railing, he emerged, chin bleeding, right cheekbone bruised and already swelling, holding the ball aloft in his glove. He went into the dugout, then took an ambulance to Columbia Presbyterian Hospital.

"I got five stitches in my chin and hit my eye socket," Jeter said later. "The first thing I checked was my teeth. I was lucky. The choppers were still there. I've fallen in before, but not that far. The photographers' pit was first and that's cement, and I knew when I caught it I was gonna fall in that. I figured if I jumped over it I could avoid the cement part, but then the chair back didn't feel too good, either."

While all this was going on, Garciaparra was sitting on the Red Sox bench, simply watching his teammates.

This night forever tainted Nomar's reputation in Boston and New York. Fans will always remember Jeter's catch . . . while Nomar sat. The awkward juxtaposition of the two star shortstops paralleled eight decades of Yankee dominance. The night that Jeter put his body on the line to make a game-saving catch, Garciaparra sat on the bench for the entire thirteen innings, resting his sore Achilles tendon. Just as Ted Williams had to live with his no-homers, .200 batting average in his only World Series, some Yankee fans will forever taunt Nomar for sitting while Jeter made a play that saved the game and landed him in the hospital.

In his pregame remarks, Francona indicated that Nomar needed a night off because the Achilles was bothering him. Noting that Garciaparra was recovering from a serious injury and had played in fifteen of the previous sixteen games, the manager said, all too typically, "It's probably my fault."

It was pretty clear that Nomar knew he wasn't playing that night. He arrived at the clubhouse with many of his teammates and didn't even bother to look at the lineup card when he walked to his locker. He already knew. It had been discussed.

In a chat with Yankee broadcaster and former pitcher Jim Kaat, Francona said that he'd given Garciaparra every opportunity to start the game, but the shortstop opted to sit. Francona told Kaat that he didn't want to "bury" Garciaparra, and thus the sanitized version was delivered to the media. But Kaat went on the YES Network during the game and told viewers that Garciaparra had made the decision to rest during this important game.

Television was not Nomar's friend that evening. Several times, particularly late in the game, when the camera panned to the Sox bench to capture the excitement, the shortstop could be seen sitting by himself while the rest of his teammates were on the top step of the dugout. ESPN's audience was bombarded with replays of the scene the next day, and the video evidence was damning.

After the game, both Francona and Garciaparra insisted that the shortstop volunteered for duty during the extra innings and spent time out of sight getting loose for a potential pinch-hitting appearance. In fact, after Jeter's kamikaze dive, Nomar told Francona he could pinch-hit, but—in a rare show of strength—the manager elected to go with the players who'd been available all night long. All parties put a good face on it afterward.

"He was trying his ass off to be available," said Francona.

"There was a time I thought I might get in," said Garciaparra. "From the ninth inning on, I was getting loose, trying to get ready."

Later, the Sox covered for Nomar by maintaining that he was a "medical scratch" for the series finale.

The loss dropped the Sox to a whopping eight and a half games behind New York, nine in the loss column. The 2003 theme of Cowboy Up felt like a few lifetimes ago.

8

No, No, Nomar

T HE NOMAR PROBLEM was officially intolerable. John Henry was livid that the onetime star shortstop had taken himself out of the finale in New York. The owner wanted him off the payroll. Theo wanted to move Nomar for other reasons. The Sox were deeply concerned with his dramatic loss of defensive skills. Before 2004, Epstein thought of Nomar in terms of "pre–wrist injury" and "post–wrist injury." Before the surgery on his right wrist in 2001, Garciaparra was a right-handed slugger on a par with Joe DiMaggio. He'd hit .372 in 2000. In a "who's better" argument about Nomar and Jeter, one could make a worthy case for Garciaparra. He was a plus on defense, though never smooth. After the surgery, the Sox still considered him a premier player, but no longer a slam-dunk Hall of Famer and certainly not worth as much money as Jeter. Defensively, he'd become little more than average, but his strong bat still made him a perennial All-Star. However, when he came back from his Achilles injury in 2004, Sox officials could not believe what they were seeing. Nomar couldn't get to many balls, and when he did, he often made throwing errors. The Red Sox hired an outside company that charts every ball hit, then rates how many balls are caught compared with an average player at each position. The numbers on Nomar in his first month back were damning. They indicated that his bat was no longer making up for his defensive liabilities. The stats were telling them that their former wonder boy was the worst defensive shortstop in baseball. It was particularly tough on a ground-ball pitcher like Lowe, and the fact that the Sox didn't have a good-fielding first baseman compounded the problem. This much was clear: Epstein's plan of 95 to 100 wins could not happen with Garciaparra at short.

The season bottomed out on the Fourth of July weekend at Atlanta's Turner Field, the ballpark situated between Little Street and Grady Memorial Hospital. The Sox lost two of the three games, capping their 1–5 road trip with a woeful 10–4 loss on July 4. It was a good time for the team to be on the road. Many fans back home were on the verge of giving up, and the team was being slaughtered on talk radio and in the newspapers.

This was when "trade Nomar" became a rallying cry across the Nation. Of six thousand readers who responded to a "Should the Sox trade Nomar?" Boston.com poll, more than 71 percent advocated such a deal. Nomar's sudden unpopularity owed to his lengthy injury, his slow start on returning, his obvious desire to get out of town when the season ended, and his no-show on the final night in New York.

I spoke to Nomar at some length about all of this before the first game in Atlanta. I'd already written (but not yet filed) a "Trade Nomar" column. In my view, it was time. More than any of the big four free agents, he was certain to be gone at the end of the year, and unlike the others, the Sox could move him without sending fans a message that the season was over.

I thought it would be only fair to tell him what was going to be in the morning *Globe.*

"I don't know what I'm supposed to say," he responded, fidgeting while he spoke, avoiding eye contact, and flashing that weird smile. "I guess it makes you feel better telling me that, but I don't know why you're telling me."

What ensued was a ten-minute conversation that was particularly fruitless and circular. I restated that I thought him wildly unhappy and that there was no chance he'd sign again with the Sox. He disputed both theories and said we never print retractions when we're wrong. He said he thought the media was "not accountable," and I argued that there was quite a bit of accountability in attaching one's name and photograph to one's opinions. I told him I could not believe that he hadn't played in the final game in New York. I said if he needed the rest, it would have been better to play one more game, then take the weekend off against the Braves. His response was to smile wickedly. It's a passive-aggressive technique he's perfected. When infuriated by a question or statement, Garciaparra will smile ("It's more like a sneer," suggested Werner), then smother his anger with one of his standard insincere answers. Ultimately, one could only conclude that here was a man who absolutely hated everything about being a public figure — other than the money and the satisfaction of succeeding at the highest level of his profession.

While this was going on, Garciaparra was locked in a petty dispute with Major League Baseball's uniform police. Nomar objected to the standard MLB logo on the back of his batting helmet and had been removing it before games. MLB officials warned him, then fined him $4,500 for three games. When the logo was put back in place, Nomar got his revenge by grinding his helmet into the dirt, effectively obliterating the logo. He was warned again and threatened with suspension.

Why would he care?

Garciaparra would not answer questions about this issue, but he was known to be sensitive about others profiting from the use of his image. He demanded compensation from the producers of *Still, We Believe,* so the movie folk reluctantly gave him a reported fee of $10,000. None of the other players thought or bothered to ask. Proceeds from the film were going to the Red Sox Charitable Foundation.

On the heels of the Yankee series, Boston's losing streak reached four games when the Red Sox dropped the opener in Atlanta. Garciaparra had three hits, raising the question Did the rest help, or could he have gotten those hits in New York? Mindful of a season on the brink of collapse, Epstein got on a plane and joined the team in Atlanta, then met with Francona. Upper management was getting a little tired of hearing about how much Terry loved the guys. Epstein said that he'd planned the visit all along. This was not entirely true, though. In fact, he went there to give the manager a pep talk and to cover for Nomar, claiming Garciaparra had been a "medical scratch" on that last night in New York.

The Sox won the day Theo arrived, but the following day Lowe imploded again, giving up seven runs on five hits and two walks in a single inning, blowing a 4–0 lead in a 10–4 loss. It was an unprofessional outing, more evidence that Lowe could set himself on fire at any moment. It also came at almost the exact midpoint (game 80 of 162) of the season.

Francona was noticeably different after the loss. For the first time all year, he was tough on a player. Everyone knew that Lowe had let the team down, and finally the manager wasn't making excuses. "It's happened too many times," he said. "That can't happen." Lowe chose to avoid the media for the first time all season.

Demonstrating again that they were not prone to panic—a trait that would serve them well in October—the Sox came home from the ragged trip and crushed the ball. It was 2003 all over again. Damon, perhaps inspired by the appearance of Matt Damon in the owners' box, went 5–6 in the first game after the trip (an 11–0 victory over Oakland), and the hitting was contagious. The top four hitters in the Sox lineup were getting three and four hits a game as the Sox ripped off five straight wins. They destroyed a good A's pitching staff and reminded Baseball America that the Red Sox would be a team to be reckoned with come October. It was a boffo home stand and carried the Sox into the All-Star break with new momentum, something they'd been lacking in the flaccid first half of 2004.

But in this strangest of seasons, another oddity arose on the final day before the midsummer hiatus: Ramirez took himself out of the lineup, claiming he had a sore left hamstring. He did so exactly one day after he was kept in a game in which the Sox were blowing out the Rangers, which was two days after Pedro was allowed to return to the Dominican Republic for an extraordinary six-day vacation.

It was another one of those only-the-Red-Sox events. Certainly no Yankee player, no player in all of baseball, was allowed to spend more time away from his teammates than Martinez. Francona and the top brass claimed that the holiday had been approved by the other players —but only because they were too savvy to squabble publicly about preferential treatment. It kindled thoughts of a dreadful September day in Philadelphia a year earlier, when Wakefield was reminded that he could have flown ahead of the team to the next city to prepare for a start. His answer: "I want to be with my teammates."

There was considerable media speculation that Ramirez was simply asking "Where's my vacation?" when he went on the shelf. It was left to Francona to sort things out—something that had already tested the patience of former Boston managers Williams, Kerrigan, and Little. Contributing to the rampant rumors was video footage of Schilling—the man with a strong stand on everything—scolding Ramirez during batting practice after Manny took himself out of the lineup. All parties later claimed that there was no discussion about Team Play 101, but it was difficult to escape the conclusion that Schilling was reading Manny the riot act. The Sox lost that final game before the break. Schilling, Manny, and Ortiz went to Houston for the All-Star Game while Pedro reclined on the beaches of the Dominican. The other Red Sox players rested for the second half of what was turning into a fairly ordinary season, which was disappointing, given the great expectations.

Manny and Ortiz hit home runs in the American League's All-Star victory, which again clinched home field advantage for the American League in the 2004 World Series. It was no small victory for Boston in October. The Sox will always have NL starter Roger Clemens to thank for this advantage. The Rocket was routed in his short All-Star stint in his hometown, and the Sox reaped the benefits three months later.

Tanned, rested, and ready to go—not unlike Richard Nixon in 1968—the Red Sox regrouped in the visitor's clubhouse at Angel Stadium on the first Thursday after the break, and Francona penciled Ramirez into the starting lineup, batting cleanup. But Manny paid a visit to the manager and said he had to sit. He could serve as designated hitter, but that was it. It was a distressing development for Francona, who was still riding the learning curve in Boston. His megastar hitter, who had just homered in the All-Star Game without a word about his hamstring, was testing him, and everybody knew it. By this point, the Sox were convinced that there was nothing wrong with Ramirez's hamstring, feeling instead that it was something he invented whenever he needed time off. Grudgingly, Francona switched Ramirez to DH. Meanwhile, Pedro strolled into the clubhouse, looking happier than he'd been all season. He high-fived his teammates, congratulated Manny and Ortiz for their All-Star homers, and said he was ready to pitch the second game of the series.

It was frustrating for some Sox fans. The highest-paid pitcher in baseball history, Martinez was getting eight days of rest at midseason, and because of the way the rotation unfolded, the extra day would take him out of the Yankee series the following weekend in Boston. When these facts were put in front of Francona, he reacted as if the questioner was speaking a foreign language: "So what's your point?"

Pedro would miss the next Yankee series. That was the point.

The Sox proceeded to go 3–3 on the trip through Anaheim and Seattle, another in a long line of mediocre stretches for this team of great expectations and greater payroll, and it raised serious questions about the ball club's ability to fulfill its destiny. The Curse of the Bambino was rearing its head in the form of unfulfilled potential. The post–All-Star trip signaled the end of eleven weeks of .500 baseball by a team that was supposed to be (with the Yankees, of course) one of the top two teams in the game. Simultaneously, there were the standard Red Sox sideshows involving the superstars.

The Ramirez situation reached a boiling point when the team arrived in Seattle and Manny again said he could only DH. Manny was toying with his new manager, perhaps because Pedro had been given the cushy holiday. To his credit, Francona elected to draw the line in the sand and told Ramirez that he could get back in the lineup only when he was well enough to play left field. When Manny had said he was ready to DH in the final game in Anaheim, Francona had made him sit. The next day, in Seattle, Manny was healthy enough to return to the outfield.

Meanwhile, the Nomar problem was worsening. There were rumors that the Sox were going to send Garciaparra to the Cubs as part of a three-way deal involving Arizona, which would bring Randy Johnson to Boston. Nomar didn't need any additional aggravation to increase his withdrawal from all things Red Sox, but certainly these rumors only made him more unhappy. He became a virtual recluse, the J. D. Salinger of the clubhouse, speaking to no one, staring into his locker, reading a magazine, and doing all the things he always did to get ready—in total isolation. He would not talk to the media and had almost nothing to do with his teammates. And he was also still locked in his ridiculous war with Major League Baseball about the logo on his batting helmet. The loco logo imbroglio went all the way to Commissioner Bud Selig. The Sox owners were not amused. Asked about Nomar's status, Werner said, "Physically, he seems to be okay. Mentally, it's another story." No one in the front office was pleased when Nomar's dad and wife sat in a radio booth at Angel Stadium and received a visit from Anaheim owner Arte Moreno. The spontaneous gathering, which bordered on tampering, was beamed back to New England, and Nomar-loving fans had another reason to wonder why their favorite was so clearly on a fast track out of town.

The Yankees went to Boston on the weekend of July 23–25, the eve of the Democratic National Convention (YANKEES AIM TO BURY DEAD SOX, trumped the *Post*).

The Red Sox lost the first game and were in a bad place when they gathered at Fenway for the second game of the weekend. Schilling had coughed up a 4–1 lead and lost the first game on Friday night, dropping the Sox to nine and a half games behind the Yankees. In the spirit of Chicago '68, the Whole World Was Watching and seemed certain that the Red Sox were going to finish second for a record seventh consecutive season. The *Herald*'s Tony Massarotti took to calling the Red Sox "the Fortune 500s": they made a fortune and they played .500 baseball. They still led the majors in unearned runs allowed.

Rain drenched Greater Boston before the Saturday matinee, and it looked as if the game would be postponed. The first order of business was an 11 A.M. meeting in the team's family room, where Henry, Lucchino, and Epstein finally met with Garciaparra and his agent, Arn Tellem. Unbeknownst to the Sox brass at the time, Nomar wanted to demand a trade at the meeting but had been talked out of it by Tellem.

"I wanted us to discuss the issue that we all seemed to be avoiding," said Lucchino. "We needed to talk about how unhappy Nomar was. Why was he still so pissed? Was there anything that could be done to change his mental state of mind, his approach to the organization, the city, and the game. We were contemplating the possibility of trading him, and we wanted to see if there was any way to take steps within our organization to make life better. Try to bring him back into the fold. The meeting lasted just about forty-five minutes, and at the end of it, we basically concluded that there was no way we were going to have a happy Nomar Garciaparra for the last couple of months of the season. There was no way to improve the situation. It wasn't a constructive session. What he told us was that the media was bothering him. He said we didn't appreciate how difficult it was to play here. He told us, 'I play three games every night. There's the media before the game, then there's the game, which is fun, then there's the media after the game.' He told us that the reason teams in Boston fade is because of the stress and strain brought on by the media. I tried to bring the conversation back to Nomar's contract or trade rumors, but he was more focused on the systemic problems of playing in Boston. He didn't want to talk about himself and his own situation."

After the meeting—which convinced the stunned Boston brass that Garciaparra must be traded—the rains continued, and the field appeared to be unplayable. At one point, word spread through the press box that the game had been called, and official scorer Joe Giuliotti made a beeline for his car to beat the rush before the inevitable announcement was made to the fans. But the announcement was never made. Behind the scenes was a debate in the ancient bowels of Fenway.

The Yankees didn't want to play that Saturday, and some of them started to change out of their uniforms when the postponement rumors circulated. One of the Yankees who was anxious to get away was catcher Jorge Posada. The focus of so many clutch and traumatic moments during the Sox-Yankee wars of 2003 and 2004, he'd had an especially disturbing experience during Friday night's game. While getting loose in the on-deck circle in the late innings, Posada was taunted in a most unspeakable fashion. A crazed, probably inebriated man wearing a Red Sox jersey crept down to the expensive seats and tossed out remarks to Posada about his four-year-old son. The child suffered from a rare birth defect, craniosynostosis, and had undergone multiple surgeries, fighting a somewhat public battle with a difficult disease, and he seemed stable that summer. But never had a patron in any city stooped to such depths. After hurling his vile message, the cowardly fan fled from the section, and Posada had to be restrained from vaulting the rail and chasing him through the stands. He spent the final two innings turning his head toward the area where the man had been. After the game, Yankee security officials were alerted, and there was a testy exchange between the Yankee brass and Red Sox security. Approached at his locker the next day, Posada declined to comment other than to say, "Please don't write about it in the paper. It will only make it worse for me."

Jeter, however, had something to say: "That's why some of us have a hard time with playing here . . . It's okay for fans to get on us about baseball, but that's crossing the line, don't you think?"

The episode speaks to the ugly side of the rivalry, the part we'd like to ignore. Too many fans develop an irrational attachment to athletes they have never met. When this passion is turned on the rival team, fans can be inexcusably cruel and obscene, attacking an athlete with language or gestures that would provoke a violent response if they were at a shopping mall or grocery store. The most cowardly fans are the loud, tough guys who feel they are safe behind the barrier that separates them from the players. We saw this boundary erased when Indiana Pacer Ron Artest and his team attacked unruly fans at the Palace in Auburn Hills, Michigan, early in the 2004–2005 NBA season. The eternal code holds that players should never go into the stands after fans — nothing good can come of it — but there are limits. It's easy to see how players can be baited into crossing the line.

While the Yankees were anxious to get dressed and leave soggy Fenway that Saturday, the Red Sox were lobbying management to stick around and play the game. According to Varitek, who emerged as the pivotal figure of the day, "The majority of our clubhouse got together and said, 'We want to do everything we can do to play this game.' We didn't want to wait and play a doubleheader later. We liked our matchup with Bronson and their starter [Tanyon Sturtze]."

Lucchino remembers, "It was one of the few times during the entire season when players, front office, manager, and coaches were all together in the manager's office, trying to make a collective decision about whether to play or not play. The players were determined. Pedro stood up and said, 'Play. If you need me to pitch in relief, I'll pitch in relief!' I remember thinking that this was a good moment. There was such unity and spirit. We'd gotten our ass handed to us the night before, and people wanted to play . . . Everyone likes to find moments which triggered the resurgence of the team. For some, that was the moment."

"We were like 'Rudy,' man," said Millar. "We wanted to play that game."

They wanted to play because of their difficult loss Friday night, and they wanted to show the fans that they were ready to take a stand against the hated New Yorkers. So the game was played. And in the third inning, with the Red Sox trailing, 3–0, A-Rod stepped in to bat against Arroyo. They had faced each other in high school when Arroyo (two grades younger) pitched for Hernando in Brooksville, Florida, and Rodriguez was hitting for Westminster Christian in Miami. Rodriguez had knocked in the winning Yankee run in the ninth the night before and said, "I felt like it was my first official big hit to make me a Yankee." Arroyo's first pitch, a sinker, hit Rodriguez near the left elbow. Instead of taking his base in silence, the quarter-billion-dollar man chose to express his umbrage. Varitek wasn't having any of it and walked beside Rodriguez as emotions escalated.

"He started yelling at my pitcher," remembers Varitek. "I knew Bronson didn't hit him intentionally. I told him to get to first base. He yelled back at me, said the F-word a couple of times and 'Come on,' and eventually it came on." Months later, urban legend held that Varitek told A-Rod, "We don't bother hitting .260 hitters," but he denied the remark, claiming he was not clever enough to think of something like that in the heat of the moment.

In the middle of one of Rodriguez's challenges to "come on!" Varitek stuffed his mitt into the Yankee's face, then lifted the quarter-billion-dollar man off the ground. It made for one of the great photos in the history of the rivalry (and wound up on the cover of Stephen King and Stewart O'Nan's best-selling Red Sox book) and triggered a donnybrook on a par with Munson-Fisk, 1973.

"I just want to know how I get some royalties out of it," Rodriguez said later. "It's unbelievable, one of the unique things that sell in this world. But I have no regrets about doing what I did. Obviously, it's not good for our game, so I'm remorseful about that, but it shows how passionate two players can be about the game and their respective teams. I have all the respect in the world for those guys, but in the heat of the moment, sometimes you've got to throw down. I don't know if he was throwing at me. Sometimes in the heat of the moment, shit happens and you do goofy shit."

Jeter was otherwise occupied when all hell broke loose: "I had been on first base, but Sheffield hit into a double play so I went into the dugout bathroom. I heard everyone running out, but I had no idea what had happened when I got back out there."

When the dust cleared, Yankee starter Tanyon Sturtze (of the Worcester Sturtzes) was bleeding from his ear; Rodriguez, Varitek, Kenny Lofton, and Kapler were ejected from the game; and the Sox were complaining about being cheap-shotted by Lofton, much as the Red Sox of yore groused about Mickey Rivers in the 1970s.

"You don't want to embarrass the game," Varitek said later (he refuses to sign copies of the famous photo). "But for whatever reason, it happened. I was just trying to protect my guy on the mound. Those things happen, and you don't know exactly what's going on. Schilling was there right away. But nobody went in to give anybody a cheap shot, at least none of our guys. They had a couple. Lofton is the one that stayed hidden. He hit at least two of our people in the head."

Three months later, Rodriguez and Arroyo would again become entangled in a memorable exchange, and again A-Rod would get the worst of things. But that was far away on July 24. The Red Sox were just trying to save some face in front of a national audience. And they did. The Varitek-Rodriguez fight would stand as the most important game moment of the Red Sox regular season. It was bigger than Ortiz's Easter homer, bigger than Mueller's walk-off winner later in the same game. It meant more than any single home run by Manny, more than any win by Pedro, and more than any save by Foulke. Even though the Sox did not start playing better until a few weeks later, most of the players and fans believed the season turned on the violent play—just as the classic 1984 NBA Finals tilted in favor of the Celtics after Kevin McHale's vicious open-floor takedown of fast-breaking Laker Kurt Rambis.

After the Varitek–A-Rod fight, the Sox still trailed, 10–9, in the bottom of the ninth, when with a man on base and one out, Mueller walked from the on-deck circle to home plate to face the indomitable Rivera. But Sox hitting coach Ron Jackson, "Papa Jack," had been working on a Rivera pitch pattern and told Mueller what to look for.

Mueller, the 5-10, 180-pound defending American League batting champ, who is so often overlooked in discussions about the miracle Red Sox, worked the count to 3–1. Papa Jack signaled—the next pitch would be a cut fastball. And it was. Mueller turned on the cutter and cranked it into the Red Sox bullpen for a walk-off, two-run homer. Mueller took off his batting helmet before reaching the mob of his teammates at home plate. It would not be the last Sox walk-off homer of 2004, and Mueller established a trend by removing his headgear for the festivities at the plate. Veterans know that exuberant teammates tend to pound on a hero's head when he's still wearing his helmet. The old ball park rocked, just as it had when Papi hit the walk-off shot on Easter Sunday. There hadn't been enough of these moments in 2004, but fans filing out of Fenway on July 24 had reason to believe something special might have begun.

The game took 3 hours and 54 minutes; featured 21 runs, 27 hits, 4 errors, and 5 ejections; and marked the first time in fifty-seven games that the Yankees had lost after leading at the end of eight innings.

The Red Sox won again the next night after John Kerry threw out the first ball and watched from Henry's box next to the Sox dugout. Hardly anyone noticed when Garciaparra popped up to Jeter (shortstop to shortstop, dust to dust) in the bottom of the eighth against Bret Prinz.

It was Garciaparra's final at-bat at Fenway Park in a Red Sox uniform.

But the Boston ball club got no bounce from these wins against the Yankees, and when the Sox reverted to their .500 form in Baltimore, Epstein renewed the attempts to trade Garciaparra. Anaheim and Los Angeles, considered obvious landing spots for Nomar, were not interested. Oakland had a brief interest but quickly backed away. The Cubs' Jim Hendry was the only GM who expressed a serious interest in Garciaparra and sent scouts to watch the Red Sox. The Sox said they needed a shortstop in return, but Epstein didn't like Chicago's Alex Gonzalez. The Cubs, meanwhile, were trying to get Orlando Cabrera from the Expos.

Then came the phone call that changed Red Sox history. Three days before the July 31 trading deadline, the Sox were in Baltimore, en route to Minnesota, when Francona called Epstein and said, "We gotta talk. I want you to hear this directly from me. Nomar's not doing well at all. He thinks he's going to need some time off and might have to go on the disabled list." Epstein was alarmed. For the first time in his short tenure, he summoned Henry and Lucchino to his office to be part of the phone call. He asked Francona to repeat what he'd just said.

That was it. Suspicious since spring training, the Sox brass was finally and firmly convinced that Garciaparra's interests were no longer in concert with the interests of the team. Henry, Lucchino, and Epstein believed that Garciaparra's only goal was being healthy at the end of the season — to make himself a stronger candidate for free agency. Nomar wasn't going to take a chance on hurting himself while helping owners he detested, men who had tried to replace him with Alex Rodriguez and send him to the Chicago White Sox.

Epstein was rattled. His hundred-win team was looking like an eighty-seven-win team out of the playoffs. Reese was out with an oblique muscle injury, and now Garciaparra was planning on more time off, maybe a trip to the disabled list. Making matters worse, the Sox would have to disclose his new injury status to prospective bidders — i.e., the Cubs. When he contacted Hendry, Epstein was surprised and happy to learn that the Cubs were still interested. Ultimately, it was Hendry who made everything come together. The Cub GM pulled Minnesota first baseman Doug Mientkiewicz into the deal and kept all the teams in the loop.

On Friday, July 30, hours before the deadline, Epstein went to the Cheesecake Factory in Newton late in the evening with his lieutenants Peter Woodfork and Jed Hoyer. They were depressed during their eleventh-hour dinner because it looked as if there was no way to make a trade that would improve the team and prove salable to the fans. Meanwhile, Hendry was still working on getting Cabrera from the Expos.

On Saturday morning, the two clubs were still discussing Cabrera and Cub starter Matt Clement for Garciaparra and Lowe, but Epstein decided he didn't like the Clement-Lowe portion of the deal. Mientkiewicz was a better fit for Boston, even though the Sox would have to part with a top prospect, outfielder Matt Murton. Hendry was told the Sox would deal Nomar if the Cubs could produce Cabrera and Mientkiewicz. Lucchino was in the Sox offices with Epstein. John Henry was at home. All were squeamish about such a deal because it might not fly with the fans.

It came together minutes before the deadline, as Chicago's Hendry started the process of contacting the commissioner's office. It was awkward. There was already a lineup card on the wall with Nomar penned into the fifth hole against the Twins that night. Watching the Philly-Cub game on the clubhouse TV, the Sox players had joked about the impending deadline. When Doug Mirabelli entered the room, he said, "Fifteen minutes to go, and we're all still here." Manny did the same thing, telling reporters, "Ten minutes to go, and I'm still here. I guess I'm not going anywhere." At 3:41 P.M. Central Time, Garciaparra answered his cell phone. In the same moment, a Red Sox publicist asked the media to vacate the clubhouse. When the reporters were gone, Francona stepped out and asked Garciaparra to come into his office. He put Nomar on the phone with Epstein. And with that, Nomar's ten-year relationship with the Red Sox organization was over. The Sox had gone a perfectly average 22–22 in the games he had played in 2004.

After the short conversation, Nomar went back into the locker room and started to say good-bye to his teammates. He had hugs for Wakefield and Ramirez. Damon said, "We just traded away Mr. Boston, a guy that meant so much to the city."

Garciaparra said, "They can take the shirt off my back, but they can't take away the memories I got. They can't take away the standing ovations that I got when I came back this season when I walked up to the plate. Or the standing ovation I got when I hit the grand slam this year. Or when I hit three home runs on my birthday [July 2002]. Every time I stepped up to the plate, the fans cheered for me. When I went deep in the hole to make a play, they'll never be able to take away that. What it's meant to me, they all know that every single day I went out there, and I was proud to put that uniform on and what it represented."

Asked about his final message to his teammates, he said, "Goodbye. I love them, I miss them, good luck, and hopefully, we'll see them in the World Series."

The Cubs' traveling secretary, Jack McCormick, arranged for Garciaparra to fly to Chicago. The Cubs were putting him up in a Hampton Inn, but McCormick did his best to stress that it was a *nice* Hampton Inn. Trailed by a single television cameraman, wearing a white

Joseph Abboud shirt hanging over his blue jeans, Garciaparra walked out of the visitor's clubhouse and caught a cab back to the Minneapolis Radisson, where the Sox were staying. He packed, took a cab to the airport, and got on a plane for Chicago.

Back in Boston, Epstein was already dealing with the frenzied fallout. He took calls from his family, informing him that he was taking a beating on sports radio. As he walked around the Sox offices, he saw panic in the faces of employees. He went upstairs for a press conference and took all the questions. He said, "The safe thing to do would have been to play it out. The safe thing to do would have been not to touch it. But in my mind, we were not going to win the World Series as it was."

In New York, the Yankees were getting ready to play the Orioles. Jeter was astonished. He thought he'd be seeing Nomar in the Boston dugout for the rest of their careers.

"I can't really picture him playing anywhere else," said Nomar's longtime pinstripe counterpart. "When I think of the Red Sox, the first thing I think about is Nomar . . . I used to wake up in the middle of the night there, and I swear I'd hear fans cheering his name."

Jeter dialed Garciaparra's cell phone and left his rival a message. "I think it's still the right number," he said two months later. "But I never heard back."

It was, by any measurement, the most significant player transaction made by the Red Sox front office since George Herman Ruth was sold to the Yankees in 1920. The Red Sox justified the deal by pointing to the potential defensive improvement offered by Cabrera (who could handle every ball) and the Gold Glover Mientkiewicz. In a second deal, Epstein acquired speedy Dave Roberts from the Dodgers in exchange for minor league outfielder Henri Stanley. Young Theo felt good about what Cabrera, Mientkiewicz, and Roberts could do for Boston. They brought defense and speed into the mix. The Sox would be able to manufacture a run now and then. Unlike Nomar, Cabrera would be able to play every day. Mientkiewicz would catch everything at first. And Roberts could steal a base.

But it was a public relations gamble of the highest order, very un-Sox-like. With the exception of Carl Yastrzemski during his triple-crown season and his 1983 retirement tour, Garciaparra had been the club's most popular everyday player since Ted Williams. Fans loved him, and he'd earned their devotion by playing hard and playing exceptionally well for seven seasons. Through the years, particularly under Yawkey, the star system had dictated the way business was done at Fenway Park. Williams was coddled. Yaz was coddled. Star players could get a manager fired. When role players like Frank Duffy and Jack Brohamer came to the star-studded Sox in the late 1970s, they were stunned by what they perceived as a clubhouse caste system. The stars ate first after games. The stars had better lockers and travel accommodations. Unable to sell championship baseball to a large fan base, the Sox front office sold stars. Ted Williams, Carl Yastrzemski, Jim Rice, Wade Boggs, Nomar. Roger Clemens and Mo Vaughn could never be traded, even when it was obvious that they were going to walk at the end of the year. The front office was afraid to alienate the fans. This is why trading Nomar was so unusual and significant. Epstein was being realistic. He knew Garciaparra was gone at the end of the year, and he remained shocked at the decline in Nomar's defense. He was taking a scientific approach, disregarding sentiment and leading the Red Sox into a brave new era.

"We were not willing to lose Nomar Garciaparra and get nothing in return," Lucchino said late Saturday night, hours after the deal was announced. "Part of it had to do with his attitude toward re-signing. He was too valuable to get nothing in return . . . He was struggling. I had a feeling his health raised uncertainty about his availability. He did seem to struggle. There was a lot of pressure with the injury. There were times the injury was reflected in this kind of pressure."

The CEO said something else that was interesting, a comment that would lead Nomar's people to believe the Sox were engaged in a smear campaign against the shortstop. Lucchino said that he'd spoken with Garciaparra briefly after the trade and that he'd asked him how his Achilles felt. Lucchino reported that Garciaparra responded, "It's fine now."

Lucchino thought it was an odd remark and didn't mind sharing it with Boston reporters. The Sox took Nomar's answer as a validation of their suspicions that his interests were no longer the same as the ball club's.

Henry thought to himself: What have we done?

The Twins beat the Red Sox, 5–4, hours after the trade. Mientkie-wicz had a few hits for Boston while Cabrera was en route to Min-neapolis. Fans watching TV at the Boston Beer Works on Brookline Avenue walked outside after the game and noticed the giant billboard on the building at the corner of Brookline and Lansdowne streets. It featured the smiling image of Nomar next to the words KEEP THE FAITH.

An exhausted Epstein flicked off the TV in his office, trudged home, met his girlfriend, and had a few beers. His mind raced. Had he really just traded Nomar Garciaparra?

He had trouble sleeping, so he took an Ambien for the first time in his life.

9

Light in August

A LITTLE GROGGY, Theo got up, fetched the Sunday morning papers, and cringed as he took in the front-page headlines. There it was in black-and-white. He really had traded Nomar Garciaparra. The columnists (myself included) were surprisingly positive toward the deal. It was, of course, different on the airwaves and in the street. Fans were flocking to the souvenir store on Yawkey Way, clearing the shelves of all things Nomar. Parents were explaining to young children about the realities of professional sports. Grown men walked the streets wearing their no. 5 jerseys.

"People were not happy about it," said Henry months later. "There was a sense that we did not get enough. People were saying we traded Nomar for two guys that were hitting .243."

Not much was known about Orlando Luis Cabrera, the man who would replace Nomar Garciaparra. Cabrera was born in Cartagena, Colombia, on November 2, 1974. A tourist city on the Caribbean coast, Cartagena had become a Red Sox town in the early 1980s when native son Jackie "the Whistler" Gutierrez played shortstop briefly in Boston. Jolbert Cabrera, Orlando's father, took his young son to visit the Red Sox player at his home in Cartagena, and the boy was impressed with Gutierrez's trophy room. Montreal Expo scout Fred Ferreira signed Cabrera when he was eighteen, and Cabrera began his professional career in Montreal's Dominican Summer League, hitting .344 in thirty-eight games. The Expos called him to the big leagues in 1997 and in 2000 he took over as the Expos' everyday shortstop. He won a Gold Glove in 2001, playing in all 162 games. He played every game again in 2003—no small statistic. The 2004 Sox were suffering because of infield instability, much of which owed to the uncertainty involving Garciaparra. Orlando Cabrera was a sure-handed, seasoned veteran, and *he played every day.* He was working on a streak of more than 280 consecutive games when he came to the Red Sox.

Cabrera was smoking a cigar in the visitor's clubhouse at Miami's Pro Player Stadium when manager Frank Robinson called him into his office to tell him he'd been traded to Boston. Cabrera had one question for Robinson: Was Garciaparra also traded? Informed that, indeed, Nomar was gone, Cabrera knew the job was his. He caught the first plane to Minneapolis and was in the Red Sox lineup on August 1. Meanwhile, his wife and two children returned to Colombia to begin the new school year. The Sox exported their television signal to Colombia to allow Cabrera's family to watch Boston's games.

He homered in his first trip to the plate for the Red Sox but made an error late in the game, and the Sox lost their second straight to the Twins. Epstein watched on television and knew the loss would make him a target. Two days after the trade, the *Globe* ran a front-page story headlined: YOUNG FANS TAKE TRADE OF GARCIAPARRA HARD. The piece was dressed up with a photo of a sad-eyed youngster surrounded by Nomar memorabilia, staring into the lens as if he'd just learned there was no Santa. The *Globe* later ran a clip-and-save story recommending the best way to discuss the Nomar trade with young children. It was more than a baseball roster transaction. In many corners of the Nation, it was the death of a family member.

Epstein remembers, "I was hearing, 'Why did they trade for a guy who hits like Pokey Reese but doesn't field as well?' It was tough. It was a challenging time. It was hard to keep my spirits up. I got on a plane to join the team [in Tampa], and when I got there a couple of players told me that it looked like my hair was falling out and like I'd aged ten years."

A few days later, when the still-struggling Sox were in Detroit, Lucchino and Epstein called Francona from the Fenway offices.

"This was the first year for Tito, and we were getting to know him," remembers Lucchino. "There were certainly recurring themes that he was not being tough enough. His method of handling players ultimately proved successful, but Theo and I called him and told him that three months of .500 baseball was just unacceptable. We were not going to talk to him about what to do differently. That was his call. But what we care about is that .500 baseball is just plain unacceptable."

Henry was not part of the phone call. "I was doing the opposite," he admitted. "I was calling Tito and saying, 'Don't worry about it. I hear you're not sleeping. You've got to sleep. This is not your fault. You're going to be here a long time. You've got to relax, and we'll get through this.' I guess we were sending him mixed messages."

When the Sox lost to the lowly Devil Rays at home, 8–3, on August 9—the first Fenway game of the No-Nomar Era, I wrote, "Hang down your heads John Henry, Larry Lucchino and Theo Epstein. You too, Terry Francona. And all you guys in uniform—you just keep telling yourselves that any day now you'll take off on a hot streak. You are 45–44 since May 1 and you have a chance to be remembered as the biggest pack of frauds ever to don the Sox uniform."

Two days later, Millar sought me out in the clubhouse. "Who are the frauds?" he asked, smiling. "Pedro? Schilling? Manny?"

I told him it would be the entire group. Every player. This team had the second-highest payroll in the major leagues. They added Schilling and Foulke to a team that came within five outs of the World Series. Playing .500 ball for five months would make them a pack of frauds.

"I like it," said Millar.

Varitek and Schilling said nothing about the column. Until much later.

It was true then, and it's true now. This team of great expectations, this team that wound up winning the World Series, throwing off the Curse of the Bambino and bringing joy to New England after eighty-six years of frustration, somehow managed to be a .500 ball club for more than half of the 2004 season. It was amazing. And had they maintained this pattern of mediocrity, they would have been detested for all time by Red Sox Nation. Too much was expected, and for too long they delivered so little. But in later months, when things went so well, all of them maintained that they knew they were going to turn things around. They never doubted themselves and dismissed the fans and media members who questioned their ability to turn it on when needed.

They did. From August 10 until the end of the regular season, the Red Sox were the best team in baseball. They went 42–19 after the trade. Including the postseason, they went 53–22 after the trade. In all the games played after the "fraud" column, they went 49–17 (.742). They put themselves in position to get to the postseason, convinced that their abilities and attitude would take care of the rest. And they delivered as no Sox team has delivered since Babe Ruth pitched on the Fenway mound.

On the morning of August 16 (the day Ruth died in 1948, and Elvis in '77), the Red Sox were a season-low ten and a half games behind the Yankees. In just a little over three miraculous weeks, they cut that margin to a mere two games, inspiring legions of Sox fans to envision revenge for the fold of 1978. The Yankees had never lost a first-place lead of more than six games, but their pitching started to collapse just when the Red Sox got hot, and there was a rare inversion of imagery as Boston fans talked about the Yankees choking. The Red Sox starters stayed in turn all season, without injury. It seemed that Ortiz and Ramirez hit homers (sometimes two) almost daily. Pedro pitched a rare nine-inning shutout. Lowe, a ground-ball pitcher, reaped the benefits of the new infield defense and turned his season around. Aided by speedster Roberts, the Sox were occasionally able to manufacture a run, and they were winning the one-run games. By the end of the month, the Sox were ahead of their 2003 pace, a fact that seemed impossible after the three months of .500 ball.

Suddenly perceived as a better manager, Francona talked about his new team: "Our bench is strong. We have a lot of ways to move people. You can defense different positions, which is what we're supposed to do. Players may not always like it, but that gives us our best team for nine innings. Plus, I think it's good when you get everyone involved. We weren't trying to make mistakes before. We weren't built the way some of us were comfortable. I thought we'd be better defensively. I care a lot about defense. Yeah, it was bothersome—the way we were wasn't perfect. We were hoping to get the matchups, but some nights we didn't. You want to play to your players' strengths. We don't necessarily want guys that can't bunt or try to bunt. If there's a guy on second base and you're not sure you can get to third on a bunt, why do it? You might make thirty thousand people think you're trying to do the right thing, but it doesn't work. If you have guys that are hitting that aren't necessarily going to hit into a double play, let 'em hit it. We are better suited to play a little more aggressive baseball right now. The philosophy I don't think has changed. I don't think we want to give outs away. You only get twenty-seven, you want to use 'em. But we're a little quicker and a little better defensively."

The Red Sox were the best team in baseball in August of 2004. They went 21–7 in the month and trailed the Yankees by only three and a half games on September 1. They established themselves as the best team in the American League, clear favorites to win the wild card, and once again threatened the Yankees. They were finally the team Theo had envisioned in the winter of 2003–2004. The Sox were no longer losing all the one-run games. They were no longer leading the majors in unearned runs. They took care of the baseball, giving the opposition twenty-seven outs per game instead of thirty. With success came happiness. The clubhouse was joyous, much as it had been in 2003. The Cowboy Up theme was gone, but the confidence was greater. This team, after all, had Curt Schilling and Keith Foulke, vital pieces that had been missing in 2003.

In Boston and across Baseball America, the debate raged. Did trading Nomar really make the Red Sox that much better? How much of the surge was simply a matter of the team's getting hot at the right moment?

The players, naturally, were reluctant to criticize their former teammate, but they gradually uttered some undeniable truths.

"We hadn't played so great before the trade happened," said Millar. "Now we're playing better. I don't know what the reason is. It would be unfair to say that trading Nomar is the reason, but is it part of it? I think so, yeah."

Schilling, who privately said that Garciaparra had been an enormous disappointment as a teammate, went on the record to say, "I don't think there's any argument against it [the trade]. Consider our recent record in one-run games . . . There isn't anybody doing their own thing now, and that's different. Nomar had a lot of things going on and he's introverted. He had the Achilles. He had the contract. And it was its own story. Every day with the trade, that changed the atmosphere immediately in here."

Varitek, a quiet loyalist who had played with Garciaparra at Georgia Tech, in the 1992 Olympics in Barcelona, and with the Red Sox for six and a half years, said, "I think we were playing good ball when he was here, before the trade happened. I don't want to discredit anything that our new shortstop has done because he's done such a phenomenal job. From the standpoint of Nomar getting blamed, I don't think he deserves the blame. He's done too much, and he's meant too much to the organization and the city to take that.

"He's a great player that did a lot of great things in that city, and he needs to be complimented for it, but we can't go on playing, wondering what life would be like with him. I very much enjoy our new guy. He's got a spunk, fire, and intelligence about him. He just plays. He plays every day."

There it was again. *He plays every day.* The Red Sox did their best not to malign their exiled star, but in effect, they damned him every time they talked about Cabrera's defensive prowess and durability. They could count on Cabrera. They couldn't count on Nomar and hadn't been able to for a long time. It seemed Nomar's mere presence had been a drag on the clubhouse karma. One couldn't help but be reminded of Dylan's closing line in "Positively 4th Street": "Yes, I wish that for just one time you could stand inside my shoes. You'd know what a drag it is to see you."

As ever, there were Curse overtones. The Cubs? Did the Sox really have to trade their signature player to the Chicago Cubs, the alter egos of the Boston Red Sox? The Cubs were the team the Sox beat when they won the World Series in 1918. Ruth beat the Cubs twice in that Series, including a 1–0 shutout in the opener. The Cubs had an old ballpark and great fans and a history of failed campaigns. The Cubs even had their own curse, the famed Billy Goat Curse, which held that the Cubs would never win because William Sianis and his goat had been denied admission into Wrigley for the 1945 World Series. Both the Sox and Cubs had come within five outs of the World Series in 2003, and it had long been suggested that a Cub–Red Sox World Series would trigger the Apocalypse. Now Nomar was a Cub. Would he lead the team to the World Series while the Sox sat at home? Or worse, would he help the Cubs beat the Red Sox in the 2004 World Series, thus creating the Curse of Nomar? The possibilities were endless.

None of the above happened, of course. Garciaparra went to the Cubs and proceeded to plague them with shoddy defense and day-to-day uncertainty. The numbers were damning. The Cubs gave up only twenty unearned runs before July 31, then yielded twenty-four the rest of the season. On balls hit in play, Cub opponents raised their average from .280 pre-Nomar to .311 after the trade.

But even though some Sox fans were reluctant to surrender their no. 5 Nomar jerseys, the Boston club was concerned only with its own standing. Which was getting better by the day. Schilling noted, "A week or two after the deal was made, we found our identity and took off."

In New York, Jeter rejected the notion. "That's not fair," he said. "They might have gone on to win forty of forty-two if he hadn't been traded."

Fair enough. When Nomar came out to defend himself, he aimed most of his barbs at Sox management, telling the *Globe*'s Edes: "This is something I had no control over. Boston was the place I bought a home in, thinking I'm going to be setting up shop here and spend the rest of my career here. I didn't trade me . . . I'm not mad at them. I'm not going to rant and rave. I'm not jabbing anybody. If they didn't want me, fine. They traded me. Why can't that be enough?"

It never is enough in Boston. Rival camps are formed, and fans line up on opposite sides. It was that way when Bill Parcells bolted the Patriots for the Jets after taking New England to the Super Bowl in 1997. The fans took sides, some blaming Parcells, others blaming owner Bob Kraft. It was the same when Clemens and Vaughn left as free agents and when an injured Drew Bledsoe was replaced by Tom Brady, he of the stardust shoulder pads. In Boston, stars are tainted when they leave and none more than Nomar Garciaparra. Two days after the deal was done, his image was removed from the KEEP THE FAITH billboard and replaced by an imposing David Ortiz delivering the same message.

After John Henry and Arn Tellem (Garciaparra's agent) had their say, Epstein called a truce in early August, saying, "It's important to stop now and not get truly ugly. These things can have a life of their own at times. It's not productive. Both sides have sort of got their stories out now. We should just move on."

WBZ-TV's Bob Lobel, a Boston broadcast legend who was sometimes involved in Sox programming, must not have gotten the memo. A few days after Theo spoke, he aired a report claiming that Garciaparra had actually injured his Achilles while playing soccer during the off-season.

On the last day of August, the Red Sox began a stretch of baseball that effectively clinched a playoff spot by beating the Angels, 10–7, at Fenway Park. During the game, Ramirez hit a hard foul ball that knocked out the two front teeth of Lee Gavin, a sixteen-year-old boy who just happened to live on Dutton Road in Sudbury in the very same house occupied by Babe Ruth when he played for the Red Sox. Some people thought it was an omen. Curse proponents were all over the kid, and he appeared on several television programs. Meanwhile, in New York, the Yankees were beaten, 22–0, by the Cleveland Indians. As the score was updated on the left field wall in Boston, the fans howled with delight. It was 9–0 in the third, 16–0 in the sixth. Sox officials decided to post the garish digits on the big board in center, which made Epstein cringe slightly in his box seat behind home plate.

"It's nice to be gaining ground on them," said Theo. "But Cash still has until midnight [the roster deadline] to make a deal. We'll see what happens. They never cease to amaze me with what they can do."

The loss to the Indians was the single worst defeat in the history of the Yankee franchise (the back page of the September 1 *Daily News* featured a photo of routed starter Javier Vazquez under the headline STINKEES), and it triggered a significant response from Steinbrenner. A day later, the Boss had signs posted inside and outside Yankee Stadium. The message was, "When the going gets tough, the tough get going." (He probably also gave a locker room pep talk, starting with, "Was it over when the Germans bombed Pearl Harbor? No, and it ain't over now!") He issued a statement: "Sure, we got punished badly last night. But winners never quit and quitters never win. We all know New Yorkers never quit, and we reflect the spirit of New York."

"This is happening to the Yankees quicker than what happened to us," said Jerry Remy, All-Star second baseman of the 1978 Boston Folders. "But when your starters win twice in seventeen games, this can happen. It's unbelievable. Just by luck your starters would win more than that."

Dennis Eckersley, a twenty-game winner for the same team, added,

"This would make up for '78 cuz they would have fucked up as bad as we did. There's a lot of pressure on them now. But there was more pressure on us in '78 because there was no wild card. These guys today can fuck up and still be in it. We didn't have that luxury."

He was right. The Red Sox were not going to catch the Yankees during the regular season. They were going to win ninety-eight games, the most since Remy and Eckersley's Sox won ninety-nine in 1978, but they were going to finish second to the Yankees for a record seventh consecutive season. Fortunately, they did have the benefit of the wild card. They knew it didn't really matter if they finished first as long as they were playing great baseball at the end of the regular season.

"We knew all along this was going to happen," said Schilling. "There was no doubt about it in the minds of the guys in this clubhouse."

Finally, it looked as if they really were going back to the playoffs, maybe even back to 161st Street in the Bronx.

10

Gypsies, Tramps, and Thieves

T HERE WAS A CONSTANT BUZZ around Fenway in the final month of the regular season. Jimmy Buffett played two shows at the ballpark, just as Springsteen had a year earlier. Like the Boss, Buffett made the requisite efforts to break the Curse, pledging all forms of exorcism and Curse-lifting. Schilling was on the cover of *Sports Illustrated*, Manny was featured in *GQ*, and *The New Yorker* carried a piece mirroring the Sox and the Yankees with the Democrats and the Republicans in the all-important election year. Stephen King attended almost every game, putting his thoughts to paper at night. The Dropkick Murphys took Fenway favorite "Tessie" (a punk rock version of a Sox rally song from the turn of the century) worldwide, and ESPN hired Alan Dershowitz to argue in a mock trial pitting the Curse of the Bambino against the Cubs' Billy Goat Curse (the Bambino won in a landslide). Meanwhile, for two weeks Fenway was overrun with stars, directors, and extras from a Farrelly brothers flick, *Fever Pitch*. The moviemakers gained unparalleled access to the ballpark, and it seemed that Sox vice president and choreographer Dr. Charles Steinberg was intent on seeing his team become the first franchise to win the World Series and the Cannes Film Festival in a span of eight months.

Meanwhile, the slovenly look of the local nine started to get national attention. Damon had been a point man for the grunge look all season, but as the playoffs neared, purists had some reservations about the team's appearance. It started in the dugout, where Francona never wore an official Red Sox uniform top, instead going with a red pullover (blue on the road), which made him look like a man preparing to change his oil every time he walked to the mound to make a pitching change. It was somehow fitting that the sloppy manager with no hair would be in charge of baseball's hair club for men. By September, Pedro's jeri-curls made him look like Eriq La Salle's Soul Glo character in Eddie Murphy's *Coming to America*. That was only the beginning. Nixon came back sporting a mohawk worthy of De Niro's Travis Bickle, and Mark Bellhorn could have been a sweathog in *Welcome Back, Kotter*. Kapler and Millar shaved their heads, then Millar grew a Lincolnesque beard. Bronson Arroyo went with the blond cornrow look, recalling Bo Derek and an early Justin Timberlake. Pokey Reese was able to unleash his cornrows and play Buckwheat from a *Rascals* episode, and Manny's goofy locks defied conventional style and gravity. Many of the Sox chose to smear pine tar over the "B" on their batting helmets, and Nixon took to powdering his cap with chalk dust, adding to the pigpen style of Francona's wild bunch. Young Theo, who pledged to get a mohawk for the playoffs, was not bothered by the sloth; he almost welcomed the contrast with the corporate Yankees.

"I think that's who we are as a team," said the GM. "It's our personnel. We couldn't do it any other way. I mean, let's say we had a policy requiring haircuts and no facial hair. The benefits would be uniformity, discipline, and perhaps a heightened sense of order. But we'd lose individuality, self-expression, and fun. Given our personalities, our players thrive when they're allowed to be themselves and have fun. When we've played our best baseball the last two years, we've looked like this. It's a pack of sloppy, fun-loving renegades. Look at us during batting practice. Guys are wearing six different kinds of hats. Four different uniform tops. We're a mess. That's the way we are."

"That's us," added Damon. "We are the total opposite of the Yankees."

Schilling, a military man at heart and a staunch Republican, didn't like the slob look but kept quiet as the wins started to mount.

Francona, who had shoulder-length hair in his youth, said, "I don't see the relevance. Nobody respects the game more than me. Our guys may look a little goofy, but they try hard to play the game right. If this were the Boy Scouts, maybe we'd try to get medals by having them cut their hair or tuck their shirts in. But this is their personality. Why take it away?"

"I never thought it was over the top," said Lucchino. "Teams that win have a personality. I tend to think the media and public make too much of these things. These guys are professional people. It's different than something you would have in high school. That stuff just didn't bother me that much. And frankly, I did like the contrast with the Yankees. They came off as Halliburton—rigid, nearly militaristic theme—and we had more free spirits and longer hair. And it's irrelevant to performance."

These were heady days for the 2004 Red Sox. A ten-game winning streak started at the end of August and carried into September before it was stopped by Chris Young, Texas's 6-10 rookie from Princeton. In what was billed as a make-or-break road trip, the Sox went to Oakland and Seattle and ripped off five wins in seven games, including three straight victories at Oakland. Their dominance over the A's was a carryover from the 2003 ALDS. Francona's men finished the 2004 season with an 8–1 record against the A's, outscoring Billy Beane's team, 76–40. The A's were the team the Sox hoped to face in the first round of the playoffs.

Toward the end of the trip, which effectively locked up a wild card playoff spot, Varitek sat in front of his locker in the visitor's clubhouse at Seattle's Safeco Field and gave some thoughtful answers to previously unthinkable questions. The Sox were only three and a half games behind the Yankees. They'd just won six straight against the Angels and A's. There were still three weeks to play, including back-to-back weekends with the Yankees. Did Varitek think his team was the best in the American League?

"Yes, I do," he said. ". . . I really think we turned it around in those last two games in New York, back in June. We lost 'em, but the effort was there. We had a little spunk. It was like 'Boom, let's go.' We still weren't winning, but it was different. Then our pitching got better with some great plays defensively, and next thing you know, we were winning a lot of games. Now that we've proven it to ourselves, there's more confidence and a better swagger to the whole team. I'm far more confident than I was last year. We have far better pitching, and we've become a very good fielding team. We do some other things better because of the way we've been coached. Little things like baserunning and talking about what's going to happen in a situation. Those things all matter."

A week later they were back in New York, and the Sox and the Nation were convinced that Boston was going to overtake the Yankees. There was considerable pre-series hype involving potential beanball wars. The rivals hadn't seen each other since Kerry sat in the Red Sox owners' box on the eve of the Democratic convention. Sheffield told the New York scribes: "I don't care if these guys hit us. We ain't gonna stand for it." Meanwhile, Ortiz said, "I betcha they're very worried. Their pitching's not very good," and Damon chirped in with: "We feel like we have a better team." Sox players walked around the clubhouse in T-shirts that read TELL 'EM WE'RE COMING AND HELL IS COMING WITH US. Others favored shirts saying SCREW THE CURSE and WHY NOT US?

Throughout baseball, because of the way the Red Sox had played since the trading deadline, there was widespread contention that Boston *was* the best team in the American League. Although the Yankees were still in first place, the Red Sox had an odd aura of invincibility about them. Reminded of this, Jeter sat in a chair in front of his locker before the first game of the series and said, "They're supposed to think that way. They probably felt that way last year, too."

"I won't say they are right or they are wrong," said Reggie Jackson. "Being the best team doesn't always pay off. Smarty Jones was the best horse. Jeff Gordon's got the best car. The Lakers had the best players. Marion Jones was the fastest runner. Michael Phelps was gonna win eight gold medals. The prettiest girl doesn't always get the crown . . ."

Mr. October finished with: "Your ball club is right back where it was last year. But they've got to get it done on the field."

The Red Sox got it done in the most impressive way possible a few hours later when they scored two runs off Rivera in the top of the ninth to win, 3–2, and close to within two and a half games of first. Suddenly, it really was looking like 1978 in reverse. The Sox were the hunters, and the Yankees were the hunted. Boston at that moment was 9–5 against the Yankees in 2004 and had a chance to overtake them in the American League East. Going back to the convention weekend, it also made for two straight blown saves for Rivera. The winning hit was a bloop to center, and Epstein compared it to Posada's hit in Game 7 of the 2003 ALCS. Meanwhile, the hit that tied the game was an opposite-field single to right by Cabrera.

There was some obvious symmetry in having Cabrera deliver the game-tying hit. Fireballing reliever Alan Embree, one of the guys who didn't get the call when He-Who-Must-Not-Be-Named failed to pull Pedro in October 2003, said, "That's what's going to break the Curse right there. The guy who gets the hit is the guy we got for Nomar. We know we can win this, and we know that there'll be twenty-five statues for the guys who finally win this in Boston."

It rained overnight in New York. A hard rain. The Northeast was feeling the final fury of Hurricane Ivan, which had submerged parts of Louisiana, and the forecast for Saturday was ominous. It's certainly possible that some Red Sox players figured there would be no game on Saturday, which might explain why some of them, especially Sox starter Lowe, did not look ready to play when the rain stopped and the game started on time early in the afternoon. With a chance to pull the Red Sox to within one game in the loss column of the Yankees, Lowe submitted a performance that fell somewhere between unprofessional and disgraceful. His head seemed to be somewhere in the swamps of Jersey as a parade of men in pinstripes rounded the bases.

Lowe walked Jeter, the first batter he faced. After A-Rod hit a sharp single, Lowe fanned Sheffield. Matsui cracked a single to left to load the bases, then Lowe walked Bernie Williams on a 3–2 pitch, scoring Jeter and effectively ending the game after it had barely started. The big righty unraveled. He threw a meatball to Posada, and the Yankee catcher smoked it to right-center for a two-run single. By this time, Lowe was gesturing in a manner reminiscent of Zero Mostel's Tevye in *Fiddler on the Roof.* Then came the mental errors. John Olerud hit a comebacker to Lowe, who turned and saw Williams stop and head back to third. With Williams clearly set to return safely, the play called for Lowe to turn and get Olerud at first. Instead, he tried to get Bernie at third. No chance. The bases were loaded. Ruben Sierra followed with a hard hopper toward the first base hole. Mientkiewicz made a diving stab and threw to second for the out. Unfortunately, Lowe over-ran first base in his attempt to cover, and Cabrera's throw for a double play sailed toward the railing for an error and an extra run.

Down 5–0, Lowe walked Jeter again to start the second. Then A-Rod hit a hard hopper that caromed off Lowe's right ankle for a hit and gave the Sox a chance to remove him from the game with a shred of dignity. Lowe's injury was revealed to be a contusion of the lower right leg. The x-rays were negative. Too bad there was no test to disclose what was going on in the big righty's head.

"I was like a rookie out there," he said after setting down a bottle of Corona. "I love to pitch against this team, but when you go out there with noncompetitive stuff, it makes for a long day. I struggled from pitch one. The biggest frustration is the noncompetitiveness of the game. It was like 8–0 before the fourth or fifth out . . . No excuses, guys. If I could find one, I'd throw something at you."

"I just thought he had a real tough outing," said Francona, again covering for his player. "I didn't think he wasn't focused. I wouldn't say that."

Focus had been a problem for Lowe throughout his career. Born and raised in Dearborn, Michigan, he was a fun guy who made everything look easy anytime he played sports. His Edsel Ford High School teammates called him a male bimbo (himbo?), and he seemed to enjoy his image as a human bobblehead toy. If Kato Kaelin had grown to be 6-6, he could have been Derek Lowe. The perfect pool boy. Think Nuke LaLoosh with less speed and more control. In Dearborn, Lowe was first-team All-State in basketball and all-league in baseball, basketball, soccer, and golf. He was easily the best all-around athlete on the Sox. Only Wakefield could match him on the links, but it was no contest in everything else.

Lowe scored forty-nine points in a single high school basketball game and was recruited as a shooter. His scholastic baseball career was less impressive. As a junior, he went 0–2, pitching rarely because of a hand infection from dunking a basketball on a rusty rim. As a senior he went 1–4, with an ERA over 6.00. He threw only 82 miles an hour. Most of the time he played shortstop. He was always able to hit .500 but reasoned, "Who doesn't hit .500 in high school?"

As if it was something we all could do on a whim.

The Mariners made him their eighth-round selection in 1991. "I could always throw strikes and had a decent delivery," he remembers.

"Seattle's philosophy at the time was to draft tall pitchers. I went to camp and they had forty of me, all 6-5, 180 pounds."

He kicked around the minors for six years before getting a cup of coffee with the Mariners in 1997. Then Dan Duquette made some history, sending inept reliever Heathcliff Slocumb to Seattle in exchange for Varitek and Lowe. Lowe still insists Duquette thought he was a left-handed pitcher when they first spoke after the trade, but whatever the Duke's designs were, no one can argue with the results. In Boston, Lowe lost his first seven starts, became an All-Star closer, then a starting pitcher who would pitch a no-hitter and win more games (fifty-two) over three seasons than any major leaguer other than Bartolo Colon. The key to his success was a sinker that induced hundreds of ground balls. Lowe didn't strike out many batters, but there weren't many hard-hit balls. What the Sox noticed, however, was his tendency to implode when one or two little things went wrong. And like Damon, Lowe had a reputation for being a late-night reveler.

Lowe and his wife, Trinka, have three children, including a teenage son from Trinka's first marriage. Lowe endured a serious bout with skin cancer on his nose before the 2003 season and devoted much time to sun safety awareness after his recovery. He was also the official Sox spokesman for the Massachusetts Teachers Association Literacy Day, a source of some amusement to folks around the club given Lowe's disinclination to read. When he was asked to name the last book he'd read, the affable Lowe offered, "Does *Barney* count?"

Throughout 2004, it was assumed that Lowe was pitching his last season with the Red Sox. His uneven performance during the regular season seemed to diminish his value on the market, but he was saving his best for October. Certainly he did not look like part of the Sox postseason plan when he choked in the Big Apple in mid-September. Rumors of his being out in New York in the wee hours before his start were rampant. It was discussed on the radio, on television, and in the Sox front office. No one bothered to ask Lowe about it until October, when he told the *Globe*'s Jackie MacMullan: "All of a sudden, there's all these reports about me going out the night before the Yankees game. I mean, it's on Fox Sports. Well, if I was out drinking that night, I'd like someone to tell me where they saw me. I don't go out the night before I pitch, but because someone floated it, it got out there . . . It was just unbelievable to me how the thing took on a life of its own. Next thing I know, I hear the reason I went out was because I thought my start was going to be rained out. What, so now I'm a weatherman? But I understand what the problem was. I pitched awful. Really awful. And I guess people had to come up with a reason why."

"We had some internal discussion about it," admitted Lucchino. "But no one thought that there was any basis to confront him about it. It's really something for the manager to deal with."

John Henry didn't want to comment on Lowe's nightlife, but he was clearly discouraged by the hurler's inconsistency. His number-crunching told him that despite all the wins, the tall sinkerballer had not pitched well in 2003 or 2004.

The Sox loss effectively put an end to the quixotic chase to dethrone the Yankees in the American League East. The Yankees routed the Red Sox again on Sunday, scoring eight earned runs off Martinez. Pedro was hooted off the mound by the Yankee fans and sounded as if he'd been lobotomized when he delivered his postgame remarks. Pedro's fire was gone, and all of New York was confident that the Yankees owned the Sox ace. It was hard for Red Sox fans not to get depressed. It seemed like a continuation of 2003 and the weird winter that led into this season of such high hopes. Once again, the Yankees were up and the Sox were down, and all the efforts of the front office and the emotions of the fans were for nothing.

On September 24, Epstein delivered some numbers to the ownership to explain what had happened since the trading deadline. The numbers showed that the Sox allowed seventy-four unearned runs before trading Nomar but only fourteen after. On balls hit in play, the Sox had shaved twenty points off opponents' batting averages. The bottom line of the thorough memo: "Team is 73–42 (.635) without Nomar at SS, 18–19 (.486) with Nomar at SS."

When the Bronx Bombers made their return visit to Boston the following Friday, New York led the Sox by four and a half games and the back page of the *Post* featured a photo of Martinez throwing, accompanied by the headline PEDRO THE PUSHOVER.

Little did they know.

This would be the game that took the Sox out of the AL East first-place chase, and it was against the Yankees with Pedro on the mound.

It was Boston baseball's Groundhog Day, conjuring the worst possible flashbacks for Red Sox fans. Pedro led, 4–3, at the end of seven and had thrown 101 pitches. The batters due up in the eighth included Matsui, Williams, and Posada, all of whom had hit safely in the eighth inning at Yankee Stadium when Grady Little took the Sox out of the World Series and got himself fired.

Timlin and Embree, the same two guys who didn't get the call in New York in 2003, started to get loose when the inning started. When Matsui homered on Pedro's second pitch of the eighth to tie the game, 4–4, Sox fans figured Francona would lift his tiring starter. So did Epstein, Lucchino, Henry, and James, the maniacal stat man.

Williams laced a ground rule double to right. Still no motion from the Sox dugout. Only after Sierra scored Williams with a single to right-center did Francona finally come out to get his erstwhile ace. Pedro turned his back on the manager while Embree ran in from the bullpen.

"In my opinion, he still had good stuff," Francona explained after the game. "If I run out there after two pitches, you understand what I'm saying, it would make it look like I wasn't making a very good decision before the inning."

In other words, rather than admit a mistake, Francona compounded it by being stubborn. One couldn't help but remember the words of the soon-to-be-fired Grady when he said, "I'll be another ghost, fully capable of haunting."

Epstein took the party line, going only so far as to say he did not always agree with his manager. Privately, he muttered, "We fucked up."

It was astounding. Bobby Valentine had claimed the "Would you have taken Pedro out?" question was part of the Red Sox managerial search. How could Francona have failed to do the one thing he was hired to do—take Pedro out after a hundred pitches when he had a lead against the Yankees?

A day later, Francona was still defending his move, saying, "I had no good reason to want to take him out of the game . . . I would not let people's emotions alter my judgment. If I'm going to let that affect what I do, they've got the wrong person managing the team."

That's what Sox fans were afraid of. They were afraid Francona was capable of a whopper blunder that would send the Sox home in October.

The bigger problem was Pedro. Boston's record in the games Martinez started against the Yankees dropped to 11–19. They were 6–17 in Pedro's last twenty-three starts against them. Worse, Pedro was a beaten man. The same slinger who once beat New York and said, "Wake up the damn Bambino and have me face him. Maybe I'll drill him in the ass," was now conceding to the Pinstripers.

"I can't find a way to beat them at this point," he admitted. "You just have to give them credit and say, 'You guys beat me, not my team.' I wish they would fucking disappear and never come back. I'd like to face any other team right now. To pitch a good game, make good pitches, and still can't beat them, it's frustrating . . . How many times am I going to have the lead and let it go? It was all me. I wanted to bury myself on the mound . . . What can I say? I just tip my hat and call the Yankees my daddy."

It was an extraordinary admission by the proud Pedro, and it set off alarms in Sox Nation. How could he lose his confidence on the cusp of the playoffs? And why? Was it a concession to diminishing skills? Was he greasing the skids for a job in New York in 2005 and beyond? Was he having trouble coping with no longer being the top dog on the staff? And the "daddy" remark? He might just as well have said, "I'm the Yankees' bitch."

The Sox came back to beat the Yankees in the final two home games of the regular season to finish 11–8 against the Bombers. The benches cleared one more time in the final game, but it was a tired dance featuring the likes of Lofton, Roberts, Brad Halsey, and Pedro Astacio.

On the morning of the final home game, Rodriguez and Jeter talked about the exhaustion of playing Boston nineteen times with perhaps seven more to go.

Still new to the Sox-Yanks rivalry but already sapped from the intensity, A-Rod said, "Watching from afar, I always thought there was nothing like East Coast baseball, and it's truly special. I love Boston. It's a great city. I love this ballpark. I love the ambiance. And I wish I was smart enough to go to college here, but unfortunately I'm not. When I walk around here, you get the joking and all, but overall there's more respect when you are a Yankee. The stuff from the fans in the ballpark doesn't count. It's just noise. It was worse for me here when I was with Texas because of the contract and because I was just one guy. Here, I'm just one of a great empire. With the fans and media, I've never seen so much passion. It's almost like a football atmosphere. Nineteen games feels like a hundred games. It's like the Super Bowl or something. But you can only build it up so many times."

Jeter nodded and added, "It's a lot of games, and I really don't like it. We pretty much know everything about them. We've seen every pitcher in every situation. We've seen Manny hit in the first, second, third, fourth, fifth, sixth, seventh, eighth, and ninth inning. So we've seen a lot."

Schilling won his twenty-first game and shut down the Torre-men in a near no-hitter in the finale, but he didn't want to hear anything about tension between himself and Pedro Martinez. He even took the trouble to call WEEI sports radio when a substitute host suggested that there was a rift between the two pitchers.

The Sox flew to Florida and clinched the American League wild card the next night with a 7–3 victory over the Devil Rays. Six games remained. Schilling said, "We spent four months being a team of— what was it?—frauds. But I think we all expected at some point to be in this position."

There was champagne in the locker room, and the cubicles were covered with cellophane, but the victory celebration was far more tame than the toga party of 2003 when WILD CARD CHAMPION T-shirts were donned and Millar and friends ran down Yawkey Way in full uniform and hopped on the bar of the Baseball Tavern, pouring drinks for the customers.

Epstein said, "We were trying to have a subdued celebration so we could demonstrate how we know this is only one step and we're really looking to the playoffs, and we are. But this team can't do anything subdued, so that's why the celebration got out of hand."

The next two nights in Florida raised new doubts about two of Boston's top three starters. Lowe was routed again, lasting only two and a third innings before taking a shower. No one said it until the end of the week, but the tall righty had officially pitched himself out of the postseason rotation. For the foreseeable future, that is.

But the decline and fall of Lowe paled compared to new concerns about Pedro. Martinez took the mound at Tropicana Field for his final regular-season turn and lost a fourth straight start for the first time in his Red Sox career. The lowly Rays pounded him for ten hits and five earned runs in five innings. He had planned on pitching only four innings, but he talked Francona into letting him go back out for the fifth. Fans watching back home were startled to see the blank look on Pedro's face as he sat in the dugout listening to pitching coach Dave Wallace.

There was a lot going on in Pedro's head. He was facing a new reality on the mound. Ordinary hitters were turning on his pitches. He was pitching with the knowledge that it might be his last regular-season start as a Red Sox. And he had already been told that Schilling was getting the ball in Game 1 of the playoffs.

Schilling blamed the media. "It's disappointing to see it be made into a lot different issue than it should be with regards to the other guys on the staff," he said. "We clinched, and the first thing everybody wanted to know was what Petey thought about who was pitching Game 1. A lot of you guys were trying to make a situation out of something that wasn't."

On the last day of September, while the Sox prepared for a four-game weekend set at Baltimore, the Yankees clinched the American League East on Bernie Williams's walk-off homer against the Twins at Yankee Stadium. It was the Yankees' hundredth win of the season, making them the fourth team in baseball history to post three consecutive hundred-win seasons. No one in Boston needed to be reminded that it marked the seventh straight time the Yankees finished first to Boston's second in the American League East. Steinbrenner issued a statement: "I am very proud of the team. They're real warriors. Now let's get ready for the playoffs."

"I think the road to the World Series is somehow going to go through New York or Boston," said A-Rod. "No matter what combination you put in there, I think somehow it's going to come to the Bronx and New England. So there's seven more that really count."

The mood in Boston was skeptical—for good reason. The Sox had beaten the Yankees eleven times in nineteen meetings, but finishing second for a seventh consecutive year was not what the fans had in mind when Schilling and Foulke were added during the historic and hysterical off-season. The post-Nomar surge was certainly encouraging, but Lowe was out of the rotation and Pedro lost his last four starts. Boston's dominant pitching seemed suddenly vulnerable. It was always something with the Sox. Teddy Ballgame had hurt his elbow before the '46 series, and Lonborg had to pitch on two days' rest in Game 7 in '67, and Rice broke a bone and missed the '75 World Series, and Schiraldi got those scared eyes in '86. What was it going to be this time? Pedro losing to his daddy? Manny or Damon dropping a fly ball after getting their hair in their eyes? A colossal brain fart for the ages by the overmatched Francona? Or a trip to the World Series and a seventh-game loss to the Cubs, with Nomar hitting a game-winning homer in the ninth at Fenway on Halloween?

Anything was possible. These were the Red Sox. They were going to the playoffs for the eleventh time since 1918. And the Curse of the Bambino was still very much alive.

11

Señor Octubre

OCTOBER IS THE BEST MONTH of the year in New England. There are select days when Greater Boston truly feels like San Diego with foliage. The air is dry, the colors splendid, and early in the month you can walk around with only a light jacket or sweater. Crunchy McIntosh apples have been harvested, the pumpkins are ripe, and the high school fields—dormant all summer—are alive with teens playing soccer, football, and field hockey. You can run for several miles without breaking into much of a sweat. Halloween caps the month with treats for all the little people.

October has also been the cruelest month for Red Sox Nation, featuring ghosts and all forms of torture. It's the month that gives "Boo!" a whole new meaning, but too often the boos have rained down on the Red Sox long before trick-or-treating starts. New England baseball fans fear the games of October the way Great Lakes seamen fear the gales of November. It's a month when bad things traditionally happen to the Sox.

In 2004, for the first time, the Red Sox had a ballplayer who owned the tenth month: David Ortiz—Señor Octubre—the new king of baseball's most important month.

Ortiz had already played in two postseasons, and he'd been remarkably mediocre. In two Division Series (one with the Twins, one with the Sox), Ortiz hit .147 with no homers and four RBI in thirty-four at-bats over nine games. In two American League Championship Series, he'd hit .286 with two homers and eight RBI in forty-two at-bats over twelve games. Overall, he was a .224 hitter in twenty-one career postseason games before 2004. Mr. October he wasn't.

But in October 2004 he was a different ballplayer in every way: relaxed, happy, healthy, and confident. He had a new contract, two seasons at Fenway under the tutelage of hitting coach Ron Jackson, and the security of knowing he was going to be in the lineup every day. When the tenth month rolled around, David Ortiz was ready to become the best and most clutch postseason hitter in the history of the Boston Red Sox.

Ortiz's road to the big leagues was not unlike that of many other Dominicans. Young David started out by playing shortstop. But he was bigger than the other kids, and he threw with his left hand. He was not going to be another Tony Fernandez. He was going to be a 6-4, 230-pound, left-handed slugger.

The oldest of four children of Angela Rosa Arias and Americo Enrique "Leo" Ortiz, he starred in baseball and basketball at Estudia Espallat High School. For a time, he wanted to be Michael Jordan, but baseball was David's game, and Seattle Mariner scout Ramon De Los Santos signed him when he finished high school, just after he turned seventeen. Under the name of David Ortiz Arias, he spent four years in the Mariners' minor league system before being traded to the Twins for Dave Hollins in September 1996. He then dropped "Arias" from the end of his name. When Twins manager Tom Kelly found out that David Arias was now David Ortiz, he quipped, "He must have gotten married." Ortiz made his debut with the Twins at the end of 1997 and a year later played half the season with them, hitting .277 with nine homers and forty-six RBI. But he kept going back to the minors, then hurt his wrist and needed surgery in 2001. A knee injury slowed him down in 2002, his final year with the Twins. Ever a home run threat, he had a hole in his swing (up and in). The Twins chided him for overswinging. If a pitcher could spot the ball, Ortiz was a player you could get out. Or he'd get himself out. When the Twins came to Fenway in the summer of 2002, Pedro struck Ortiz out three times in one game, then took him home for dinner. Minnesota did not tender him a contract after the 2002 season. He was not yet twenty-seven years old.

George Steinbrenner still tries to claim he wanted Cashman to sign Ortiz in the winter of 2002–2003, but any team could have had him for short money, and no one stopped the presses when Theo Epstein signed him to a one-year, $1.25 million deal just a few weeks before the start of spring training. Epstein made the signing on the recommendation of Sox scout Dave Jauss, who'd been watching Ortiz tear up the winter league in the Dominican Republic (where the nameplate over his locker read DAVID ORTIZ ARIAS). Jauss had played baseball at Amherst with Dan Duquette and was one of the few holdovers from the Duke's regime.

Epstein remembers, "We had a list, and Ortiz was at the top of the list. Like a lot of young hitters, he was evolving. We'd liked him for a long time, going back to when I was in San Diego. His performance in triple-A was outstanding for his age. There was almost no urgency because there was a surplus that winter of left-handed hitting, first base–DH types. You could kind of take your pick."

There was support for Ortiz in the Sox clubhouse.

"We got calls from Pedro and Manny saying that we should sign David," said Lucchino. "That was unusual. I don't remember ever getting a call from a player on behalf of another player. It was pretty powerful stuff."

"I'm happy to be playing here," Ortiz said the day the Sox signed him. "I hope we can get something going and beat the Yankees."

He was lined up to battle for the Red Sox first base job along with Shea Hillenbrand and Jeremy Giambi, another free agent signee. In Boston, Ortiz was viewed as a younger and cheaper version of Brian Daubach. His health and personal life were in good shape when he went to Fort Myers for the start of the season. His wrist and knee injuries were healed, and more than a year had passed since his mother, only forty-seven, was killed in a traffic accident on New Year's Day, 2002. David had been having a house built for her in Santo Domingo at the time. His dad, who owns a gas station and two auto parts stores, moved into the new home in 2002.

Given all that happened subsequently, it's strange to look at Red Sox box scores in the early part of the 2003 season. Ortiz appeared in only thirty-one of the first fifty-four games and had only two homers at the end of May. His teammates were calling him Juan Pierre—Pierre was the flyswatter with the Florida Marlins who already had three homers. In Boston, Ortiz was on the bench beside backup catcher

Doug Mirabelli. His agent was calling Epstein to complain. One day the agent spoke with Epstein in the Sox players' parking lot. Epstein told them to remain patient. Then he traded Hillenbrand to Arizona, and Ortiz moved into the lineup, hitting .293 with a whopping twenty-nine homers and eighty-two RBI over the final ninety-seven games. He finished fifth in voting for the 2003 American League Most Valuable Player Award.

"Sometimes trades have unintended consequences," Lucchino said with a chuckle.

In 2004 Ortiz demonstrated what he could do when he played every day. He hit .301 with 47 doubles, 41 homers, 139 RBI, and a .603 slugging percentage—all career highs. He emerged as "the Big Papi" (pronounced "Poppi" by Pedro and friends), the lovable bear in the middle of the Sox lineup. His wife, Tiffany, whom he met while playing in the minors in Appleton, Wisconsin, gave birth to his first son, their third child, in midseason. Big Papi was a favorite in and out of the clubhouse. He went to the Jimmy Fund Clinic to cheer up sick kids, and he rolled baseballs across the dugout roof, to the delight of young fans. Kids loved his pajama look, with uniform pants that extended to the tops of his shoes. He was huge and happy, the big man with the infectious smile. And it turned out that his walk-off game winner on Easter Sunday was a harbinger. By October, people were walking around wearing T-shirts that read THE CURSE OF THE BIG PAPI.

As always, there was a playoff seeding scramble in the final days of the regular season, and the Sox sat around the visitor's clubhouse in Baltimore, wondering which team would be their first-round opponent. Much to their surprise, the Anaheim Angels made a late season run, winning the American League West by eliminating Oakland on the next to last day of the season. Still, the playoff seeding was unclear since the Angels and Twins were locked in a battle for the right to host the first round.

With less than twenty-four hours remaining in the regular season, Red Sox traveling secretary Jack McCormick still had three hotels reserved in three cities for the first round. When the Angels beat the A's late Saturday, McCormick canceled the rooms at the San Francisco Westin St. Francis. But he was still holding space in Minneapolis and

Anaheim when the Sox arrived at Camden Yards on Sunday, October 3, for the regular-season finale. The Sox lost the final game, 3–2, finishing with ninety-eight wins, the most by any Boston team since the 1978 Don Zimmer Red Sox won ninety-nine. After allowing seventy-four unearned runs in the first 102 games, they allowed only eighteen in the final sixty games.

After the final game, the Sox watched the clubhouse TV and saw the Twins lose to Cleveland in the Metrodome, which meant that the Sons of Terry Francona would be winging their way to California.

"We wanted to play Oakland," admitted Epstein. "I think they're a great team . . . To win ninety games five years in a row with that payroll is incredible, but I just thought that their pitching was starting to crumble down the stretch, and I thought we matched up really well with them. Minnesota and Anaheim was pretty much a dead heat, with a slight preference to avoiding Minnesota because of Johan Santana." Southpaw Santana was a twenty-game winner who won his last thirteen in a row and would go on to win the Cy Young Award unanimously.

"The Angels were a team that exposed our weakness in the first half of the season," continued Theo. "We didn't make the Nomar trade because we knew we'd play Anaheim, but that was because they were the example we kept using when we talked about trading him. Who cares how many component runs you're going to score and allow when you have to go up against a team like Anaheim, that's going to make life crazy on you and force you to make mistakes? Before the trade, we were just not really equipped to play them. We didn't match up well with them. They were a good example to demonstrate what was wrong with our team. They put so much pressure on you—if you're capable of making defensive mistakes, you will. They ensure that they'll find your weakest link defensively."

The Sox settled into the Hyatt Hotel in Anaheim late Sunday (it took some time because some members of the Sox were originally assigned rooms with bunk beds) and went through a light workout on Monday afternoon. Schilling met with the national media and said, "These guys were five outs away from the World Series last year, so I think anything short of being in the World Series this year will mean they have fallen short of where we should go. I understand that if I don't go out and do the things I have done in the past in October that the season will be a wash in a lot of people's minds as far as my contributions here. I understand that."

Monday night, almost half the Red Sox players went to dinner at the Outback Steakhouse, a two-minute walk from the hotel. In many ways it was like going back to Fort Myers, where the Outback had witnessed so many meals in the spring. Same layout, same cuts of beef. Only this time there was Monday Night Football on the tube instead of the NCAA basketball tournament, and the next day's game was going to be slightly more significant.

At the ballpark before Game 1, Pedro declined a request to participate in a standard press conference for the Game 2 starters. When approached by Sox PR man Glenn Geffner, Pedro smiled, did the Manny double-point, and said, "Tomorrow's starting pitcher is not going to do the press conference!" He also missed the pregame introductions, fueling speculation that he was pouting about not being named to start the first game.

In Pedro's place, the Sox sent Damon to the interview room, and Hollywood Johnny engaged in a memorable session in which he said, "You know, we are not the Cowboys anymore, we are just the idiots this year . . . We feel like we can win every game, we feel like we have to have fun, and I think that's why this team is liked by so many people out there. You know, the kids watching us out there, you know, we got the long hair, we got the cornrows, we got guys just acting like idiots. And I think the fans out there like it."

It was pure Damon. He was liable to say anything. On national television he'd said that Jack Daniel's helped him recover from tough losses. He'd admitted that He-Who-Must-Not-Be-Named had warned him about staying out too late too often. He'd sung background vocals for the Dropkick Murphys and performed in a scene with Drew Barrymore for the Farrelly brothers flick. He was a baseball player who wanted to be a rock star. He was also one of the most talented, genuine, and kind members of the Boston ball club, and before the first game of the postseason he'd stumbled into a new nickname for his teammates: Johnny and the Idiots. How very punk.

When asked about Damon's idiotic manifesto, Francona said, "As a group, they are borderline nuts, but when they get out on the field,

I think they try to play the game right, and I don't see that changing today at all. I don't want them to show up and be different. I want them to be themselves because I think we are a good team like that."

Schilling, the anti-idiot, got the ball for the first game and delivered. He was not overpowering, but his teammates staked him to an 8–0 lead with a seven-run fourth inning as all the life was sucked out of Angel Stadium. ThunderStix and a Rally Monkey aren't much good when you're trailing Curt Schilling by seven runs in the fourth inning of a big game. The Red Sox won, 9–3, thanks to some jittery play by Angel infielder Chone Figgins. Millar and Manny both hit homers. Schilling was limping a little bit in his final inning, and there was talk that he'd reinjured his right ankle, which bothered him in the spring, but not much was made of it after the first game. He had precautionary x-rays taken at the ballpark, and Francona said, "Everything came back negative."

Things changed in the next twenty-four hours as Schilling went to the hospital for a second set of x-rays. Francona admitted, "He's got a problem in a slightly different area of his ankle. It's higher. It's a tendon problem . . . I think our trainers and medical staff are really confident that he can make his next start, whenever that is, without any problems."

Back in Boston, there was plenty of chest-thumping over the rout, but those nattering nabobs of negativity wondered if maybe the larger forces were at work again. First Lowe tanked in September and pitched himself out of the rotation. Then Pedro lost four straight games for the first time since his rookie year. Now Schilling was shaky. Was the big Bambino fellow giggling at the Sox again? Was he a little fed up with the T-shirts and banners claiming his Curse was dead?

Martinez put a stop to any irrational fears with a strong outing in Game 2, an 8–3 Red Sox victory that was close until the Sox blew it open with four runs in the ninth.

Only Pedro seemed to know what to expect, and he was keeping his thoughts to himself. He'd finished the season with four straight losses. He'd made the incredible "daddy" remark. He'd dissed the media. He was facing the possibility that this would be his final appearance in a Red Sox uniform, and there was concern that he was tired and suddenly mortal.

As summer turned to fall, the Red Sox became the laughing gashouse gang, erasing almost all of a 10½-game deficit to the Yankees and smiling all the way. Manny Ramirez (*above*) and David Ortiz and Terry ("Tito") Francona (*below*).

The low point. Down two games to the Yankees, who seemed destined to repeat history, the Red Sox lost Game 3 of the ALCS in desultory fashion, a hideous 19–8. Only a few fans remained that night to see the writing on the wall. The Sox were going to be swept in the playoffs. But then Señor Octubre (*above*) came to the rescue.

Opposite, top: In the key play of the entire season, pinch runner Dave Roberts stole second in the bottom of the ninth of Game 4 against the Yankees. *Opposite, bottom:* Meanwhile, frustration built in the Yankee dugout as the Red Sox roared back. *Above:* With blood seeping into his white sock, Curt Schilling beat the Yankees in Game 6 to force Game 7 in the Bronx.

Left: Cardinal Jeff Suppan's base-running blunder in Game 3 effectively clinched the World Series for Boston. *Below:* The curse was lifted after eighty-six years. *Opposite, top:* Jason Varitek and Gabe Kapler played poker while the Holy Grail was strapped into a middle seat on the flight home from St. Louis. *Opposite, bottom:* World champion Pedro Martinez returned with his teammates to Fenway by dawn's early light.

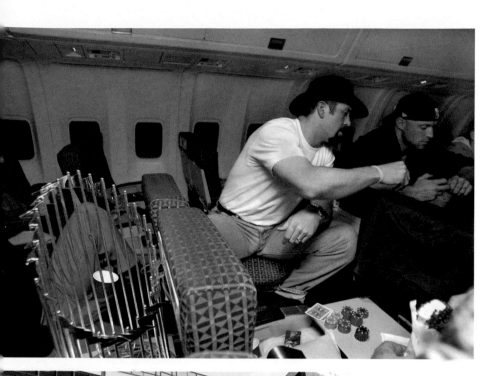

Red Sox Nation finally got their parade, by both land and sea. *Above:* Big Papi wore his life jacket and saluted fans. *Below:* Shortstop Orlando Cabrera was never spooked by ghosts.

Certainly no one in the Sox organization was going to say anything negative about the diva righty, although the candid Arroyo told the *Globe*'s Jackie MacMullan, "I think a few of the guys wish he'd come on time. They feel like he'd be more professional if he did . . . Sometimes he's not in the dugout until the seventh inning."

Pedro was there in the first inning of Game 2, and he came through with a solid seven innings, holding the Angels to three runs on six hits and two walks while throwing 116 pitches. When he fanned Figgins, to end the seventh, he pointed to the heavens and walked to the dugout, where he was hugged by his teammates, including Schilling. It was a scene not unlike the end of the seventh in Yankee Stadium the year before, but this time Pedro wasn't coming back out to pitch the eighth.

It was 2:30 A.M. back in Boston when Martinez made it to the interview room in Anaheim after the win, and he had a lot to say:

"You know, I was number one today. That's all that matters to me. I don't believe in what experts from out here have to say . . . I actually shut my mouth. I ate my ego . . . and I swallowed it, because to me, anytime they give me the ball, I am special. I am the number one. It doesn't matter how many days I have to wait. And to me it was an honor to see Curt Schilling win. He pitched better than me: I am admitting it. I respect that as well, so enough with the trash talking. We get along really well. I have never been mad because he pitches any game . . . We get along great. Please don't try to break that up, making up trash talking—or making up stuff that's not true."

Leading the Angels, 2–0, the Sox returned home for the first time in eleven days and enjoyed an off-day before trying to close it out in a game that started just after 4 P.M. on Friday afternoon.

As they would do so many times in the postseason, the Sox broke it open early, scoring a combined five runs in the third and fourth innings (both rallies buoyed by Ortiz doubles) and taking a 6–1 lead into the seventh. For most teams it would have been a remarkable output, but the Red Sox and their fans were accustomed to heavy thunder from the Sox bats. The Sox in 2004 led the majors in runs, on-base percentage, and slugging percentage. They were the first team to accomplish the feat in back-to-back seasons since the 1953–1954 Yankees. The Sox led the majors in pitches per plate appearance, an important stat to Theo. They also led the majors in doubles, extra-base hits, and total bases. This team could mash, and it wasn't just Big Papi and Manny. It was a 1–9 operation. The Red Sox bat rack housed weapons of mass destruction.

The big lead wasn't quite enough in the late innings of Game 3. Francona lifted Arroyo after a leadoff walk in the seventh. Mike Myers came on and walked the only batter he faced, which brought Francona back out to summon Mike Timlin. Before you could say "Aaron Boone," Fenway was funeral home quiet, and the indomitable Vlad Guerrero was circling the bases after crashing a game-tying grand slam into the Red Sox bullpen.

Yikes. Was it going to be another classic fall? Would Francona get roasted for doing the exact opposite of what Grady had done one year earlier? Would Game 3 of the Division Series be enshrined in the Sox Hall of Shame?

No, no, and no. Ortiz made it all go away.

Arroyo, Myers, Timlin, Embree, and Foulke were spent when Lowe shook off the cobwebs and came out of the bullpen to shut down the Angels in the top of the tenth. Fans chanted, "D-Lowe." It was a nice, redemptive moment and put Lowe in position to win the game if the Sox could score in the bottom of the inning.

Angel wunderkind Frankie Rodriguez was into his third inning of relief when Damon came to lead off the tenth, and it was clear that right-handed hitters weren't going to have much of a shot against the 2002 World Series hero. Damon led with a single but was erased when Figgins threw him out on Mark Bellhorn's bad bunt. Reese, running for Bellhorn, watched helplessly as Manny struck out. Rodriguez was at thirty-eight pitches, and Angel manager Mike Scioscia came out to replace him with lefty starter Jarrod Washburn.

As Washburn wound up to pitch to Ortiz, Francona turned to Millar in the dugout and said, "Can he hit one out here?"

As the words left the manager's mouth, Ortiz opened up on a high slider and drove it high and far to left-center, into the Green Monster seats.

Walk-off. It's a relatively new term, made popular by Dennis Eckersley after he was victimized by Kirk Gibson's pinch-hit, game-winning homer in the 1988 World Series. Bobby Thomson and Bill Mazeroski hit the two most famous walk-off homers in baseball history, but that was before they were so named. Carlton Fisk's 1975 moonball for the ages off the left field foul pole wasn't called a walk-off homer until years later, after Gibson beat Eckersley. Today "walk-off" shots are catalogued like hits, runs, and errors. The 2004 postseason was a walk-off wonderland for Ortiz, starting at 8:21 P.M. on October 8 at Fenway.

Ortiz was still wearing his late afternoon, glare-reducing eye black when he struck the historic blow, vaulting the Sox into the American League Championship Series. He raised his right hand and signaled "number one" as he circled the bases, then swept the helmet off his head before stomping on home plate in the middle of a hooting huddle of teammates. It was one of the most electrifying moments in the history of a ballpark that's almost older than household electricity— and it was only the beginning in 2004.

Champagne again, this time Great Western. Ortiz wore swimmer's goggles in the clubhouse. Embree poured a beer over the head of John Henry. ("He did it slowly, while we were talking," said Henry. "I take that as a sign of respect.") While the beer and the bubbly flowed in the ancient room, the Sox players went back out to celebrate with Fenway fans who'd lingered long after hearing the Standells' "Dirty Water" and the Dropkick Murphys' "Tessie." The Red Sox were going to lift the Curse of the Bambino, but this would be the only champagne celebration at Fenway in October of 2004.

Across the way, Darin Erstad, a gracious Angel with a championship ring in his drawer at home, said, "These boys are winning the World Series, by the way. That's the deepest team I've ever seen. They have every piece of the puzzle. I don't see anybody beating them."

Francona again downplayed Schilling's ankle injury: "He's getting better. I don't think it's anything that can't be managed. In fact, I know it isn't."

A few hours after the Sox victory, the Yankees beat the Twins, 8–4, to take a 2–1 lead in their Division Series. The rematch that Baseball America hoped for was only one game away.

Fenway Park was quiet the next day except for the Sox expressing concerns about Schilling for the first time. Team medical director Bill Morgan said Schilling was battling an inflammation of tendons in his ankle. All agreed it was not a big deal. Hardly worth mentioning.

Henry made the most of the off-day, frolicking on the field with a couple of employees from his company in Florida. In the empty stands, he took a few moments to comment on all that had happened thus far:

"Can you imagine what it would have been like here if that [Garciaparra] trade had gone the other way? These guys play the game the way it should be played. They have as much fun probably as any team that ever played baseball. They love each other. It's a great team. We're healthy now. We weren't healthy most of the season, but now we were a lot healthier than the Angels were. I thought it was just a matter of time before this team put it together. I said that during some of the darker hours of the season. I felt we were going to be fine. I don't feel that there are any idiots in that clubhouse. They are just guys having fun. I prefer it [idiots] to Cowboy Up, but that's not my term. I would never use that term. These are guys that love the game. It's a big love-in now."

Looking ahead, he turned to me and said, "Can you imagine, Dan, Halloween? It's gonna be a full moon. And you know what, if we close it out before that time, we have to come here anyway. You and I will talk about 'What do we do now?'"

He would not say much about Boston's next opponent. The Yankees were scheduled to start against the Twins in a few hours, and there were plenty of competitive reasons for Boston folk to want Minnesota in the next round. The Sox were going to have three full days to rest their pitching staff. The Twins were pitching Santana on three days' rest in Game 4. If New York and Minnesota went to a fifth game on Sunday, whichever team won would be at a decided disadvantage playing against rested Boston the following Tuesday. Henry referred to the Metrodome as a "loud gymnasium" but would not pick a favorite. He kept saying he just wanted to play a National League team.

Diplomacy is important at times like this, but Red Sox fans could afford to differ. Certainly there were practical souls who could see the wisdom of rooting for the Twins. It would be less stressful: the Sox might escape without facing Santana more than once, and there would be nothing to offend genteel fans. Nobody was going to chant "Twins Suck!"

But all red-blooded Red Sox fans wanted the Yankees. The front page of the *Herald* called for the matchup before the Sox and Angels were finished playing, and I wrote "Bring on the Yankees" after the Sox went ahead of the Angels, 2–0. It was premature and insulting to the Anaheim gang, but sometimes you've got to play to the crowd, and the crowd wanted the Yankees. We all knew that. The *Herald* was slightly less subtle, leading its front page with GO YANKS! the day the Sox came home from Anaheim, still readying to play a third game against the Angels. The subhead in the *Herald* was "We want to kick your butts on our way to the Series!" It was bold stuff, and when the New York papers got hold of it, they bombarded Boston with stories themed "Be careful what you wish for."

It didn't matter. All reason was out the window on this issue. Going to the World Series, winning it all, just wouldn't be the same unless the Sox did it by romping through Yankee Stadium, scene of the heartache in 2003. The sweetest way to reverse the Curse would include a Big Bite out of the Big Apple. Obviously, Boston sports talk radio ran hard with the topic. It must have been difficult to be an Angel, waiting to play a third game against the Red Sox yet hearing about the Yankees every hour of the day.

The day after the Sox clinched, a few hours after John Henry sauntered around an empty Fenway Park, the Yankees and Twins started their fourth game, and New York trailed, 5–1, in the eighth inning at Minnesota. It seemed certain that they were going to need a fifth game, which would be another advantage for Boston. But five outs from defeat—sound familiar?—New York rallied for four runs to tie the game in the eighth. A three-run homer by thirty-nine-year-old Ruben Sierra capped the comeback before the Yankees won it on a wild pitch in the eleventh. No surprise for pinstripe fans. Joe Torre's team enjoyed sixty-one come-from-behind victories in 2004, a major league record.

It was official. Red Sox–Yankees. Game on.

"Is it special?" asked Sheffield. "I guess I'm going to find out pretty soon. It took me sixteen years to get to this point. I couldn't ask for anything more."

Torre, the most experienced postseason veteran of all, simply said, "It's going to be nuts."

12

When the Yankees Really Did Suck

O N SUNDAY, OCTOBER 10, the Red Sox gathered in their club-house at Fenway Park, enjoying a second consecutive off-day. Still bothered by his balky right ankle, Schilling threw in the bullpen under the watchful eyes of Francona, Epstein, trainer Jim Rowe, physical therapist Chris Correnti, and team doctor Bill Morgan. All parties said the session was successful.

When it came to the Yankees, the players and front office said the predictable things.

"No one is expecting us to win because of history, but we feel like we've had the best team since day one," said Damon.

Epstein divulged what they had all been thinking: "Now that it's here, we can admit that if we're able to win a World Series and go through New York along the way, it will mean that much more."

Meanwhile, Henry paid the standard lip service, citing the rivalry and how evenly matched the Sox and Yankees had been over the last two years, but that's not what he was thinking. He'd gotten into this baseball business for the fun of it, but it wasn't any fun. Not at all.

"It was the first time in my life that sporting events were torturous for me," he said a month later, when it was all over. "I didn't really want to go to Game 1 in New York. I had been looking forward to playing the Twins. I really had had enough of the Yankee–Red Sox nonsense. I wasn't looking forward to going to Yankee Stadium again."

Late in the afternoon, the Sox boarded buses at the corner of Van Ness Street and Yawkey Way to get to Logan Airport, took a chartered flight to La Guardia, then rode luxury coaches to the Westin Hotel in Times Square.

Monday's *New York Times* featured a column by Murray Chass, headlined LIKE AUTUMN'S LEAVES, THE RED SOX WILL FALL. Workout day at Yankee Stadium drew hundreds of media members, and the nonstop din in the Sox clubhouse did nothing to discourage the notion that Francona was in charge of a fraternity—MLB's Delta House. The manager made the reference himself when he talked about the motivational films his players watched. "Usually you see guys watching *Hoosiers* or something like that," said Francona. "But the other day I walked in on our guys, and up on the screen I saw John Belushi breaking a guitar over a guy's head in one of the *Animal House* scenes. That's just us."

Kapler, the muscular, thoughtful, part-time outfielder who had been part of the Sox Cowboy Up clubhouse in 2003, sat on a chair in front of his locker before the workout and said: "It's been a long and winding road, but one that was always headed in this direction. We were always in a position where we could make a run. I never felt like there was a lack of confidence or resolve. We're a goofy group, but it's a good goofy. I can't express enough how important our ability to have fun and enjoy each other's company and spend time together off the field is. We hang out and laugh and joke and play. The silly, stupid stuff is important to us because we maintain a level of sanity through it. You can be in a tough spot if you don't enjoy the passion that the city of Boston brings to baseball. I think win or lose, good or bad, the attention is always good. When people stop paying attention, you know you're up shit's creek. So I think that the people here spend a lot of time analyzing what goes on with our team. Obviously. But I appreciate it. There are some who don't, but the bottom line is, we found a way to distract ourselves when we needed to distract ourselves. It works when everybody in the clubhouse is human and real. So if Johnny calls us idiots, there's no one guy who takes offense at it. We know that it's all in jest. This feels a little different this year. I can't put my finger on it yet, but it feels a little different."

Some of his zany teammates were making barnyard sounds in other parts of the room while Kapler spoke softly. There were more than a hundred media members prowling about, looking for stories, and the Sox were feeding the hungry press. What Kapler didn't say, what none would say, was: "It would have been tough for this to happen with Nomar sitting around, sulking and angry all the time."

Schilling wore his WHY NOT US? T-shirt to a formal press conference in the underbelly of Yankee Stadium. Three years earlier, as part of the Arizona Diamondback team that dethroned the Yankees in the 2001 World Series, he'd delighted the New York press by dismissing "aura" and "mystique"—allegedly key ingredients in the Yanks' success in their home park—as nothing more than names of exotic dancers. He was no less bold this time around.

"I want to be a part of a team that does something that has not been done in almost a century," he said. "I'm not sure I can think of any scenario more enjoyable than making fifty-five thousand people from New York shut up."

At that moment, Schilling's career postseason record was 6–1 with a 1.74 ERA in twelve starts—an October line worthy of Whitey Ford, Sandy Koufax, or Bob Gibson.

Yankee GM Brian Cashman held his own press conference and said, "I think Boston likes to pretend they are not in the same market as the Yankees, but I think they really are. They are a mirror image of us in terms of finance and aggressiveness and desire to win. I think with this new ownership group they have assembled up there, we are a lot more similar than the 'Evil Empire' comment would lead you to believe."

On the long-awaited morning of Game 1, the vaunted *New York Times* (which had $75 million invested in the Red Sox partnership) made the Sox quest a page one story. But the *Times* couldn't top the *Daily News,* which splashed a hilarious cartoon on its back page: a papa-like Babe Ruth cartoon figure gathered his Red Sox children next to the headline COME TO DADDY!—PEDRO'S BOSOX POP IN FOR ANNUAL SPANKING.

Borrowing from the best elements and emotions of Achilles-Hector, Kennedy-Nixon, Russell-Chamberlain, Leno-Letterman, and Red States–Blue States, the Red Sox–Yankee rivalry had officially superseded all traditional boundaries. After a winter of cutthroat backroom moves by both front offices, 162 regular-season games, and 101 years of history, they braced to battle again. The first game of the 2004

ALCS was the forty-sixth meeting between the two teams in seventeen months.

To the surprise of Red Sox Nation, which had been assured that Schilling's ankle problem was no big deal, the big righty had nothing in Game 1 and was routed for six runs in three innings of a 10–7 loss. It was clear from the outset that he couldn't push off or land properly on his right leg.

"I was shocked," said Epstein. "He looked like a horse with a broken leg. It was hard to watch."

It was Schilling's shortest outing of the season, his quickest hook in seven years. Curtis "the Mechanic" Leskanic, a few days shy of retirement, was on the mound to start the fourth inning, and the Yankees led, 8–0, in the top of the seventh. Yankee stopper Mike Mussina retired the first nineteen Red Sox batters (Damon went 0–4, all strikeouts) before the Sox finally rallied.

The Sox cut the lead to 8–7 in the eighth, which prompted yet another tale of Yankee glory. New York relief ace Mariano Rivera, who only hours earlier had been in Panama, at the funeral of two relatives, came on to slam the door as he had done so many times in previous years. Rivera was not yet at the ballpark when the game began, and his trip to the bullpen in the middle innings was an emotional lift for his team and the sellout crowd in attendance. Certainly none of the Yankee fans had been "shut up" by Schilling, and when the game was over, Schilling said he would not pitch again unless his ankle felt better.

By any measure, it was a deflating night for Red Sox Nation. Lucchino and Company were upset with the Sox medical team. Why had Schilling been allowed to take the mound when he couldn't compete? He was pitching with a torn tendon sheath in his ankle. The result was a painful flapping of the tendon over his anklebone every time he threw a pitch. A shot of Marcaine failed to help. In hindsight, it was clear that Schilling could not perform unless the tendon could be stabilized. Why had he been asked to try?

Lucchino admitted, "It's fair to say that we were a bit upset that we didn't have a better handle on it, that we didn't have a little more sense of the potential severity at an earlier stage. We knew that there was an issue going into New York. In my experience, it's always worse than what we are told by team doctors and trainers. They tend to put an optimistic projection on things. But we didn't get much of a preliminary warning about how bad this was. We didn't know about the tear until just before the Yankee game. We knew there was a clicking issue. I remember him telling us that there was some modest concern, but the issue was really joined after his performance and people were saying, 'What the hell was that? How did that happen?'"

Walking around Manhattan the next day, a discouraged John Henry answered his cell phone. It was Werner.

"He started talking about Curt's injury," recalls Henry. "He said, 'Maybe we are cursed,' and I said, 'Don't you start with that!'"

Lucchino is one of the more superstitious people on the planet. He's maniacally sensitive about the number 13 and will not sit in seat 13, row 13, section 13, or take a room on the thirteenth floor of any hotel. His mentor, the great Edward Bennett Williams, died on a Friday the thirteenth in 1988, and Lucchino has had to face his fears of working with an owner, John Henry, who was born on September 13. Wednesday, October 13, 2004, was not a good day for Lucchino or anyone else associated with the Red Sox. On that day, the Sox revealed that Schilling needed surgery and could not make his next scheduled start. The bad news was compounded when Pedro Martinez took the mound in Yankee Stadium while fifty-five thousand chanted, "Who's your daddy?" and once again lost. New York's 3–1 victory was sealed when John Olerud cranked a two-run homer just as Pedro was hitting the Bill James pitch-count limit in the sixth. Olerud hit pitch 106. This time it was unheralded Jon Lieber smothering the Sox bats, allowing just one run on three hits in seven innings. The indomitable Rivera got the save again.

Going home, down 0–2 after Schilling and Pedro both lost, was not exactly what the Nation had in mind for the final scene of the season. Gone was so much of the hope for revenge against the Yankees.

It was suggested (by me) that instead of traditional red, white, and blue bunting, the Sox hang black crepe on the ancient Fenway facade for Game 3. George Vecsey of the *Times* wrote: "What once looked like a classic series between these old rivals now looks like a mismatch because of Curt Schilling's ankle injury."

It was a double shot of Absolute Trouble.

Martinez's woes typified the Sox plight. He hadn't pitched badly, but for the twentieth time in his thirty-one career starts against the Yankees, the Sox did not win. And the "daddy" stuff was out of control. Major League Baseball had sanctioned T-shirts that featured HEY RED SOX . . . WHO'S YOUR DADDY? beside a Yankee logo and red pacifier with a "B" on it. When the Sox complained, it was pulled from the shelves, but not in time to prevent hundreds of the shirts and assorted knockoffs from making it into Yankee Stadium for Game 2. Afterward, Martinez participated in yet another weird press conference, saying, "You know what, it actually made me feel really, really good . . . I actually realized that I was somebody important, because I caught the attention of sixty thousand people, plus the whole world watching a guy that if you reverse time back fifteen years ago, I was sitting under a mango tree without fifty cents to pay for a bus." He added, "I can't do anything else if we don't score runs."

Another Sox pitcher, the overlooked Lowe, had spoken in frustration before Game 2, saying, "My mindset right now? To pitch one inning in this series at some point, as crazy as that sounds . . . I'd love to get an opportunity to contribute in a game, but . . . What kills me about the whole thing is not being able to contribute. The postseason sucks in a way if you are not contributing."

Boston batters were the ones not contributing in the first two games. Damon was an idiotic 0–8 with five strikeouts. In the first six innings of the first two games, the Sox amassed one hit.

I flew from New York to Boston after Game 2. Imagine my surprise when I heard the gate agent announce: "Last call for Flight 1918 to Boston."

Yeesh. Of all the flights in all the terminals in all the world, I have to get on Flight 1918 in the middle of yet another Red Sox crushing defeat by the Yankees? Initially, my crack reporter instincts took over and I realized, "Hmmm. Imagine if this plane goes down. Dan Shaughnessy, the author of *The Curse of the Bambino*, perishes on Delta Flight 1918 in the middle of the ALCS between the Yankees and Red Sox." Just for the sake of the story, it almost would have been worth it. *Almost.*

Boston had an off-day on Thursday, and Ortiz had a moment when he saw the KEEP THE FAITH billboard as he drove to Fenway. The boards were featured around town all season, including the infamous Nomar edition. Seeing the image of Manny, his smiling, double-pointing, Dominican countryman, Ortiz stopped and thought about what was happening to a once great season. He took the message into the clubhouse. But it was a few days before the fellows responded.

Game 3 was rained out on Friday, October 15, a gift from the hardball god and an indication that things might go Boston's way just once. Instead of playing on Friday, Saturday, and Sunday, they were going to play on Saturday, Sunday, and Monday, which meant the Game 5 starter would have an extra day of rest. Martinez could pitch the fifth game on his normal four days of rest. And then there was Schilling, who threw in the bullpen while it rained before Game 3 was officially postponed. After the side session, the Sox left open a window that Schilling's season might not be over. They were thinking he might be able to pitch Game 6 in New York on Tuesday if the Sox could somehow extend the series that far. There was much talk about a specially made, high-top shoe, which might be able to stabilize the flapping tendon. The Sox had yet to turn to the final option—surgical experimentation.

Another small but telling measure of the fierce competition between the respective front offices presented itself when the scribes went to eat at Fenway before the rainout was announced. A media army marches on its substantial stomach, and for the second straight year the Red Sox crushed the Yankees in the area of media hospitality. After two days of box lunches in New York—entries of mysterious substance, raising the old George Carlin question "Is it meat or is it maybe cake?"—the folks from the Fenway press box were offered unlimited shrimp, top-shelf Legal Sea Foods clam chowder, and a variety of hot foods. Maestro Steinberg was behind this maneuver, and the Sox truly enjoyed making the Yankees look cheap in the eyes of the national media. Small surprise that the Sox became America's team. Check the glowing coverage from the well-fed masses.

Arroyo took the hill in Game 3 on Saturday night and looked like a pitcher who had only nineteen big league wins under his belt. The Yankees jumped on him for three runs in the first and three more in the third. It was 11–6 after four, 13–6 after five, and 17–6 in the seventh inning. Sheffield, A-Rod, and Matsui looked as of they were taking batting practice off Boston pitchers. The Yankees cracked twenty-two hits en route to a 19–8 victory, which certainly seemed to draw a curtain on the Red Sox season. Matsui was 5–6 with five RBI. A-Rod was 3–5 with three RBI, and Sheffield was 4–5 with four RBI. All of them homered, Matsui twice.

Nineteen to eight. Why not 19–18? As the game droned toward its inevitable conclusion, the scene in the Red Sox owners' box was not pretty. With the score 17–6, Werner turned to the suite steward, Bill Teseira, and said, "Do we have any whiskey?" Lucchino joined Werner in a shot of Glenlivet on the rocks. It was hardly a rally shot, but Werner admitted, "I nursed the drink for the last three innings, and it really did help with the pain of that game." It was the first hard liquor either one had consumed in Fenway all season.

It was cold and late, and most of the sad faces of the Red Sox were wrapped in hooded sweatshirts as they sat slumped in the dugout. They knew what this was. It was an ass-kicking. The hole was too deep. It was no way to end such a season of high hopes. They were going down without a shred of dignity against the team they hated most. And it was happening in their own house, a ballpark that was almost empty for the final innings of a must-win playoff game.

In her season-ticket seat in the lower boxes, historian Doris Kearns Goodwin stopped keeping score, breaking what she called "an almost religious habit my father had instilled in me when I was six years old." During the meaningless late innings, three customers walked into the Twins Enterprise Souvenir Store on Yawkey Way and switched allegiance. They bought Yankee caps. The unbearable heaviness of being a Red Sox fan had simply become too much. In the press box, veteran *Globe* writer John Powers spoke over the phone with his twenty-three-year-old son, Evan, who was watching from his Eighty-second Street apartment in New York. Evan had witnessed Game 2 in Yankee Stadium, but he said it was simply too hard to keep rooting for the Red Sox. He was done.

"They have broken my spirit," he told his dad.

As the game lurched toward its brutal, inevitable conclusion, John Henry went to his best friend, his computer. Undaunted, ever optimistic, and hopelessly innocent (in other words, he was a newcomer to the Red Sox), he started crunching numbers. A philosophy major who never graduated from college, Henry made his billions calculating odds. He was a commodities man. It was easy to calculate that the odds were 16–1 that the Sox could come back from an 0–3 deficit to win four straight. Henry turned to Rich Levin of the commissioner's office and said, "Someone is going to do it. Someday. Absolutely. Why not us? It's going to happen sooner or later. It's overdue."

Maybe. But in a century of professional baseball, hockey, and basketball seven-game series, only 2 of 236 teams ever came back from a 3–0 deficit—the 1942 Toronto Maple Leafs (vs. Detroit) and the 1975 New York Islanders (vs. Pittsburgh). This wasn't a hedge fund. The Sox weren't pork bellies. Swept up in his childhood love of baseball, Henry was letting his heart get in the way of his head. He was dreaming.

The Yankee blowout lasted four hours and twenty minutes, the longest nine-inning game in postseason history. It did not end until 12:25 A.M. on Sunday, and there were barely five thousand fans in the ballpark for the final pitch. Who would have guessed it would wind up being the shortest of the three Fenway games of the 2004 ALCS?

Few noticed, but something important happened in the middle of the horrible loss. Watching Arroyo, Ramiro Mendoza, and Leskanic take their beating, Tim Wakefield went to Francona and volunteered to pitch. Typical Wakefield. He was the man who gave up the homer to Aaron Boone in 2003 and feared he'd be Buckner. He'd pitched an inning of relief in Game 1 and been rocked for two runs on three hits, including a Kenny Lofton homer. He was slated to be Game 4's starting pitcher, but there he was, raising his hand to save the beleaguered bullpen in a game the Sox were certain to lose. By the time Wakefield got into Game 3, the Sox were out of it and already thinking about how they could salvage Game 4. So Wakefield, who prided himself on always wearing his spikes, came into Game 3 and took his beating, giving up five runs on five hits in 3.1 innings. It was the 3.1 innings that counted. Wakefield finished the ALCS with an awful ERA of 8.59, but his willingness to take one for the team lined up the Sox pitching for the final four games. He was the silent MVP with the ugly numbers.

Francona made a point of Wakefield's contribution in his postmortem, er, postgame remarks, noting, "We got ourselves into a bind. You saw what was going on. It was getting ugly. Because Wake did what he did, we were able to stay away from Timlin and Foulke . . . He's a professional, and when we win tomorrow, we'll have Wake to thank for that." The manager also mentioned that Lowe, not Wakefield, would be starting Game 4. Lowe, who had yet to pitch in the series, was 2–3 with a 9.28 ERA against the Yankees in 2004. In thirty-nine career games against New York, he was 8–10 with a 6.07 ERA. He was certainly no Yankee killer, but he was all the Sox had left.

Game 3 drove a stake through the heart of the Nation, and tales of woe were legion. My son, seventeen-year-old Sam Shaughnessy, who lives for all things baseball, gave his Game 4 ticket to his aunt Ann. He claimed it was because Game 3 had ended after midnight and he had a history test the morning after Game 4. A ruse. Sam loves the Red Sox and hates history. But he couldn't bear to watch the Yankees celebrate at Fenway after a four-game sweep.

It wasn't much different on the other side of the world, where New Hampshire's Captain Tilton officially surrendered in Tikrit. For the first time in the postseason, Captain Tilton did not rise at an ungodly hour to trek to the morale welfare center for the Red Sox telecast. "I was pretty much at the end of my wits after Game 3 as far as loyalty to the Red Sox," he admitted.

Epstein had an interesting few hours after the blowout.

"I was pissed," he remembers. "That was probably our worst game of the year, including spring training. You hate to play your worst game of the year at the most important time. We were faced with our own mortality. I was thinking, 'God, is this the way this team is going to be remembered? This team should have won it all.' After the game I sat in Tito's office, even after Tito left."

Epstein was rescued by Jonathan Gilula, Peter Woodfork, and Jed Hoyer, three of his young friends from the front office, part of the Real World Fort Myers from March. In the late 1980s, a young Lucchino had been rescued in a similar manner by his mentor, Williams. Both men were battling cancer at the time, and one day, when Lucchino was feeling sorry for himself, his boss grabbed him and said, "Let's go out for some real chemotherapy!" An afternoon of drinking ensued. In the hours after the sickening loss to the Yankees, Epstein went to the apartment of his three pals—above the Baseball Tavern a block from the park—and downed four or five vodka tonics. They even watched an ESPN broadcast of Game 7 of the 2003 ALCS, the Aaron Boone game.

"They said they didn't want me to be alone, they were worried about what I might do," remembers Epstein. "We sat and talked about the series. I said we just needed one miracle in Game 4. Then we could come back with Pedro and Schilling, and anything can happen in a Game 7. We were flipping channels, forcing ourselves to watch highlights, then we came across last year's Game 7. I hadn't watched it all year. So I said, 'That's it, I'm watching it! We need a cleansing.' I ended up passing out on their couch. So I spent the night in my sports coat."

He bounced back and was at the park plenty early for Game 4. He took tough questions from a bloodthirsty media for half an hour during batting practice. Everyone could see that it was going to be especially tough on Epstein, who had boldly traded the wildly popular Garciaparra hours before the midsummer trading deadline. Ever mindful of my book, Epstein looked at me and said, "You look kind of pale. How's that book going?"

Easy answer. Susan Canavan, a Sox fan and the editor of this book, had already summed things up early Sunday, saying, "There's no book anymore. No one wants to read about these guys now."

She was right. We all knew it was over. And it was ugly. Under my byline on the front page of the *Boston Sunday Globe* it read, "So there. For the eighty-sixth consecutive autumn, the Red Sox are not going to win the World Series. No baseball team in history has recovered from a 3–0 deficit, and this most promising Sox season in eighteen years could be officially over tonight. Mercy."

Fastidious about admitting and correcting factual errors, the *Globe* has yet to retract this incorrect declaration in its October 17, 2004, edition.

Tommy McLaughlin, a longtime Sox employee who served as equipment manager in the visitor's clubhouse, was forced into the dirty deed of procuring champagne for the Yankee victory celebration. A Brighton native, he went to ever-trusted Dorr's Liquor in Brighton Center and picked up ten cases of Great Western. The stuff was iced and stored in a back room near the Yankee clubhouse on Sunday afternoon. McLaughlin and his helpers also had to put the plastic covering in front of the Yankee lockers, then disguise it above the stalls before the team arrived at Fenway.

Kevin Millar never gave up. Speaking for all of his teammates when the world expected the Sox to fold and go home, Millar corralled me near the first base dugout during batting practice and warned, "Don't let us win tonight. This is a big game. They've got to win, because if we win we've got Pedro coming back in Game 5 and Schilling in 6, and then you can take that fraud stuff and put it to bed. Don't let the Sox win this game." He said the same thing to just about every person he saw before Sunday's game.

They were surprisingly composed and confident while perched on the brink of extinction. They truly believed they could dig out of this hole, and there was odd comfort in the knowledge that no one outside the clubhouse thought they could do it.

Meanwhile, the message on the Sox clubhouse door read WE CAN CHANGE HISTORY. BELIEVE IT.

Francona, he of the intestinal woes, kept a jar of Metamucil handy at all times. He was downing a large chalky glass of the stuff before every game, always offering some to his young GM. Before Game 4, Epstein joined the manager in the odd ritual. It was the ultimate gesture of solidarity. So to speak.

Lowe gets credit for slowing down the Yankee lineup in Game 4. He gave up a two-run homer to A-Rod in the third inning but wasn't charged with another run until the sixth, and the Red Sox led, 3–2, when he was lifted in favor of Timlin. The thumpers in the middle of the Yankee lineup, Messrs. Sheffield, Rodriguez, Matsui, and Bernie Williams, were finally stifled in Game 4, and they never found their hitting shoes after Lowe put a stop to the batting practice madness that had marked Game 3. Meanwhile, Wakefield's Game 3 sacrifice paid the predicted dividends, as Foulke was able to hold the Yanks scoreless for 2.2 innings when the game groaned past midnight.

The key play of Game 4 — indeed, probably the key play of the series and the season — came in the bottom of the ninth inning. It was a stolen base by Dave Roberts.

Odd that a stolen base would wind up being one of the most important plays in Red Sox history. It's like MIT winning the Rose Bowl or Legal Sea Foods earning a citation for the best steak in Boston. Red Sox and base stealing go together like Danny DeVito and Arnold Schwarzenegger.

The Yankees were leading, 4–3, in the top of the ninth, and the sand was truly running out on another Fenway summer. Rivera, without question the greatest closer in the history of October, needed only three outs to clinch New York's fortieth pennant and send the Sox into yet another cold winter without a ring.

Upstairs in L-1, Lucchino took out a yellow notepad and starting composing some thoughts. He was joined by Werner, Dr. Steinberg, and former Maine senator George Mitchell, one of the many limited partners of the Sox.

"I didn't trust my instincts to say the right thing," Lucchino said. "I wanted to talk about what a bitter pill it was—having this phenomenal, exciting, great second half of the season—and how we would redouble our efforts to come back again."

While Lucchino scribbled, Werner looked toward the third base dugout and saw Cashman, Randy Levine, and former New York mayor Rudy Giuliani. "The idea that we are going to be defeated by the Yankees at Fenway Park and have the American League trophy handed to them in this clubhouse was a little more than I could stomach," Werner remembers. "It had been a very good season for us. We'd won ninety-eight games and swept the Angels, but clearly losing four in a row to the Yankees was going to be a pretty harsh blow. You couldn't help but come to the conclusion that once again the Yankees had proven they were the stronger team. And could you ever beat them? This was just such an embarrassment. So we wrote some notes."

When Millar led off with a walk—on five pitches—Lucchino put the pad into a drawer. His wife, Stacey, fumbled with a tiny no. 11 rubber pool ball, the same orb that Grady Little had apparently jinxed the year before. She'd left it at home for the first three games of the series but figured there was nothing to lose when the Sox went down, 0–3. Sort of like a shot of Metamucil.

With Millar on board and nobody out, Francona sent Roberts in to run for him. Thirty-two years old, Roberts was born in Okinawa (where Damon lived briefly). His dad was a Marine for thirty years, his mom Japanese. Roberts graduated from UCLA, majoring in history, and broke into the big leagues with the Indians in 1999. Along with Cabrera and Mientkiewicz, he'd been part of Theo's trading deadline harvest—the least celebrated of the July 31 newcomers.

The 5-10 Roberts looked over his shoulder at Francona as he

walked toward first. The manager winked at him. Green light. Francona was trusting his player, as he had trusted all of his players all season. He was leaving the game and the season in the hands (okay, feet) of a .256 career hitter who'd stolen thirty-eight bases and been caught only three times in 2004.

"Dave's one of the few guys in the league who can steal a base when everyone knows he's going to try," said Francona. "We had talked after the inning. When I winked, he knew that meant, 'Go when you can go.' I wouldn't pick a pitch for him because that's hard to do. But he knew if he got a jump, he had my blessing to go, and if he got thrown out, I would take the bullet."

It was a bold move. With Mueller at the plate—the same Mueller who'd beaten Rivera in July with a two-run walk-off homer—Rivera threw to first base three times before delivering a pitch to the plate. When the Hall of Fame closer finally fired toward home, Roberts was off and running. The pitch to Mueller was high and away. Mueller took the pitch. Posada uncoiled from his crouch and came up firing. It was an ideal pitch for a catcher to handle with a runner stealing. However, Posada's strong throw to Jeter was a shade to the shortstop side of second, and it allowed Roberts to beat the tag with a headfirst slide. Mueller squared to bunt the next pitch, then took it for a strike. Francona lifted the bunt sign and Mueller made contact with the 1–1 pitch, shooting it past a sprawling Rivera and into center field. Roberts scored easily. Game saved. Series saved. Season saved. Finally, something went Boston's way. It was 4–4.

With former Red Sox Paul Quantrill on the mound in the bottom of the twelfth, Manny led off with a single to left. Ortiz strode to the plate, dragging the magic black bat that had done so much damage all year. It was long after midnight, just as it had been when Carlton Fisk walked to the same home plate in Game 6 of the 1975 World Series. It was the twelfth inning. Just as it had been for Fisk. Ortiz worked the count to 2–1. When Quantrill tried to sneak a fastball past him, Ortiz sent it into the Yankee bullpen. It was 1:22 A.M. in Boston, and Fox's Joe Buck told the world: "We'll see you later today."

Even at that hideous hour, there was hardly an empty seat in old Fenway. Like the players, the fans were not ready for winter. Not yet. There would be other days to cut cordwood and hang storm windows.

It was still baseball season in New England. Theo went back to the couch and the vodka tonics at his friends' apartment above the Baseball Tavern.

Not much work or studying got done in New England on Monday, October 18. The fans, who had watched the game through their fingers, didn't roll into bed until 2 or 3 A.M. It seemed that by the time they finally woke up, it was almost time for the next game.

Dr. Morgan, the youthful orthopedic specialist who served as medical director of the entire Sox system, could ill afford to be sleepy. He spent part of Sunday at the University of Massachusetts Medical School in Worcester, practicing an unprecedented procedure in hopes that he could get Schilling back on the mound. Shots of Marcaine hadn't worked—Schilling needed to feel his foot push and land. The special hightop shoe hadn't worked—it put too much pressure on the ankle. Morgan was forced to be more creative. He wanted to stabilize the flapping tendon by attaching the skin around the tendon to the deep tissue, thus creating a makeshift sheath to hold the tendon in place. He went to UMass to find a human cadaver leg on which he could practice.

"I was able to get an ankle there and open it up and look at the anatomy again," said Morgan. "It was an amputated specimen, cut just below the knee."

Male or female? we wondered.

"Let's just say it was kind of a big, hairy foot," said Morgan. "No nail polish. I'd say it was a guy."

Yeesh. The ultimate sacrifice. A dead man breathed life into Curt Schilling to get him back on the mound.

"Fans didn't actually give their lives for the Red Sox," noted Lucchino. "This was after the fact. But it did help us win."

Before Game 5, Morgan gathered with trainer Jim Rowe and assistant trainer Chris Correnti and performed the procedure on Schilling in the back training room of the Sox clubhouse. It required local anesthesia and took approximately twenty minutes. Boston University's Dr. Timothy Foster, associate editor of the *American Journal of Sports Medicine,* later told the *Globe:* "This is the first time I've seen or heard of this." Schilling was able to walk around with his numb foot before the game.

Fifteen hours and forty-nine minutes after Ortiz rounded the bases to end Game 4, Pedro Martinez threw the first pitch of Game 5 to Jeter. It would turn out to be the longest postseason game in history—five hours and fourteen minutes over fourteen innings.

Pedro was long gone and the Yankees led, 4–2, in the top of the eighth when A-Rod muffed a chance to bury the Sox. Miguel Cairo led off with a double, and Jeter (acting on his own) bunted him to third. Facing Timlin, with only one out, Rodriguez was expected to get Cairo in from third. But A-Rod struck out swinging, a sin for which Yankee fans will punish him forever.

In the bottom of the eighth, with the Red Sox down to their final six outs. Lucchino again was scribbling concession notes in the owners' box. Then Ortiz—officially replacing the great Carl Yastrzemski as Boston's best clutch postseason hitter—started the inning with a home run off Tom Gordon. Lucchino put his notes back in the drawer. Millar walked again. Roberts pinch-ran again and took third on a single to center by Nixon. Rivera replaced Gordon, and for a second straight night he was unable to hold the lead as Varitek—doing what A-Rod failed to do—tied the game with a sacrifice fly to center. The Red Sox would never trail again in 2004. The idiot savants played their final sixty innings without ever needing to come from behind.

In the top of the ninth, something happened that gave pause to those who might have believed in the Curse of the Bambino. With Sierra on first base and two out, Tony Clark (like Quantrill and Gordon, another former Sox) roped a double down the right field line. Running on contact with two out, Sierra was a lock to score from first, but the ball somehow hit the right field wall beyond Pesky's pole and crawled up the green facade into the stands for a ground rule double. Sierra had to hold at third. In a typical Red Sox unlucky time, the ball would have stayed in play and Sierra would have scored. Joe Morgan's flare dropped in front of Fred Lynn in Game 7 in '75, and Posada's pop-up landed in front of Damon in the fateful eighth in New York in 2003. Not this time. This year was different. Cairo, the next batter, popped up, and it was on to the bottom of the ninth.

With two on and two out in the fourteenth, Ortiz had a memorable at-bat against Esteban Loaiza. He fouled off six pitches before dumping the game-winning single into center on Loaiza's tenth pitch, scoring Damon from second. Kapler described Ortiz's feat as "Jordan-esque." Fittingly, Wakefield got the win in relief. Games 4 and 5 both ended on October 18, a rare "morning-night" doubleheader.

Wakefield said, "Being down, 3–0, and being down the last two nights shows the depth, the character, the heart, the guts of our ball club. And it took every ounce of whatever we had left to win tonight's game and to win last night's game."

Epstein said, "I'll take nominations. I might be in sort of a haze, but I think that was one of the greatest games ever played, if not the greatest." Then he was back to the vodka tonics and the couch in his friends' apartment.

In the next day's *Herald,* Mike Barnicle wrote: "The Yankees are about history, achievement and the corporate monotony of nearly automatic victory. The Olde Towne Team, however, is a constantly exposed nerve ending, an athletic mirror reflecting life in New England: the slush of February, the engine that won't turn over on early January mornings, the built-in municipal inferiority complex that is Boston, the negativism that can be erased by the sunlight of a single splendid spring day and the realization that we thrive and wrestle and live in a comfortable parochial village where a lot of our dreams are wrapped around the fortunes of this one baseball team, always have been, too."

McLaughlin, the veteran visitor's clubhouse manager, smiled when it was over, and returned the ten cases of Great Western to Skip Dervishian, the owner of Dorr's Liquor in Brighton. McLaughlin also clipped a small piece of the plastic that he'd prepared for the Yankee lockers. He put it in his wallet and carried it with him the rest of the season.

In three games in three days in Boston, the Sox and Yankees had gradually progressed from nine . . . to twelve . . . to fourteen innings — from 4:20 . . . to 5:02 . . . to 5:49. They played fifteen hours and eleven minutes of baseball, throwing 1,299 pitches. There were twenty-nine pitching changes. And the Red Sox, reeling after the 19–8 beating, had recovered from a 4–3 deficit in the ninth in Game 4 and a 4–2 deficit in the eighth in Game 5. They'd forced Rivera to blow saves in each of the last two games and won them both in extra innings on hits by Big Papi. The magic was back. This was the stuff of folklore. It was beginning to feel as if they might be able to beat the Yankees four straight times.

Damon said, "Unless I'm mistaken, we've won four straight before."

Back to New York, where the Sox had lost seven of the last eight games. The two-year total, however, was now dead even. In fifty meetings since the start of 2003, it was 25–25. And all the momentum belonged to Boston. Not to mention the Schilling factor.

The Sox owners did not make the trip to New York for Game 6. The weather forecast was bleak, and Lucchino spoke for them all when he said, "Yankee Stadium is a very inhospitable place." But hundreds, perhaps thousands, of Red Sox fans trekked back to the scene of the crime—putting up with all manner of insult in the stands.

Pedro Martinez also chose to stay at home and, incredibly, was given permission. It was an extraordinary request. It meant that if the season ended in Game 6, Martinez would not be with his teammates for the final game. Not available. Not there for moral support. He said he could get more work done in Boston than in New York and offered that he would be ready to pitch in relief in Game 7 if needed.

"Not a big deal," explained Lucchino. "This isn't fucking high school sports!"

Lucchino and Epstein resented the image put forth by the media that the Sox were too soft on their stars. The new management team had inherited most of the prima donnas on their roster and saw themselves powerless to change things as long as the divas remained under contract. Part of the price of doing sports business in the new century involved putting up with petulant stars, and the Sox brass consistently resisted the temptation to chide their own players when they acted like babies. In this area, Francona took most of the heat for the front office and the players.

It was 49 degrees and windy at Yankee Stadium when Game 6 started at 8:19 P.M. According to Millar, the Sox did something unusual to stay warm. He told WBZ-TV's Dan Roche after the World Series, "It was freezing in New York. It was about 35 degrees with misty rain. So I grabbed a bottle of Jack Daniel's out of the clubhouse and I said, 'Boys, it's time to Cowboy Up. We need to do some shots.' We went around the locker room, and everybody did just a little shot of Jack Daniel's to go through his system."

Millar told the same story on *The Best Damn Sports Show Period*. His teammates were not amused, and Damon and Timlin went to some lengths to dispute the notion. There is probably a grain (grain alcohol?) of truth to the story, but most of the Sox said Millar was exaggerating. Metamucil was one thing, but Jack Daniel's?

It's doubtful that Schilling would have imbibed. He had scoffed at Damon's idiot theme and bristled at the sloppy appearance of his teammates. But on this night he was just trying to hold his ankle together and do what he had not been able to do in Game 1: give his team a chance to win. While he warmed up in the bullpen, some of the stitches in his ankle tore and blood seeped into the white sanitary hose under his stirruped crimson sock. Naturally Fox TV was all over it. If it bleeds it leads. Schilling would bring a whole new meaning to red sock that night. He buzzed A-Rod in the first inning and set the first eight Yankees down in order. He was working on a one-hit shutout when Mark Bellhorn crashed a three-run homer off Lieber in the top of the fourth.

Bellhorn was another Francona success story. He drove fans crazy all season, walking and striking out at an alarming rate. But he got on base and scored runs and knocked in runs. Fans were booing him with gusto at Fenway during the dark hours of 19–8, and he was 3–21 for the series when he stepped in to face Lieber in Game 6—and became a hero.

It took a few minutes for Bellhorn's homer to register. Everyone in the park and all the fans watching at home on television saw it strike the chest of a fan in the first row of the left field seats, but left field umpire Jim Joyce initially ruled that it bounced off the wall. After a conference involving all six umpires, the call was changed. The Sox led, 4–0.

Again, there were echoes of Red Sox seasons past. In 1975, umpire Larry Barnett made the wrong call on the Ed Armbrister bunt, but the ruling stood and the Red Sox lost. Twice in 1999 the Sox were violated by incorrect umpiring calls in the ALCS against the Yankees. Both rulings triggered postgame apologies from the umpires, but the calls stood, and the Sox lost. But this was 2004. This was the year that the calls, like the Curse, would be reversed.

It happened again in the eighth inning, a play that forever tainted Alex Rodriguez (inspiring some to suggest that there's a Curse of A-Rod) and convinced Sox cynics that this was in fact The Year.

Schilling, bloody sock and all, had left after seven, leading, 4–1, and secure in the knowledge that he would forever be the Audie Murphy of Boston sports. Mr. "I guess I hate the Yankees now" gave up only four hits and walked none. It was gritty. Even Willis Reed tipped his cap to the Sox ace. Schilling had given new definition to playing in pain. By the time he came off, Francona had already sent Lowe back to the Times Square Westin to get ready for Game 7.

But it looked as if Schilling's win and the Sox season might be in jeopardy when Arroyo got into trouble in the eighth. A-Rod stepped to the plate after a one-out, RBI single by Jeter had cut the Sox lead to 4–2. Rodriguez represented the tying run, and he was facing the same kid he'd faced in high school, the same pitcher who had plunked him in July, igniting the latest brawl between the two teams. This time, A-Rod hit a dribbler to Arroyo's left. The tall hurler scooped the ball on the run and easily caught up with A-Rod, who was streaking down the line. Ball in glove, Arroyo applied the tag, but the baseball suddenly squirted toward the right field tarp down the line in foul territory. Yankee Stadium shook as Jeter scored from first and A-Rod wound up on second.

A collective panic engulfed Sox Nation. Sitting on a couch in Lucchino's home theater in Brookline, Werner thought to himself, "This is Bill Buckner all over again. Maybe there really is a Curse." He was not alone. It was one of those rare instances when fans and ownership, paupers and princes, shared the exact same feelings.

But no. Again there was a conference of all six umps. First base arbiter Randy Marsh had been screened by Sox first baseman Mientkiewicz. The other umpires saw what the replay clearly showed: Rodriguez had karate-chopped Arroyo's glove, forcing the ball loose. It was a cheap stunt. It was cheating. By definition, it was interference. Rodriguez was ruled out, and Jeter was instructed to return to first base. When the call was changed, A-Rod hurt his reputation further by standing on second, raising his arms, and folding his hands on top of his helmet as if to say "What did I do?" It was transparent. In baseball parlance, it was horseshit. Schilling made no attempt to disguise his disgust the next day when he went on the radio and said, "That was junior high school baseball right there, at its best."

Again, it was more evidence that the Curse, like the call, might be going the other way this year. Not privy to the conclusive replay, Yankee fans littered the field with debris, and the game was interrupted while riot police were summoned to keep the fans at bay.

It was still 4–2 when Foulke came on to pitch the ninth. Oriole manager Lee Mazzilli, who coached and played in New York for many seasons, likes to say, "The toughest six outs in baseball are when you face the Yankees in the bottom of the ninth at Yankee Stadium."

It was no different this time. Foulke created trouble with a couple of walks, and there were some shaky moments—moments that made Red Sox Nation think of Aaron Boone—before Clark finally struck out to end it.

Kapler said, "What's been so special about this is the fashion in which we've won games. It hasn't been easy for us. It never has been easy for us. I'm just so proud of my teammates right now. I think a lot of guys right now are proud of each other."

"Nobody gave up and nobody quit," added Embree. "The whole time we kept saying we could do it, take it one game at a time. We put ourselves in a position to have a chance to win this series, and that says something about the true grit of this team."

And playing the role of John Wayne in this version of *True Grit* was Schilling, who had his stitches removed after the game. The Sox and Yankees had already played for twenty-five hours and thirty-six minutes—more time on the field than any two teams in any postseason series. And they hadn't even started the seventh game.

It was set. After a hundred years of bare-knuckle brawls, a record fifty-one games over two seasons, and twelve months of front office squalls, the Sox and Yankees were again going to play one game to decide who would represent the American League in the World Series. The game would begin on the seventy-third birthday of the late Mickey Mantle and end on the seventy-sixth birthday of Whitey Ford. Bucky Dent would throw the ceremonial first pitch to Yogi Berra—

a low blow by the desperate New Yorkers. And the Red Sox owners, finally making the trip back to the dreaded stadium, would be offered sanctuary in the Babe Ruth suite. The *Babe Ruth* suite.

"It's in Joe Torre's hands," said Steinbrenner. "Sure, I'm worried. The whole team should be worried. We've got to win it."

After Game 6, in the midnight press conferences, neither manager would name a Game 7 starter. Wakefield's name had been floated, but Lowe was already sleeping at the Westin, sure that he was getting the ball. Torre ultimately would go with sour Kevin Brown, who had lasted all of two innings in Game 3. The Yankees had not lost four straight games since April 22–25. The front page of the next day's *Post* featured a giant photo of Babe Ruth next to the headline PUT ME IN—YANKS NEED BABE'S CURSE IN GAME 7. The back page featured a photo of Clark whiffing and the headline CHOKERS OR CHAMPS?

For all that was at stake, for all the drama that had already taken place, there was no drama in Game 7. Series MVP Ortiz (who else?) hit a two-run homer off Brown in the first. When the Sox loaded the bases in the second, Vazquez came on in relief, and Damon, who had come into the game hitting .103 (3–29) for the series, crushed the first pitch, driving it barely over the lower wall in right to make it 6–0. Lowe, working on two days of rest (like Jim Lonborg in '67), was cruising.

Having abandoned the Babe Ruth suite, the Sox ownership troika sat in a box to the right of the Sox dugout. Epstein watched in Francona's office. Due in some part to the Metamucil routine, Young Theo suddenly needed to be near a bathroom during games. In the middle of the game, with the Sox leading, 8–1, Henry left his seat in the stands and went to find his general manager.

"He was in Terry's office, shoes off, sitting back on a chair with the lights out, watching the TV," recalls Henry. "He couldn't go far from a bathroom. I knew that. I asked him if he could get a message to Derek and [pitching coach] Dave Wallace to make sure not to walk anybody. Theo said they already knew that and that it would be a bad breach of baseball protocol to go down there."

Yankee Stadium was like a tomb through the middle innings. The pregame euphoria and anticipation had been sapped out of the crowd as the small contingent of Red Sox fans gained a toehold in the Bronx beachhead. The hometown fans were stunned. Gone were the Yankee arrogance and entitlement. This time there was no sense that the Yanks could come back and break the Red Sox hearts. Boston's lead was too big.

Pedro came on for a curious inning of ineffective relief in the seventh, awakening the quiet Yankee crowd and igniting a new flurry of "Who's your daddy?" chants. But it didn't matter by then. The Yankees had stopped hitting. They were going down. Sheffield managed only one hit in his final seventeen at-bats. In Game 7, the great A-Rod hit three feeble grounders, then struck out and was booed by the New York fans. A home run by Bellhorn made it 9–3 in the eighth (the Sox were going to win this thing without an RBI from Manny or a win from Pedro), and Henry started to relax.

"That one run seemed important," Henry said. "That's how snake-bitten we felt. After that loss last year, and having spent two and a half years here, I'd never had that kind of thinking. But until we had beaten them, I was nervous up until the third out."

Lucchino was also jittery at the end: "In the ninth inning, with one out, I turned to John and Tom and said, 'Everybody in America knows we're going to win except the three of us. What's wrong with us? In California they're out there and they know this game is over, and we're right here and we don't know it.' Maybe that was a sign we had become real Red Sox people with that sense of negativity and fatalism."

Embree—who had talked about all of the Sox players getting statues a month earlier—was on the mound at the end. As the clock struck 12:01, Sierra hit a routine grounder to Reese at second. Reese swallowed the ball and fired to Mientkiewicz. It was over. Baseball's greatest comeback. Baseball's greatest choke. With the most unlikely reversal of starring roles.

October 20 should be marked on New England calendars as Boston Baseball's Bastille Day. It should be an official holiday—no school, no work, no mail delivery. It's the day that Sox fans were liberated from eight and a half decades of torture and torment at the hands of the Yankees and their fans. In the haunted House That Ruth Built, the sloppy men wearing red socks embarrassed and eliminated the $182-million-payroll Yankees.

It is impossible to understate the psychological fallout and abject magnitude of the Red Sox conquest of the Evil Empire in October 2004. No matter how many future World Series are won or lost, no matter how many indignities New York may yet heap on the doorstep of Sox fans, what the Red Sox did to the Yankees in October 2004 stands forever as the answer to any Gotham taunts about Bambinos or 1918. Sox fans can simply smile and cite four straight wins after falling behind, 3–0. It was both the greatest comeback and the greatest choke in baseball history. In other words, gentle Red Sox fans, you can always look at each other like Bogey and Bergman and utter those words scripted by Theo Epstein's forebears . . .

"We'll always have Paris."

"Unbelievable" is a word tossed about too freely in modern times, but it was truly hard to believe that the Boston Red Sox were dancing on the infield of Yankee Stadium after completing the greatest comeback the sport has ever known. That they could do it at the expense of the Yankees made the victory exponentially greater for anyone who has ever been associated with or rooted for the Red Sox. Those fortunate enough to be on the scene made every effort to immerse themselves in the moment. Champagne was hardly necessary. Nobody needed Millar's bottle of Jack, either. Sheer happiness—something you'd normally associate with the birth of a child or maybe a million-dollar lottery ticket—washed over Red Sox Nation. While the Boston players and executives took pictures and celebrated on the sacred sod of Steinbrenner, a Boston fan in the stands held a sign: HISTORY STARTS NOW.

Millar said, "How many times can you honestly say you have a chance to shock the world? It might happen once in your life, or it might never happen. But we had a chance and we did it. It's an amazing storybook."

They had shocked the baseball world and in the process expanded Red Sox Nation. Across the land, casual sports fans who never gave a damn about Boston baseball suddenly became Red Sox rooters. To the uninitiated, the Red Sox were the classic underdogs, making less money and looking less professional than the Yankees. They had a history of losing after coming close, and the Yankees were their nemesis. Nationally, the Yankees were a trademark, like U.S. Steel. Beating them was like beating the IRS. It was a victory for the little guy, the younger brother, the eternal underdog. Frank Capra and Steven Spielberg couldn't make up this stuff.

After the American League championship trophy was presented in the visitor's clubhouse, the same room in which Wakefield wept a year earlier, the ever-classy Brian Cashman came and congratulated the Sox brass. Pedro looked into a television camera and said, "The Bambino is a good man. He did a lot of things for the community. He's not a bad man. Why would he put a curse on anybody? Right now, he should be drunk around here."

Across the way, Rodriguez said, "I'm embarrassed . . . I don't think I'm even going to watch another baseball game until spring training."

Epstein, blessed with a wonderful sense of history despite his tender age, raised a can of Budweiser (did he already know the Sox would be playing the Cardinals in the Series?) and said, "We did this for all the great Red Sox players who never found a way to beat the Yankees. The '49 team with Ted Williams and Bobby Doerr and Johnny Pesky. The '78 team that should have won the playoff game. For our team last year, that should have won the game and gone to the World Series. I can't really put this in historical terms, but it's taken a long time to beat the Yankees."

He then checked his cell phone voicemail. It was overloaded. A Yankee fan had gotten hold of the phone number and urged all his friends to call Theo and leave a message. (Theo had the number changed the next day.) Henry and Lucchino received messages from Yankee officials. Henry got a short letter from Steinbrenner, and Levine sent a two-sentence congratulations letter to Lucchino's office.

It would always be difficult for Lucchino to be gracious toward the Yankees. He was the one who'd refueled the rivalry with his "Evil Empire" remark. In the summer of 2004 he'd said, "I hope George has a good libel lawyer" after Steinbrenner made negative remarks about him in *Sports Illustrated*.

"Before we played them," said Lucchino, "I had been asked about who we'd rather play and I said I was agnostic. I said I didn't care who we played as long as we made it to the World Series. But then after we beat them, I thought, 'This is the way it was meant to be.' It was much better that we did it that way. If we had won the thing by beating

Minnesota, it wouldn't have had the same feeling, the same hormonal satisfaction."

At 1:20 A.M., after the Red Sox buses had pulled away from Yankee Stadium, Steinbrenner emerged and said, "I want to congratulate the Boston team. They did very well and played very well. They are a great team."

Rodriguez didn't leave the park until 3 A.M. A month later he told the *New York Times:* "I'll never forgive myself or my team. As good as we were, there's no way we should have lost four games in a row to anyone. That disappointed me. That shouldn't have happened."

The next day's front-page headline in the *Daily News* read THE CHOKE'S ON US. The back page featured a photo of Pedro pointing toward the sky under the headline HELL FREEZES OVER. The *Boston Herald* went with BABE, YOU'RE HISTORY!

Bob Ryan, a history major at Boston College and a *Globe* sportswriter since 1968, took a deep breath, went to his keyboard, and labeled the experience "the single most alternatingly stressful and exhilarating week in Boston sports history . . ."

And to think it was all *before* the World Series.

14

No More Curse

THERE IS NO CHAPTER 13. This is the year of the happy ending.

The Red Sox enjoyed a true off-day on Thursday, October 21. They didn't get home and into bed until between 5 and 6 A.M.; among the few players who made it back to Fenway later that day were Wakefield, the Game 1 starter, catcher Doug Mirabelli, and Foulke, who said he needed to throw. Most of the fellows slept all day, then got up in time to watch the Houston Astros and St. Louis Cardinals play a seventh game to determine the National League's entry in the hundredth World Series.

In Boston, there was plenty of sentiment for Houston. A date with the Astros meant that the Sox would get to face Clemens and Jeff Bagwell, who'd been traded by Boston for the immortal Larry Andersen in 1990. The 'Stros had been managed by former Sox skipper Jimy Williams until the All-Star break of 2004, and a trip to Houston would have conjured up memories of February, when the New England Patriots won their second Super Bowl in three years at Reliant Stadium. The Celtics had won two of their last three NBA titles against the Houston Rockets. Houston just seemed like a good-luck place for New England sports teams. And the thought of beating Clemens to win a World Series was delicious to all members of Red Sox Nation.

But St. Louis beat Clemens and the Astros, 5–2, in Game 7, so for the third time in fifty-eight years, the Red Sox and Cardinals were matched in a World Series. The pairing carried significant history and tradition. Boston and St. Louis were the only two cities that have played each other in all four major sports championships. The Boston Bruins won a Stanley Cup against the St. Louis Blues in 1970, clinching the fourth and final game when Bobby Orr flew through the air after scoring an overtime goal on Mother's Day to complete the sweep. The Celtics won the first of their sixteen World Championships against the St. Louis Hawks in 1957, thanks to some nifty play from a couple of rookies named Bill Russell and Tommy Heinsohn. The Patriots won their first Super Bowl in February 2002 when Adam Vinatieri beat the St. Louis Rams with a last-second, 48-yard field goal. And the Red Sox and Cardinals met in two World Series, 1946 and 1967, both won by the Cardinals in seven games.

In 1946 the Sox were almost 3–1 favorites to beat St. Louis. It was Boston's first World Series in twenty-eight years and would be the only postseason opportunity in the Hall of Fame career of Theodore Samuel Williams. However, Williams was hit in the right elbow while participating in a warm-up exhibition for the World Series and never got his stroke back. He wound up batting only .200 in the Series, with no homers, one RBI, and no extra-base hits. St. Louis's 160-pound lefty, Harry Brecheen, proved too tough for the Sox and won three games as the Cardinals beat the Sox in seven. More bad luck visited the Sox in Game 7 when Dom DiMaggio suffered a charley horse running the bases as Boston tied the game in the eighth inning. Leon Culberson replaced DiMaggio in the bottom of the eighth and was slow getting to a double by Harry Walker. It was on Walker's hit that Enos "Country" Slaughter scored from first base with the winning run. Sox shortstop Johnny Pesky has been blamed for more than half a century for hesitating after catching Culberson's throw to the infield. His peg to the plate was way late, and the Sox were beaten, 4–3. Video replays are inconclusive, and Pesky's teammates have lined up to defend his play, but in 1989 Pesky admitted, "Even to this day, some people look at me like I'm a piece of shit."

Pesky has long been a victim of the Curse of the Bambino. He was born on September 27, 1919, the same day Ruth played his final game with the Red Sox. In 1945 Pesky married the woman he would love for the rest of his days, Ruth Hickey. *Ruth*. Johnny and Ruth celebrated their sixtieth wedding anniversary in January 2005.

In 1967 the Red Sox were sentimental favorites against a power-house Cardinal team that included Bob Gibson, Lou Brock, Orlando Cepeda, and Roger Maris. The '67 Red Sox forever changed Boston baseball, rescuing a moribund franchise and making the Sox winners and a big drawing card for the remainder of the century and beyond. They fell behind the Cardinals, 3–1, but took the Series to a seventh game, only to lose at Fenway as Gibson beat them for a third time. Carl Yastrzemski won baseball's last triple crown and continued his torrid hitting in the World Series. He got help from Jim Lonborg, who threw two of the greatest games in Series history, but was unable to win in Game 7, working with just two days of rest. There was no talk of the Curse in 1967. The fans forgave the Cinderella Sox even though they failed to finish the job. The only bad luck anyone could find that year was the tragic beaning of Tony Conigliaro in August. Conigliaro, who was perhaps on a path to matching Ruth's 714 homers, was done for the rest of the year. His vision never fully returned, prompting an early retirement. He suffered a massive heart attack in 1982 and died at the age of forty-five in 1990.

Incredibly, the euphoria of the 2004 conquest of the Yankees inspired some fans and media members to declare that the Curse of the Bambino had been lifted. It came as quite a surprise to me. Having written the book that triggered the whole thing in 1990, it was clear that there was another job to do. Certainly what happened in New York was magical and would forever enable Sox fans to hold up their heads in Yankee Stadium, but it fell short of erasing the Curse. Since 1918, the Red Sox had finished ahead of the Yankees eighteen times, but in none of those years did they win the World Series. The Sox beat the Yanks in '46, '67, and again in 1986, but no one was happy about the end of the season after Buckner and friends let the World Series slip between their ankles. The object of any major league season is to win the World Series, and it was almost pathetic to hear Sox fans say that the mission had been accomplished simply because of the miracle in New York.

Francona knew. His message on the day after the New York series was: "There's more baseball to be played."

This might be the place to give the manager his props. Terry "Tito"

Francona took a lot of heat in his first year with the Red Sox. He certainly ran a loose ship, and it could have blown up in his face if the Sox had been swept by the Yankees. But they were not. In the final eight games, his deployment of the Sox pitchers turned out to be brilliant. He protected Foulke in the 19–8 Yankee blowout, then had Lowe ready in Game 4 against New York. He made the risky decision to let Dave Roberts steal in Game 4. He somehow had Pedro, Schilling, and Lowe lined up for 5–6–7 against the Yankees. He kept the hobbling Schilling out of the batter's box in the World Series and allowed Pedro to pitch where it was warm (65 degrees for his Game 3 start in St. Louis). He dealt with the egos of Manny, Pedro, and Schilling. He got the max out of Foulke and maybe inspired Lowe. The idiots, the men of Delta House, responded to his free rein. Francona was considered the second-best manager going into all three postseason series—not nearly as good as Anaheim's Scioscia, New York's Torre, or St. Louis's La Russa. But he beat them all to the ballpark for every game. Francona never lost a game because of lack of preparation. He was at Fenway at 10:10 A.M. for the first game of the World Series, which started more than ten hours later. And the preparation paid off. He beat Scioscia, Torre, and La Russa. In succession. He did something no Red Sox manager had done since Eddie Barrow in 1918. Not bad for the bald guy with the big nose and the wad in his cheek.

The St. Louis Cardinals won 105 games in 2004, more than any other team in baseball. In the second, third, fourth, and fifth spots in their lineup, the Cards featured Larry Walker, Albert Pujols, Scott Rolen, and Jim Edmonds. The latter three all finished in the top five in the National League Most Valuable Player balloting. It was a true murderer's row, equal to the 2004 or even the 1927 Yankees on any level. But the Cardinal pitching staff was ordinary and depleted. They'd played seven hard games against Houston, not wrapping it up until less than forty-eight hours before the start of the World Series. Chris Carpenter, who'd gone 15–5, was on the shelf with a strain of his right biceps. Woody Williams, Matt Morris, Jason Marquis, and Jeff Suppan didn't scare anybody. Still, they were the vaunted Cardinals, winners of the most World Series (nine) of any National League team.

Lucchino admitted, "There was something appealing about playing

St. Louis—one of the great old franchises in baseball. If we were going to do this, it was nice to do this against someone other than an expansion team, against one of the traditional powerhouses."

Henry, who had grown up a Cardinal fan in Ford City, Arkansas, and Quincy, Illinois, said, "My entire being was invested in the Cardinals at a very young age. I had a radio with me all the time. Kids called me 'St. Louis.' I grew up about a hundred miles from there, and it was split between the Cubs and the Cardinals. My favorite player was Stan the Man. He was the man. He was the National League equivalent to the guy here [Ted Williams]. But then I started thinking . . . In 2001 I almost bought the Angels and then they won. Then I sold the Marlins and then they won. Now we're playing St. Louis, my boyhood team. I've always been extremely fortunate in my life. This World Series thing can't just be going around me, can it?"

The Sox and Cardinals worked out at Fenway on Friday, October 22, and there was some amusement at the sight of the Red Sox ground crew spray-painting the 2004 World Series logo behind home plate. Only a year after their premature move before the end of the 2003 ALCS, Boston's lawn men waited until the last possible moment before putting the finishing touches on the sacred emblem. Schilling threw in the bullpen and made plans with the medical staff to have the stitches put back in place the next day. He was scheduled to start Game 2, on Sunday.

After the groundbreaking bombast of the Yankee series, there was almost no way the World Series could be anything but anticlimactic. Epstein encapsulated the situation and demonstrated his sense of history before the first game when he said, "Time to play Finland now."

Though slightly dismissive of the Cardinals, it was a perfect analogy. In 1980, the United States hockey team made history by defeating the Soviets on a late goal by Mike Eruzione in the medal semifinal game of the Lake Placid Olympics. Considered perhaps the grandest upset in sports history, the event has been immortalized on the big screen and in many books. Eruzione and friends haven't paid for a meal in a quarter of a century. What is commonly forgotten is the small detail that the victory over the USSR was not the gold medal game. The U.S. team still had to win one more game, against Finland, to clinch the gold. And that's how St. Louis became Finland in the eyes of Red Sox Nation. Eruzione, who is from Winthrop, Massachusetts, sent MIRACLE hats to the Sox for additional inspiration. As if anything was needed.

The Red Sox served as hosts of a World Series gala at the John Fitzgerald Kennedy Library the night before Game 1. A lavish affair, it received glowing reviews from baseball officials, the fans, and the media. When asked how the Sox were able to throw together a bash on such short notice, Lucchino had an easy answer: "We had all this planned last year. We just took out the World Series party file from 2003. It was easy to resurrect the plan."

Not everyone went to the gala. Back on Yawkey Way, Young Theo and his staff joined Francona, the coaching staff, and catchers Varitek and Mirabelli to go over the Cardinal scouting report that had been prepared by Dave Jauss (a Duquette holdover), Jerry DiPoto, Alan Regier, and Galen Carr (Theo minions), and David Chadd (a John Henry loyalist). They met in the underground conference room outside Epstein's office, an area that had formerly been part of the Fenway Park Bowling Alley. The twenty-lane alley and adjacent game rooms had been gutted and rebuilt as offices. In the meeting, the scouts used two projectors and two computers to show how to attack the Cardinal hitters and pitchers. They dissected the Cardinal lineup Friday night, then returned Saturday to go over the subs and pitchers.

The scouts were not afraid of the St. Louis pitchers. "Not an intimidating staff," read the report. "Their hole is their inability to consistently shut down your offense." It warned about St. Louis's early-inning quick-strike capability, including a number of first-pitch, fastball hitters. It recommended that the Sox pitchers throw curveballs to Pujols, balls that broke back on the inside corner of the plate. The plan on Rolen was changeups on the inner half of the plate. The strategy on Edmonds was to start out by coming up and in, then work him high and away from the plate. At the end of the Series, St. Louis's dynamic trio would be 6–45 (.133), with one RBI. Small wonder that Francona and his group were confident after reviewing the material supplied by All of Theo's Men.

Everything the Sox ownership did, it did thoroughly. In October, the theme around the front office and the clubhouse was "Share the gold." Folks from the Red Sox minor league affiliates were flown into

Boston and put up at hotels for the World Series games at Fenway. *All of them.* Mike Stelmach, the clubhouse equipment manager in Fort Myers, got the same treatment as Carl Yastrzemski and Johnny Pesky. Stelmach even got to bring his girlfriend to Boston, all expenses paid. Meanwhile, Maestro Steinberg upped the ante in the dining room: the national media feasted on lobster tails, fresh shrimp, and London broil before the games in Boston. The Sox would be winners again when tired box lunches were wheeled out in St. Louis.

Several hours before the first game, Dr. Morgan, this time accompanied by Mass. General's Dr. George Theodore, again performed the tendon-stabilizing procedure on Schilling, who was scheduled to pitch the next night.

Minutes before the game, there was a moment of silence for twenty-one-year-old Victoria Snelgrove, an Emerson College student who was killed when Boston police fired supposedly nonlethal pepper-powder-filled pellets into a crowd outside Fenway's left field wall in the early morning hours after the Game 7 ALCS win. The tragedy subdued subsequent Boston celebrations and prompted extra patrols and vigilance for the remainder of the Red Sox victory tour.

Yastrzemski, the greatest living Red Sox, the man who almost carried the team to a World Series win over the Cardinals in 1967, threw out the first pitch, but he, too, labored with a heavy heart. A month earlier, his only son, Mike, still in his mid-forties, died while undergoing surgery in western Massachusetts. His dad, the intensely private Hall of Famer, wanted no part of any condolences or festivities in October 2004. He just wanted to be left alone. He came in from left field, threw the pitch, and left the park, speaking only to a few Sox staff members. Few in the sellout crowd were aware of his family crisis.

The Sox won Game 1, 11–9, when second baseman Mark Bellhorn clanged a two-run homer off the right field foul pole in the bottom of the eighth inning. Only 302 feet from home plate, the pole is called "Pesky's pole" because the light-hitting Pesky managed to curl a number of his seventeen career homers around the yellow stanchion. The idea that Pesky's pole would play a role in a World Series win by the Sox over the Cardinals was fitting for those who sought to clear the name of the resident Mr. Red Sox. In addition, the homer reminded Fenway folk of Carlton Fisk's shot off the yellow tower in left that won what many consider the greatest World Series game ever played. The homer also redeemed a player who had been loudly booed when he slumped badly in the early postseason games, and it enabled the Sox to win a game in which they committed four errors and saw their starter (Wakefield) routed.

"Every little boy dreams of playing in Game 7 of the World Series and winning the game," said Bellhorn. "I'm not trying to be a hero, just trying to win four games."

Ortiz knocked in four more runs, giving him an unworldly nineteen postseason RBI. He was on his own planet. Meanwhile, Manny made errors on two straight balls in the eighth inning when the Sox gave up the lead. The first error came when he overran a single to left, allowing a run to score. The second came on a flair that Manny had to charge. He chased the ball intently, but just as he seemed to be going into a pop-up slide, his leg got caught, making him lurch forward and fall awkwardly (not unlike Chevy Chase playing Gerald Ford in an early *Saturday Night Live* skit). As always, everyone laughed. Even in the Sox dugout. Even in left field. When Manny returned to the dugout after the disastrous inning, he told Roberts, "Snipers got me."

The tone was set. The Cardinals knew they had blown it when they lost the first game. They would never hold a lead in the entire World Series. The 9–9 tie in the eighth inning of Game 1 was their only sniff of victory.

Lucchino had left a bottle of Dom Pérignon on his desk during Game 1. A Fenway cleaning woman had commented on it as she dusted off its label during the afternoon, and Lucchino said she could take it home if the Sox won. When he got back to his office after the game, the bottle was gone. Share the gold.

The Sox were supremely confident from the start of the World Series. The ever-nervous Henry was getting a good vibe from his young general manager.

"When the World Series began, Theo was a completely different person," remembers Henry. "He was so confident. I have never seen a man in the game of baseball that was as confident as Theo was. He said that we knew how to stop three of the four big guys [Pujols, Rolen, and Edmonds] and we knew how to hit their pitchers. He said that all of them are essentially the same pitcher in different forms. He said this was because of the scouting and preparation. But I know it's one thing to scout, it's another thing to execute. Well, Jason Varitek was determined to execute, and our pitchers were able to hit the spots. Theo knew. He was telling me from Game 1, 'Don't worry, we're gonna beat these guys.' It was just amazing how confident both Theo and Tito were."

Francona could feel it. He had never seen or felt anything like what he was feeling in the dugout every game. Every inning, his players were saying, "Let's go win this inning! Don't let up!" It was Little League stuff, and it was working.

When it was all over, the manager admitted, "Starting in the Yankee series, from that fourth game on, I have never seen a team go pitch-to-pitch . . . I loved it. When you are a manager or a coach and your team is playing like that, it is the most awesome thing. It was Tek. Dave Roberts. Mirabelli. It was everybody."

Nixon remembers, "It was constant. It wasn't like some big, hoop-hoop-hurrah. But what was said was the right thing to ignite us. A guy like Ellis Burks knew what to say to keep the guys loose and keep them plugging away. The rest of it was just going out there and performing."

"They came together for each other, unlike any team I had ever seen before," said Epstein.

The last Fenway game of 2004 was played on Sunday night, October 24, and Schilling made it a night folks would remember. Bleeding again from his ruptured sutures, he pitched six innings of four-hit ball without allowing an earned run in a 6–2 victory, making it abundantly clear that the Red Sox were really going to win the World Series this time. All of Boston's runs were scored on two-out hits. The angst of seasons past and the folds of other Octobers were not on the minds of anyone in Red Sox Nation. This felt nothing like '46 or '78 or '86. It didn't feel like Cowboy Up either. This team had two weapons the 2003 team didn't have: Schilling and Foulke. They were Damon's happy idiots, the Laughing Gashouse Gang. Simultaneously, a team of destiny and density. And they were not going to come back from St. Louis without the World Series trophy.

Schilling's performances in Game 6 of the Yankee series and Game 2 of the World Series immediately elevated him into the pantheon of

Boston sports greats alongside Russell, Orr, Bird, and Brady, the guys who came to Boston and delivered championships. But more than any of them, Schilling won the ring by overcoming an injury that had threatened to shut down his season. He underwent an unprecedented medical procedure, and he bled on the mound for the Boston Red Sox. Embellishment and hyperbole weren't needed. By the time Schilling (aptly described by the *Washington Post*'s Tom Boswell as a "glory hog") got through telling his story, book agents and screenwriters were chasing him home to Medfield.

Schilling's postgame press conference perhaps would have best been headlined as FENWAY FATIMA.

"I don't have the time to explain today," Schilling started. "I just wish everybody on this planet could experience the day that I just experienced. I will never use the words 'unbelievable' and 'the Lord' again in the same sentence. Just the most amazing day of my life . . . Just so many things happened today. I promise you that when I walked out of that dugout today and headed to the bullpen, the most shocked person in this stadium was my wife, because I woke up at seven o'clock this morning, which is a tip-off right there. I mean, I've never woke up at seven o'clock in the morning for anything in my life. I wasn't going to pitch. I couldn't walk, I couldn't move. I don't know when it happened, but I knew that when I woke up there was a problem. I called Chris and I talked to Jimmy and I left for the park, and I told her that it was not going to happen. I wasn't going to go out on the mound with the way I felt today. There's no way. And that's kind of when everything just started. I left my house. I'm driving to the park, and anybody here that knows where Medfield is, it's a pretty long haul. There were signs every mile from my house to this ballpark on fire stations, on telephone poles, wishing me luck. And I mean it, I can't explain it. I got here, and got out of the car, and I got into the trainer's room, and Doc was here . . . But I didn't—I honest to God did not think I was going to take the ball today because I didn't think I could. And then everything starts happening. You start looking at your teammates and understanding what you've been through over the last eight months, what it means to me. And I did what I did last time: I went to the Lord for help, because I knew, again, I wasn't going to be able to do this myself."

God must not like the Cardinals. Schilling was sensational, throwing ninety-four pitches over his six innings. The Red Sox made four more errors, giving them a whopping eight over two games, but it didn't matter. At the end of the game, per tradition, "Dirty Water" blared over the Fenway loudspeakers. The Standells, who first recorded the song in the 1960s, had performed their signature tune before the game.

The Sox ownership took just about everyone who ever worked at Fenway Park to St. Louis. By this time the Sox were certainly America's team. They had a lot going for them: attempting to reverse the Curse, the great comeback against the Yankees, transplanted fans around the world, and the hip, loopy players who forgot to tuck in their shirts. Oscar winner Tom Hanks, a Californian, was interviewed by Fox during a Series game at Fenway and said, "I'm an American. There's nothing wrong with the city of St. Louis. They are lovely people, and they have lovely colors on their baseball uniforms—but come on! I want Billy Buckner to have a good night's sleep, for crying out loud!"

These sentiments were not lost on the folks in St. Louis. *Post-Dispatch* columnist Bernie Miklasz wrote: "National sentiment is against the Cardinals. We're the fly in the soup . . . I mean chowder. Boston is America's latest team."

Including the playoffs, the Cardinals were 59–28 at home. But they were in no position to stop the Boston steamrollers. St. Louis had Suppan on the mound for Game 3. The latest in a line of former Sox (Eckstein, Quantrill, Clark, Gordon) to play opposite Boston in the 2004 postseason, Suppan had been one of Theo's July 31 acquisitions in 2003, but he did not work out nearly as well as the people Epstein got at the 2004 deadline. He went 3–4 with a 5.57 ERA for He-Who-Must-Not-Be-Named, but he was deemed unworthy of a roster spot when the Sox played the Oakland A's in October 2003. He was added to the roster for the Yankee series and was in the bullpen when Boone's homer crash-landed in the left field seats in Yankee Stadium. Suppan was originally drafted by the Red Sox in 1993, when Lou Gorman picked him after selecting Trot Nixon. Suppan made twenty-nine starts for the Red Sox before he was left unprotected and selected by the Diamondbacks in the 1997 expansion draft. He'd pitched in part of ten major league seasons but didn't make it to the playoffs until his 16–9 season with the Cardinals in 2004. It's important to note that he pitched for Arizona, Pittsburgh, and St. Louis—three National League teams. He was a relatively experienced base runner.

The usual themes about pitchers hitting and the American League team giving up its designated hitters were replayed before Game 3. The main story concerned Big Papi, playing first base instead of serving as DH. Ortiz had played only thirty-four games at first all year, only one since July 22. Fans remembered the night in New York when Tony Clark's hard hopper apparently tore through the webbing of Ortiz's glove, costing the Sox a ball game.

Game 3 marked the first time the Sox had played at Busch Stadium since October 9, 1967, when Lonborg beat the Cardinals, 3–1, in Game 5, surrendering a home run to Roger Maris—a game that lasted only two hours and twenty minutes.

Making his first World Series appearance in what might have been his last game for the Red Sox, Martinez pitched seven innings of shutout ball in Game 3, retiring the final fourteen batters he faced in a 4–1 victory. He got a solo home run from Manny in the top of the first, his fourth homer in his last six at-bats against Suppan. Francona lifted Pedro after ninety-eight pitches.

The Cardinals knew they were in trouble when they failed to win the first game after knocking out Wakefield and coming back to tie the game in the top of the eighth. They knew they were in trouble when they couldn't win in Boston even though the Sox made four errors in each game. And they knew they were in trouble when Pujols, Rolen, and Edmonds stopped hitting. But they still had a chance to get back into the Series.

The book on Martinez in 2004 was: get to him early. The Cardinals had their chance in Game 3. With the help of two walks, Pedro loaded the bases in the first, but Edmonds hit a one-out fly to left field and Manny gunned down Walker, who'd tagged and tried to score from third. Varitek helped the situation by standing up nonchalantly, acting as if there wasn't going to be a throw. At the last moment, he snatched Manny's throw, blocked the plate, and tagged out a stunned Walker.

With the Sox still leading in the third, Suppan led off and reached on a scratch single toward third. He moved around to third when Renteria followed with a booming double to right. Five of the first ten St. Louis batters had reached base. It was a 1–0 game, and the Cardinals had runners on second and third with none out. They also had four of the best hitters in the National League ready to hit. Francona conceded the run and had the infield play back. Pedro was on the ropes. The World Series was about to get close again.

Then it happened. One of those plays that alter the course of a playoff series. Walker rapped a hard grounder, which Bellhorn gloved while standing on the lip of the outfield grass. Suppan was supposed to run home on any grounder to the right side. There was no need for a coach, a signal, or a yell. It was automatic. Baseball 101. When the ball was hit, Suppan started, then froze. Then he started back toward third. Seeing that Bellhorn hadn't even looked toward home but had merely relayed to Ortiz at first, he started for home again. Then he froze again. That's when Ortiz saw him and gunned the ball over to Mueller, who made the easy tag on the dizzy pitcher trying to return to third. Renteria, who had almost been all the way to third, retreated to second. Ortiz's throw was right on the money, which was somewhat interesting, given how much had been said and written about the Sox disadvantage with Big Papi forced to play defense in the National League park.

For all practical purposes, Suppan's baserunning blunder signaled the end of the 2004 World Series.

Once again, the Curse was being reversed. Suppan's gaffe was exactly the kind of mistake that marked Boston's eight decades of frustration and convinced the Nation that the planets truly were aligned for Boston this time. La Russa's and Suppan's postgame explanations represented an almost identical-yet-inverted version of a memorable Sox moment from Game 6 in 1975. In that game, eventually won on Fisk's home run for the ages, the Sox had the bases loaded with no outs in the ninth when Denny Doyle tagged up from third and tried to score on a lazy fly to the Reds' leftfielder George Foster. That night, Doyle said he heard coach Don Zimmer yelling, "Go, go, go," when it turned out Zimmer was saying, "No, no, no." This time the Cardinals were saying the opposite words. Suppan heard "no" when coach Jose Oquendo was yelling "go."

In some ways, the Suppan gaffe was the evil twin to Slaughter's mad dash, which beat Boston in Game 7 in '46.

This was Bizarro World. John Henry's alternate universe. Reversing the Curse.

Ever intent on making it about himself, Martinez one last time launched into contract negotiations in his midnight postgame press conference.

"It's been great," said Pedro. "I hope everybody enjoyed it as much as I did. Even with the struggles up and down during the season, I enjoyed every moment of the season. I enjoyed my career in Boston. I hope I can have a chance to come back with this team. I hope people understand that I wasn't the one that wanted to leave. If they don't get me, it's because they probably didn't try hard enough. I consider Boston my house. I hope everything works out okay."

There wasn't any hope for St. Louis. Only one team in more than a century of postseason baseball had recovered from an 0–3 deficit in a best-of-seven series—the 2004 Boston Red Sox. That's little comfort when your only inspiration sits in the visitor's dugout of your own park.

The thirty-eight-year-old Timlin, who'd won two World Series with the Blue Jays, said, "I think we were a little more prepared than they were. They were kind of on a downslide. They had clinched a month early. In athletics, you don't just turn it on, and at that point, we were on. Not only were we on, we were rolling at full steam. We came into the World Series full tilt. We had just faced the Yankees. Their first five hitters are All-Stars. To face a lineup like that and beat 'em, your confidence is high. The Cardinals, their first five hitters, are tremendous, but their first hitter [Renteria] is not as good as Jeter by any means. We were more prepared to face them than they were to face us."

The final game, a 3–0 Sox win, was more coronation than contest. It was the night of simultaneous celestial events—a total lunar eclipse and the Red Sox winning a World Series. Damon homered to right on the fourth pitch of the night from Jason Marquis, and everyone could have gone home then. It marked the fourth consecutive Series game in which the Red Sox scored in the first inning. Damon's swat was all the scoring the Sox would need as the suddenly unhittable Lowe and his bullpen friends mowed down the anemic Cardinals one final time.

Nixon added a pair of insurance runs with a two-out double in the third, swinging at a 3–0 pitch. It was another demonstration of the Curse reversing itself. Nixon swung at the 3–0 pitch because he missed the sign.

"When I saw the sign, I assumed, 'Man, these guys really want me to hit!' So I'm gonna swing, then I found out from Dave Wallace and Tito that it was a take sign, and I freaked. It worked out, though."

Sure did. Nixon's blast was almost a grand slam and turned a 1–0 game into a 3–0 blowout thanks to the mastery of Lowe, the ultimate redemption story in a Sox season of redemption. Winning his third straight clinching game, the big floppy righty pitched seven innings of three-hit, shutout ball. Foulke, who got the last out in all four World Series games, picked up the save with fourteen pitches in the ninth.

In the sweep, no St. Louis pitcher lasted more than six innings, and Boston batters swung and missed only thirty-seven times. Ramirez, who stretched his postseason hitting streak to seventeen games, batted .412 with a homer and four RBI and was named World Series MVP, an award that could as easily have been awarded to Foulke, Schilling, or even Dr. Morgan. Or Theo. Or Tito. Or Dr. Charles. And everyone knew that Big Papi was the MVP of October.

The cloud cover in St. Louis prevented the fans at Busch from seeing the blood-red moon, but around the country, Red Sox alumni watched and celebrated under the red ball in the October sky. Men who had come close but been unable to win in Boston felt connected to the victory. It was bigger than the 2004 Red Sox. It was about anyone who ever rooted for the team and anyone who ever wore the Boston uniform.

Wade Boggs, who sat in the third base dugout in Shea Stadium in 1986 and cried long after Game 7 was lost, was at home in Tampa, in bed with his wife, Debbie.

"It's fate, destiny, all those things rolled into one," Boggs said. "I felt such a warm glow. It was a nice feeling that now New Englanders can walk around with their chests pumped out a little bit. It put a lot more smiles on their faces. It just changed the whole attitude of New England. The big black cloud was lifted."

Fred Lynn, the MVP–Rookie of the Year from 1975, the man who almost won it all in his first year in Boston, watched with his wife and family in his living room in La Costa, California.

"It's hard to describe that feeling from after it ended," said Lynn. "Everything seemed to be moving in slow motion. I felt disbelief. I still thought back to the Yankee series, though. Winning the World Series, obviously, was the pinnacle, but the way the Sox dispatched the Yankees was delicious."

Jim Lonborg, the Cy Young winner from '67 who beat the Cardinals twice in the World Series but lost Game 7 to Bob Gibson, was home in Scituate, Massachusetts, watching the game with his daughter Nora, one of his six grown children.

"Nora had jumped into my arms when we beat the Yankees, and she bruised me, so I was staying away from her when we beat the Cardinals," said Lonborg. "It's wonderful. I thought about all the great players that passed through the doors of Fenway over the years."

And then there was Pesky, class of '46, along with Ted Williams, Bobby Doerr, and Dominic DiMaggio, one of the famous teammates who served the Sox organization so well for so many years. He was the man who got blamed when the Sox lost Game 7 in St. Louis, and now he was back in that same city seeing something that had never happened in his eighty-five years on earth. After the final out, Dr. Steinberg grabbed Pesky and took him down to the clubhouse.

"Schilling almost broke my neck when he picked me up," said Pesky, welling up in tears weeks later at the mere thought of the moment. "I was waiting my whole life, and I was glad to be there to celebrate it. I never had so many guys tell me they loved me. I've been with the ball club sixty years, and being in St. Louis when we won the thing was great. It was the highlight of my life. And I felt for number 9, and Bobby and Dominic."

Lucchino stood outside the clubhouse, took a deep breath and said, "Halle-fucking-lujah."

Varitek and Schilling, drenched in champagne, walked by me, smiling.

"Frauds now?" asked the catcher.

No. They were merely the team that perpetrated the greatest comeback and won the most important championship in the history of Boston sports.

Pesky wasn't the only celebrant who was almost hurt in the frenzy. John Henry apparently lingered too long on the field and was grabbed and whisked away by an MLB official. He was late for the TV trophy presentation, and the MLB functionary roughed him up as he yanked him toward the clubhouse. Henry looked like a U.S. president being whisked to safety by a zealous Secret Service agent.

"There was no part of the season that was not remarkable," Henry said later. "We played .500 ball for so long. Then we went something like 45–14. Was it because we traded Nomar? It's just a remarkable season. From the moment the ball went over the fence in the eleventh inning in New York last year up until that ball was hit back to Foulke, it was just incredible."

After the trophy presentation, the Sox went back to the field, sprayed champagne, took pictures, and hugged one another and their families. They celebrated and toasted with the thousands of Sox fans still gathered behind the third base dugout. Mike Barnicle, tough-guy columnist for the *Herald*, bent down at third base and scooped up some dirt, which he put in his pockets. The dirt is now in a box in the room of twelve-year-old Tim Barnicle in Lincoln, Massachusetts.

While all the celebration was going on, the generosity and courtesy of the St. Louis fans and club officials seemed boundless. Cardinal fans were forgiving of their own team and gracious toward everyone in Red Sox garb. Late during Game 4, when the gates were opened to allow discouraged Cardinal fans to beat the traffic, ballpark officials allowed Bostonians without tickets to enter Busch Stadium for the celebration. Small wonder that the first "Yankees Suck" chant broke out only six minutes after the Red Sox won.

One of the Cardinal security folk even made a little joke when Lucchino was setting up photos on the field with the World Series trophy. "He told me they weren't going to rush us since we only get to do this once every eighty-six years," said the Sox CEO.

The Red Sox went back to their hotel, the Adams Mark, just a few blocks from Busch Stadium. It would have been too cocky to have packed everything and checked out before the game, even though they had been confident there would not be a Game 5 in St. Louis. Hundreds of Sox fans stood outside at the intersection of Pine and Fourth streets, cheering, chanting, and waiting until the players and their families boarded buses after 2:30 A.M.

They eventually got on a Delta charter in St. Louis and left at 3:22 A.M., with the thirty-pound World Series trophy strapped into a middle seat next to Pedro. Wakefield sat in the cockpit for some of the flight. Varitek played cards with Kapler, Bellhorn, and reliever Mike Myers. Schilling made announcements over the plane's public-address system.

The World Champion Boston Red Sox landed in the Hub just after 6:30 A.M. Boston time. Burks carried the trophy off the plane as about a hundred Massport workers, state troopers, and firefighters greeted them. Then the Sox piled into more buses and followed a police escort to Fenway through the morning commute. The scene from Logan to Fenway is something that stayed with all on the championship buses. They saw early morning Boston come to a standstill as their motorcade made its way out of the airport. There was some apt symbolism at the start of the route as the airport exit road steered the bus directly into the mouth of the Ted Williams Tunnel, under the harbor, and into the city.

Timlin stood in the front of his bus and videotaped the entire trip. As the buses rolled on the clogged highways and side streets, cars were forced to pull over to make way for them. Instantly aware of what was passing before them, commuters got out of their cars and cheered. The sun was rising, and the full moon was finally dropping below the horizon in sleepy Boston. The early morning light was golden and so was the moment. In East Boston, a truck driver from Hudson General got out of his rig, climbed up on top of his tanker, and bowed repeatedly to the Sox. The rest of the way, people were standing on the hoods of their cars. Guys in hard hats — Big Dig sandhogs — flashed the thumbs-up sign. People in row houses came out in bathrobes and slippers. Some held out the morning papers and pointed to the gigantic headlines (*USA Today,* the Nation's Newspaper, led its front page with SOX REVERSE CURSE). Children walking to school started to run beside the buses, breathlessly trying to make the historic passage last a little longer. Helicopters hovered above. When the motorcade turned down

Van Ness Street and into Fenway, Pedro told the *Globe*'s Stan Gross-feld, "Nobody's going to work. The Sox are here. Blow them kisses. I could die now. I'm at peace."

There was a formal parade in downtown Boston more than forty-eight hours later that would draw an estimated 3.2 million Sox fans on a rainy Saturday morning. It was the largest celebration in the 374-year history of Boston, but for many of the men and women on the buses, nothing was more special than the spontaneous celebration they saw from Bostonians on the way to work. Everyone was smiling.

Finally, Boston once again knew how it felt to win the World Series.

15

Now What?

S TILL RUMPLED AND STINKING of dried champagne, Lucchino went straight to his office after getting off the magic bus Thursday morning. He then went to Boston City Hall, posed for some photos, and helped plan the parade route for Saturday. He felt shorthanded without Maestro Steinberg at his side and wrestled with the city hall gang about parade details. At the same time, Governor Mitt Romney was perched in the bucket of a cherry picker on Storrow Drive, wielding a torch to remove the REVERSE CURVE sign from the overpass. Years earlier, pranksters had spraypainted the sign to read REVERSE THE CURSE, and like-minded officials let the graffiti stay. It had become something of an inadvertent civic landmark, like the Leaning Tower of Pisa. With the Curse officially reversed, the governor seized the moment, stalling traffic for a phony photo op. The historic green beam was removed, and the governor promised it would be auctioned off, with all proceeds going to charity.

Meanwhile, Schilling was everywhere, first appearing on *Good Morning America,* where he finished his interview by telling everyone to vote for George Bush (the presidential election was five days away), then off to Disney World a day before Pedro was scheduled to appear at the Magic Kingdom. Assorted radio, television, and charity appearances, plus ankle surgery, were on deck for the big righty. The crutches and wheelchair only added to his glory.

At the end of a long Thursday, Lucchino went out to dinner with his partners at Grill 23, on Stuart Street in Boston. Much to his surprise, the meal was not on the house.

"There was always this fable about how if you win the World Series in Boston, you'll never have to pay for a meal again for the rest of your life," Lucchino said with a smile. "Well, there we were the next night, and we got this gigantic check. I was a little surprised. It had been less than a day. One night, and they couldn't buy us one meal? Then, when we were leaving, another customer asked if we got the bottle of 1918 wine he'd sent over . . . We never saw that bottle. Too bad."

Lucchino was back in the office on Friday, and that was the day Dr. Charles Steinberg suggested that the Red Sox victory parade be extended onto the Charles River. Nice touch. The World Champs and Dr. Charles on the Charles. Mayor Menino later took credit for the aquatic portion of the parade, and Lucchino said, "I like the river idea. There's something poetic, romantic, something Boston about that."

The Sox offices were flooded with phone calls as they prepared for Saturday's massive celebration, but small details were not overlooked. Lucchino got a call on behalf of thirteen-year-old cancer patient Patrick White, a Babe Ruth ballplayer from Quincy. White had relapsed earlier in the year and spent a midsummer night at Fenway with his family as guests of the Red Sox. On that occasion, Lucchino, a former patient himself (non-Hodgkin's lymphoma) at the Dana-Farber Cancer Institute, had told the boy's parents, "If there's anything we can ever do . . ."

It's a standard offer, too often uttered without sincerity when people don't know what else to say. But when Lucchino got a call the day before the parade asking if perhaps Patrick White could be on one of the floats, he put his best people on the case, and young Patrick and his family wound up on the Red Sox Foundation Float, sponsored by Home Depot.

Share the gold.

On Saturday morning, the day before Halloween, the World Champion Red Sox were hardball heroes in the middle of a slowly moving rally. Then they were rolling on a river, the same muddy water that inspired the Standells all those years ago. And if you listened carefully, the World Series trophy could be heard finally singing: "Boston, you're my home!" These Red Sox would ride forever—not on the streets or waterways of Boston—but in the hearts and minds of New Englanders who waited eighty-six years for a World Series championship. Manny held up a sign, handed to him by a fan, which read JETER IS PLAYING GOLF. THIS IS BETTER. The suddenly cuddly slugger reached out and touched as many hands as he could until his fingers and wrists ached. He didn't want the parade to end. When the Duck boat carrying Ortiz waded into the Charles, the big DH put a tiny life preserver around his neck and said, "I can't swim, and we got too many fat asses on this boat!"

During the river ride, more than a few Sox fans jumped from the shores and were baptized in the championship waters. Amazing. Winning a World Series was a cleansing experience, even in the muddy Charles.

Pesky, who rode with Rich Gedman, Oil Can Boyd, Joe Morgan, and so many other former Red Sox heroes, said, "I could go tomorrow and I'd die happy, but I don't intend to. I want to see it a couple of more times. Especially for our fans."

Unfortunately, not all former Red Sox were similarly caught up in the euphoria. Appearing on *The James Brown Show* on Sporting News Radio, Bill Buckner said, "Personally, on my end of it, I'm just a little disappointed with the whole thing. This idea of being forgiven and clearing my name, you know. I mean . . . cleared from what? What did I do wrong? It's almost like being in a prison for thirty years, and then they come up with a DNA test to prove that you weren't guilty."

There were other occasional reminders of past failures. According to police in Salem, on the day of the parade a wedding was interrupted when a busboy chanted, "Yankees Suck!" and threatened to beat up the groom, who was from Staten Island.

But for the most part it was hardball heaven in the Hub. And the Sox players, it seemed, were everywhere, and they always had the World Series trophy with them. Timlin, Ortiz, Embree, Roberts, and Lowe went on *Letterman* after Damon went on Leno. Damon also appeared in *People* magazine, where he talked about doing naked pullups. Damon later reappeared in the America's Sexiest Man Alive issue. Ortiz hit the set with Ellen DeGeneres. Schilling campaigned with President Bush in Ohio. Varitek was feted at Children's Hospital in Boston. There was Derek Lowe Day in Quincy. Arroyo was ubiquitous, hitting more spots around Boston than Ben Affleck during the Democratic convention. Schilling and Damon were honored at a Patriot game. Ortiz, Lowe, Kapler, and Youkilis were guests at a Celtic game. Lowe and Millar went on an ESPN broadcast with former Sox outfielder Fred Lynn. *Sports Illustrated* named the 2004 Red Sox Sportsmen of the Year, the first such award for a major professional sports team.

The World Series winners turned out to be champions of generosity as well. Unlike the 1986 Sox, these players spread the wealth when they carved up the playoff shares. Close to sixty full shares were awarded (the cheapo Marlins awarded only thirty-seven full shares in 2003). The Sox largesse lowered each player's individual harvest but more than quadrupled the annual salaries of clubhouse workers, groundskeepers, trainers, and video aides, who toiled long hours for the love of the game. Damon, Nixon, and Wakefield were in charge of the shares meeting, and the players took care of the parking lot attendants and lawn-mower men who had worked so hard for so many years. When the prior regime owned the Red Sox, Edward "Pookie" Jackson, a longtime assistant equipment manager, did not have health insurance and could not afford necessary medications. In 2004 Pookie replaced Harold Reynolds for a night on ESPN. He wound up getting a check for more than $200,000, thanks to the generosity of the Red Sox players. Club publicists Glenn Geffner and Peter Chase got partial shares, unthinkable in an earlier time, when players regarded publicity men as the enemy.

Share the gold.

Francona signed a $75,000 contract to promote Metamucil, which paid almost as much for a full-page ad in the *Globe* with the memorable headline way to go! and a subhead, "Congratulations Boston on your World Championship. Let's hope it becomes a regular thing."

"It's been busier than before," said the underrated, oft-maligned manager. "But when you get home and you do gutters and take the laundry out, you're kind of back to normal. Still, every time someone introduces me as 'World Series Champion,' that hits me like you can't believe, and I love that. I loved living through it. I really did. But when it was over, it was kind of like Christmas. You rush up to it and then it's gone. It's hard to put it into words."

Lives were changed. Joseph Mazzone, the Pine Street Inn official who had coined He-Who-Must-Not-Be-Named, heard his true calling during the magical Red Sox summer and joined the seminary. He was already wearing a priestly collar when the Sox won, but he said he did not feel the events were related. John, Melvin, Pablo, and David, the elderly homeless men who'd watched Sox games together at the shelter, left Nomar's TV at the Pine Street Inn and were living on their own by the time the Sox won it all. Ever the wise guy, John said, "After they won, I had a dream that some other ball club decided Francona was a genius and came here and hired him away from the Red Sox. It was like winning the World Series twice!"

There were lines to get into the Twins Enterprise Souvenir Store on Yawkey Way. The *Boston Globe* put out a pair of instant books; both were on local bestseller lists by late November. Stephen King and Stewart O'Nan came out with a four-hundred-plus-page fan tome; the *Globe*'s review concluded with Howard Frank Mosher saying, "Go, Sox!"

Congressman Ed Markey rewrote "Casey at the Bat," applying modern Red Sox lyrics, and read it into the *Congressional Record*. In the Senate, Ted Kennedy sponsored a resolution; it held that "The Curse of the Bambino, as it is called, was finally lifted after eighty-six long years; we had a World Series victory to celebrate at long last."

It's always about history when it comes to the Red Sox. Kennedy's grandfather, Boston mayor John "Honey Fitz" Fitzgerald, threw out the first ball in the World Series when the Sox won it all in Fenway's first year, 1912. And, of course, Dr. Charles Steinberg, the Sox vice president in charge of everything, the man who planned the parade, was first brought into baseball by the grandson of the man who signed Babe Ruth.

Manny finished third in the MVP balloting, Ortiz fourth. Guerrero and Sheffield were 1–2. Schilling finished second to Santana in the Cy Young voting, and Francona was almost off the map, finishing fifth and appearing on only four of the twenty-eight ballots. Kapler was the first of more than a dozen Sox to file for free agency; he was the first to leave when he signed to play in Japan on November 22. The Sox signed former nemesis David Wells and Matt Clement, the Cub righty Theo rejected in July. Pedro went to Tampa for a date with Daddy

Steinbrenner, then signed with the Mets. The sensitive and petty Pedro ripped Epstein, Francona, and Schilling on his way out the door, and his graceless exit tarnished his seven years of stellar service in Boston.

Renteria, who made the final out, signed a four-year contract with the Red Sox. Varitek eventually signed with the Sox and was made captain. Lowe signed with the Dodgers. Roberts was traded to the Padres. Reese went to the Mariners.

No one would ever forget the band of idiots who won it all and broke the Curse in 2004, but the new reality was that the defending World Champion Red Sox were going to have a different look when they got to Fort Myers in February 2005. It wasn't like the 1950s, when Yogi and Mickey and Whitey came back and won again, year after year.

Better not to think about that. Better to continue to bask in the warm glow of October 2004. Most fans needed a calendar and some old newspapers to remember the specifics of the most exhausting and exhilarating month in the history of Boston sports.

"The whole sleep deprivation thing needs to be noted," said Lucchino. "I told our front office people that November was for sleep, but then it turned out they had to wait until December. The whole experience was somewhat muted as you were going through it because you were operating on so little sleep. It kind of all merges together, this amalgamation of events and moments."

On Friday, November 19, Fred Hale Sr., the world's oldest man, died at the age of 113 in Syracuse. His obituary in the *Globe* included a photograph of him sitting in his wheelchair, watching Ortiz bat during the final game of the World Series. Originally from Maine, Hale had been twenty-seven years old, married for eight years, when the Sox won in 1918. He was one of the few who actually remembered that day.

"It's an incredible feeling to drive past cemeteries and see Red Sox pennants on the gravestones," remarked Epstein. "It makes you think about how meaningful it must be to the family to do something like that. People are happy and proud. There's a little different way people are carrying themselves now."

Why this team? Why did it happen with these players?

"I think there are two reasons," said Theo. "One is, there was a lot of luck and good fortune involved. Dave Roberts gets thrown out by six inches, we're done. So many things could have gone the other way. Tony Clark's ball hits off the fence and hops into the stands. And that ties into our organizational philosophy, which is that our goal is to make the playoffs every single year. We don't necessarily design a team to win the World Series. You can't say, 'Well, I want this guy because he can pitch the eighth inning in Game 7.' You've got to build your team to win 95 to 100 games every year to get us in there. We figure you have a 12 percent chance of winning the World Series every year you get in the postseason. Let's get in there every year, and sooner or later, we're going to win one.

"The second reason is that the group of twenty-five guys we had worked. They worked as human beings, and they worked as a roster. They functioned well under pressure. It all came together. I don't think you come back from 3–0 against the Yankees for yourself. I think you do it for your teammates. Guys like Bill Mueller look around and see Dave Roberts and say, 'He's busting his ass. He's an awesome guy. I don't want his season to end. I want to do it for him.' They all look around at each other. There was some selflessness to this team, which is not a trait usually associated with the Red Sox."

Does it change the Red Sox?

Historian Halberstam predicted, "It will certainly change things. It will fragment. With the civil rights movement, all these great black leaders were pulled together and were loyal to each other as they were ascending, struggling against the white supremacists. The moment they won, everything fragmented because it went on to individual ambition. There's always a difference in a revolution. When you finally get it, the strength that bonds you together changes and you put private ambition over group ambition, and that's something the Red Sox will have to think about. Will success and winning spoil this unique sense of community and passion and this mystique of being close but never quite getting there?"

Young Theo preferred to put a more positive slant on what winning will do to the players and their fans.

"I think it does change the Red Sox," he answered. "I think we really feel the challenge to get back to where we expect to compete for the World Series on an annual basis. Nineteen eighteen had always been the number that sort of characterized our failures. It could also come to symbolize the end of an era of Red Sox dominance. Now we have 2004, which could either come to symbolize a year which was an aberration, or it could be the start of a new period of Red Sox excellence."

In the end, it was never about digging up the Babe's bones and making a public apology, or exorcisms, or Salem witches, or pianos in ponds, or planting a Sox flag on the top of Mount Everest. It wasn't about the missing teeth of a young man who lives in the Babe's house in Sudbury, and it wasn't about Reverse the Curse cookies or ice cream flavors. The Curse was there only to give some fans a reason for all the bad luck and near misses. It was like Santa Claus or the tooth fairy or the Easter bunny. It was a bloody joke, one that some fans took far too seriously. But as the 2004 Red Sox proved, what really mattered was having the best pitching and a clubhouse full of players who believed in one another and cared nothing about Boston baseball's past.

That said, great as they were, the Sox are not quite as special as they have been for the last several decades. New England loves its championship teams, and America exhaled with the rest of Red Sox Nation when the boys from Boston finally won, but now the Red Sox are a little bit more like the Phillies, Orioles, Cardinals, and Dodgers. No longer part of a quixotic quest, the Sox are a team with a championship trophy in the lobby of its executive offices, a team with a chance to win every year. New Englanders still love the Red Sox but will never think of them in quite the same way. The "unique sense of community and passion" is inalterably changed. No matter what happens next to the Red Sox, it's probably not going to be as good as it was in the autumn of 2004. We all remember Neil Armstrong and his "giant leap for mankind" on July 20, 1969, but few can recite anything about NASA's second successful walk on the moon.

The Curse of the Bambino has been lifted. Never more will the Red Sox hear about 1918, Bucky Dent, Bill Buckner, or Aaron Boone. No more will New Englanders spend the winter complaining about how the Red Sox just blew it and wondering if maybe, just maybe, next year is going to be The Year. No more waiting to see them win it just once before we die. It happened. Two thousand and four was The Year . . . the year that pigs flew and cows jumped over a giant red moon in the late October sky.

ACKNOWLEDGMENTS

All these years later, it goes back to the beginning, back to 1988, when Meg Blackstone and the folks at E. P. Dutton hired me to write a book that they wanted to call *The Curse of the Bambino*. That was sixteen years, several Sox collapses, and a couple of dozen printings ago. Never meant to be taken seriously, the Curse became part of the language and, ultimately, part of the amazing story of the 2004 World Series Champion Boston Red Sox. It even became an ice cream flavor.

So thanks again to Meg and Al Silverman, Dick McGrath and Clifford Corcoran at Dutton and Viking Penguin. And to those who got me started in this business: Bill Tanton, Dave Smith, Vince Doria, and later bosses Don Skwar and Joe Sullivan. Thanks to Ken Nigro and Peter Pascarelli, Dream Team reporters from Baltimore. To Dave O'Hara, who helped me get started, and Kevin Dupont and Lesley Visser from the old days. And to Peter May, Tim Kurkjian, John Lowe, Laurel and Wendy Selig-Prieb, and Phyllis Merhige, who is always happy if I don't have her crying anywhere in the text. To Ernie Roberts, the late Jerry Nason, and the late, great Ray Fitzgerald. And of course Will McDonough, who always treated me as if I was one of his kids. Thanks to Bob Hohler and Gordon Edes, who wrote the amazing story of the 2004 Red Sox every day on the pages of the *Boston Globe*.

Thanks to Bob Ryan, Jackie MacMullan, Larry Whiteside, John Powers, Mike Barnicle, Marty Nolan, Tom Mulvoy, Bud Collins, Bill Griffith, Nick Cafardo, Steve Krasner, Charlie Scoggins, Joe Giuliotti, Jonny Miller, Sean McAdam, Steve Buckley, Bill Ballou, Rob Bradford, Art Davidson, Phil O'Neill, Brian Cashman, Rick Cerrone, Jason Zillo, Arthur Richman, Bill Madden, Christy Lemire, Kevin Kernan, Roger Angell, Mike Lupica, Jim Kaat, Jerry Remy, Joe Castiglione, Jerry Trupiano, Don Orsillo, Sean McDonough,

Clark Booth, Ed Kleven, Dick Johnson, Eddie Andelman, Stephen Stills, Steve Sheppard, David Halberstam, John Iannacci, and John Horn. Thanks to John Henry, Tom Werner, Larry Lucchino, Theo Epstein, Dr. Charles Steinberg, Larry Cancro, Dick Bresciani, Mike Port, Lou Gorman, Janet Marie Smith, Kerri Moore, Glenn Geffner, Peter Chase, Mark Rogoff, Andrew Merle, Colleen Moore, Pam Ganley, John Carter, Al Forester, Jerry Kapstein, Danny Kischel, Vanessa Leyvas, Debbie Matson, Meghan McClure, Sarah McKenna, Joe Mooney, Dave Mellor, Fay Scheer, Joe Cochran, Pookie Jackson, Tommy McLaughlin, Brita Meng Outzen, Carl Beane, Arthur D'Angelo, Tim Samway, Peter Gammons, Guy Spina, Bob Lobel, Alice Cook, Steve Burton, Dan Roche, Jackie Connally, Joe Amorosino, Wendi Nix, Gary Gillis, Dave Briggs, Mike Lynch, Uri Berenguer, Reid Laymance, Tony Massarotti, Jeff Horrigan, Mike Silverman, Len Megliola, Dave Heuschkel, Alan Greenwood, Ian Browne, Garry Brown, Bob Levin, Eric Monroe, Mike McHugh, Sue Callaghan, Paul Comerford, Jim Davis, Michael LaVigne, Marty Baron, Jack McCormick, Hank Morse, Ken Fratus, Sean Sullivan, Bob Norcross, Alan Waugh, Tom Verducci, and everyone in the *Boston Globe* library. Thanks to Ed Jesser, Mayor Thomas Menino, Ed Carpenter, Roger Berkowitz, Maria Cigravino, and Sylvia Moon.

Systems whiz Sean Mullin gets his own paragraph. He knows why.

Stan Grossfeld is my second brother. His work on these covers and pages brings the book to life.

Susan Canavan and the people at Houghton Mifflin signed off on the project in February, when no one was certain what was going to happen to the 2004 Red Sox. None of us knew what we were going to do after ALCS Game 3, the 19–8 Red Sox loss to the Yankees. So let's not even go there. Susan is a great editor and a wonderful Skipjacks lunch companion, and she should be running Houghton Mifflin in a few years. Thanks also to Teri Kelly, Janet Silver, Megan Wilson, Suzanne Cope, Luise Erdmann, Becky Saikia-Wilson, Martha Kennedy, and Bill McCormick. Sean Smith saved me with his fact-checking.

As always, thanks to Bill, Mary, Joan, and Ann. Once again, the Hunnewell Hill home team provided great support, and I look forward to many more years of watching Sarah, Kate, and Sam getting a good pitch to hit. Dr. Marilou Shaughnessy has the professional and personal skills to deal with a sleep-deprived, deadline-looming author. It is appreciated.

DAN SHAUGHNESSY
Newton, Massachusetts
December 14, 2004

BIBLIOGRAPHY

Boston Globe articles, 1919–2004.

Boston Herald articles, 2003–2004.

The Boston Red Sox. Official Media Guides, 2003, 2004.

Bradford, Rob. *Chasing Steinbrenner.* Washington, D.C.: Brassey's Inc., 2004.

Creamer, Robert. *Babe.* New York: Simon & Schuster, 1974.

Kettmann, Steve. *One Day at Fenway.* New York: Atria Books, 2004.

Loverro, Thom. *Home of the Game.* Dallas: Taylor Publishing, 1999.

New York Daily News articles, 2003–2004.

New York Newsday articles, 2003–2004.

New York Post articles, 2003–2004.

New York Times articles, 2003–2004.

Olney, Buster. *The Last Night of the Yankee Dynasty.* New York: HarperCollins, 2004.

The Rivals, Red Sox vs. Yankees: An Inside History. New York: St. Martin's Press, 2004.

Shaughnessy, Dan. *The Curse of the Bambino.* New York: Dutton, 1990.

Sports Illustrated World Series Commemorative. New York: Time Inc., November 10, 2004.

Stout, Glenn, and Richard A. Johnson, *Red Sox Century.* Boston: Houghton Mifflin, 2000.

———. *Yankees Century.* Boston: Houghton Mifflin, 2002.

USA Today articles, 2003–2004.

INDEX